To June Hancock Catron
and
Segundo Virgilio
Vicente Eliecer Chiriboga B:
separated from us by death, continuing in spirit

DIVORCE

CRISIS, CHALLENGE OR RELIEF?

David A. Chiriboga, Linda S. Catron
and Associates

NEW YORK UNIVERSITY PRESS
New York and London

Library of Congress Cataloging-in-Publication Data
Chiriboga, David Anthony.
    Divorce : crisis, challenge or relief? / David A. Chiriboga,
  Linda S. Catron and associates.
        p.   cm.
    Includes bibliographical references (p.   ) and index.
    ISBN 0-8147-1450-1 (alk.paper)
    1. Divorce—California—Longitudinal studies.   2. Divorce—
California—Psychological aspects—Longitudinal studies.
I. Catron, Linda S., 1948–   . II. Title.
HQ835.C2C45   1991
306.89—dc20   90-22219
                                                       CIP

New York University Press books are printed on acid-free paper,
and their binding materials are chosen for strength and durability.

Book design by Ken Venezio

CONTENTS

PREFACE

The past two decades bear witness to dramatic increases not only in the rates of divorce but in the number of popular and scholarly works devoted to the subject. In book after book we are offered glimpses of empty-eyed men staring at bare motel walls, or desperate single mothers struggling to reestablish careers and lives while juggling bank balances and the social opportunities of their children. There is no doubt concerning the import of these words and stories, for divorce can be a fearful business, just as it can be a window of opportunity and salvation.

There is also no doubt that many gaps remain in our knowledge concerning the impact of divorce on the lives of ordinary men and women. This book describes a research project designed from its inception to address one overarching concern: the need to better understand the stress context represented by divorce. Its intent was to translate empirical research into information useful for both academics and those in the health professions. Of particular interest was whether it is possible, using information available at the time a petition for divorce is filed, to identify those in short- and long-term need of assistance.

A FOCUSED STUDY

The project upon which this text is based examined a host of very specific questions, such as what kinds of stresses people going through a divorce are exposed to, but also sought to address several rather critical needs in the field of divorce. Perhaps the most important of these needs were for life span studies, since we know surprisingly little concerning age differences in the impact of divorce, and for randomly drawn samples of ordinary people who may or may not have sought therapeutic intervention. In the following paragraphs we will describe some of the unique features of the study, and discuss why each seemed to warrant inclusion. In brief, we developed a life span study from a nonclinical population, sampled for men as well as women, included a comparison group of persons who were not undergoing a divorce, and made a special effort to include members of minority groups. We sought to avoid a static or mechanistic view of divorce and employed instead a more process-oriented model that clarified the relevance of transitional perspectives on role change and introduced procedures drawn from stress research.

Life-Span Studies

The majority of divorce research has concerned itself with persons in the younger adult years, and yet we know that increasing numbers of middle-aged and older adults are divorcing. In one pioneering study, Goode (1956) reported that older women seemed more distressed by divorce. Although by "older" Goode was referring to women in their late thirties, the idea that age might bring with it increased vulnerabilities has been supported by scholars in more recent studies (e.g., Hagestad, Smyer and Stierman 1984; Payne and Pittard 1969; Rice and Rice 1986).

Random Studies in the Community

For a variety of reasons, divorce researchers tend to draw samples from persons either seeking treatment in some sort of clinical intervention program or who are members of self-help groups such as Parents Without Partners. While the results are often highly informative, these samples represent somewhat special populations whose problems and concerns may not entirely reflect those of the general population. To provide an example of sampling bias that occurred in another context, many early clinical studies of the impact of children leaving home overemphasized parental reactions, when compared to later community studies (Lowenthal and Chiriboga 1972). Rather than reacting with the proverbial "empty nest" syndrome, the majority of parents were relishing their newfound freedom!

Men as Well as Women

It is clear that divorcing women have special vulnerabilities evolving both from economic hardships and the fact that women ordinarily are the ones who obtain custody of children. At the same time, there is growing evidence that men's vulnerabilities are equally deserving of study. Overall, there is a need for the kind of balanced perspective afforded by studying both sexes.

Comparison Groups

Most studies of divorce are limited in their ability to generalize since they lack any control or comparison group. Our research team was fortunate to have available a sample of individuals from the same geographic area who were comparable to the divorce sample on most if not all demographic criteria. Unlike the nonnormative transition facing our Divorce Study participants, those in the comparison group were experiencing more normative transitions such as parenthood, the so-called empty nest and retirement. Hence, the changes they faced were more likely to have been anticipated for some time.

Minority Issues in Divorce

Although excellent studies exist of family issues concerning African Americans and Hispanic Americans, rarely considered is how minority family members deal with divorce. In our study the sample was sufficiently large that we could anticipate recruiting meaningful numbers of African and Hispanic Americans. Since the study was conducted in an area with an unusually large proportion of Asian Americans, but recruiting them might be particularly difficult, we worked closely with several Asian community leaders and hired a number of Asian interviewers. These interviewers made the initial contacts with all potential subjects with Asian surnames or maiden names, and also conducted the actual interviews.

Divorce as Process

With a few marked exceptions, such as the work of Wallerstein, Hetherington and Bloom, research on divorce has depended on cross-sectional or "one-shot" contacts with persons. Moreover, the point at which people are contacted is highly variable, with some being contacted one or more years after the legal act of marital dissolution, and others being interviewed at varying points before the legal process of divorce is completed. In the present study we sought to interview people more than once at potentially critical periods.

The literature and our own work on stress indicated that two basic periods are of concern to those in the helping professions. The first is what might be called the "impact" phase of divorce, a phase that commonly starts when the couple separates and marital conflict "goes public." The second is much later and involves the person's long-term adaptation. In order to capture functioning during these two phases, our first contacts with participants took place an average of six months after marital separation and our follow-up interviews were approximately three and a half years later (or about four years after the separation).

The Relevance of Transitional Perspectives

Divorce is often referred to as a transition. Used in a colloquial manner, the word "transition" is simply a synonym for role change. In our work, transition has a different meaning and involves a series of demands or "developmental tasks" facing persons undergoing divorce. We used the concept of transition as a guide in formulating and conducting the study.

The Value of Approaches from Stress Research

Marital separation and divorce are generally portrayed as major life events or social stressors (see, for example, Holmes and Rahe 1967). Divorce researchers also note the importance of considering divorce as a stress condition (e.g., Bloom, White and Asher 1979; Hetherington, Cox and Cox 1976; Ilfeld 1982), but this recognition frequently does not extend beyond the observation that divorce is a devastating event whose consequences therefore deserve investigation. Application of current stress methodologies and theoretical perspectives has been limited, but should prove rewarding since stressors and mediators are implicated in the evolution of mental illness. Price-Bonham and Balswick (1980, 968) take a strong position on this issue:

Stress theory and crisis theory could provide useful frameworks for conceptualizing people's reactions to divorce. These frameworks could be used to explain both short-term and long-term reactions to a stressful situation.

Studies of stress factors in divorce are now appearing in the literature. For example, Bloom and his colleagues (e.g., White and Bloom 1981; Caldwell, Bloom and Hodges 1983) have considered the range of stress responses evoked by divorce, while Ilfeld (1982) has explored the importance for mental health of coping strategies and personality. We hoped to avoid the blanket assumption that separation and divorce are stressful by looking at what participants themselves had to say about how stressful their life had been.

A UNIQUE STUDY OF A COMMON PROBLEM

The probability sampling of men and women who ranged widely in age, a two-interview panel design and the other characteristics described in the last section provided us with an opportunity to focus on issues and processes that seemed, early on, to have tremendous significance for how well people deal with divorce. A broad-ranging model of stress and coping guided the selection of the topics to be covered in this book. After chapter 1, in which we introduce the study, each of the ensuing chapters is devoted to some issue or question that is salient to the stress of divorce. As some topics, such as childhood stress and locus of control, may not be especially familiar to all readers, we begin each chapter with brief literature reviews of the particular content area to be covered. Towards the end of each chapter, we present two or more case histories in order to highlight key points.

The chapters in part one present an in-depth consideration of topics related to stress and adaptation. In chapter 2, "Childhood Stress and Adaptation to Divorce: A Shaping Condition," we introduce a measure of childhood stress that not only is significantly associated with adult adaptation but also demonstrates reasonable measurement properties. In chapter 3, "Divorce Stress and Adaptation," we introduce the basic model of stress and adaptation that guided the study from its initiation. Our focus is on the many ways in which divorcing persons encounter stress, and we consider not only their levels of stress exposure but also compare these levels with those of our comparison group. Chapter 4, "Coping Strategies in Divorce," expands upon the stress chapter by looking at some of the ways in which people attempt to deal with stress, for better or worse.

With part two we move to a topic with substantial overlap to stress: the topic of transitions. Chapter 5, "Passage through Divorce: A Transitions Perspective," traces the history of transitions and demonstrates that divorce in the modern world produces its own set of transition-related tasks. Chapter 6, "Passage through Divorce: Timing Issues," develops the concept of transitions still further. It introduces the innovative notion that the speed with which the individual proceeds from one marker point of divorce to another may provide a good indication of psychological well-being.

In part three we look at how study participants viewed themselves and others. Chapter 7, "The Self-Concept of Divorcing Persons," focuses specifically on their self-image. In chapter 8, "Views of the Other: Issues of Self-Image and Identification," we continue with the same theme of self-image, this time employing semantic differential techniques to determine the significance of perceived similarities between views of oneself and one's ex-spouse, present partner (if any) and parents.

Part four explores a variety of factors that may mediate the relationship between the experience and the consequence of divorce. Chapter 9, "Social Supports in the Context of Divorce," takes the position that support is a multidimensional concept with its own particular role to play. "Who Leaves Whom: The Importance of Control" is the title of chapter 10, and we here explore the significance of several different ways in which control can be defined. In chapter 11, "Minority Issues in the Study of Divorce," we examine the special vulnerabilities and strengths of several groups that rarely have been examined in the context of divorce. As noted previously, we made an effort to include not only black Americans, Hispanic Americans and Asian Americans; we also identified a small group of men and women in heterosexual marriages who subsequently adopted a more homosexual lifestyle.

In chapter 12, "Risk Factors in Divorce: A Life Course Perspective," we review the topics we have covered and the essence of what we have learned. Given that we sampled people at a relatively early point in the divorce process and followed them over a period of years, our approach allowed us to identify risk factors associated with problems in both the short and long run. We also identified factors that may be associated with better outcomes.

ACKNOWLEDGMENTS

The inspiration for this book came from the doctoral theses of five very talented and creative students from a variety of disciplines: Linda Catron (Anthropology), Ann Coho (Counseling Psychology), Cathy Birtley Fenn (Health Psychology), Leah Friedman (Counseling Psychology), and H. B. Wilder (Clinical Psychology). Linda Catron and Dave Chiriboga spearheaded the effort to turn highly technical and quantitative theses into readable book chapters. They added rich qualitative materials from case studies to help illustrate key points in each chapter. Readers interested in learning more of the technical details may wish to read one or more of the dissertations; these, and an additional one by Hal Rogers whose content area fell outside the scope of this book, are cited in the references. In the process of creating the final product we recognized the need and value of highlighting minority issues in divorce, and recruited Barbara Yee to prepare a chapter on these issues.

In a study spanning nearly four years of data collection and 10 years of data analysis, it is impossible to mention all our wonderful friends and colleagues from the University of California, San Francisco. A few are particularly deserving of recognition. Marjorie Fiske and Majda Thurnher, who together masterminded the companion Longitudinal Study of Transitions, brought intellectual rigor and human kindness to the research process in both studies. Phyllis Olsen, as chief administrator to the graduate program in which we all worked, was the benevolent orchestrator of all those details without which everything fails. Robert Pierce, Judith Stein, Lorie Cutler, Lance Pollack, Sherry Spitzer and the whole multidisciplinary team of researchers that together constituted the Department of Psychiatry's Human Development Program provided an intellectual context that made our research experience more satisfying. New friends at the University of Texas Medical Branch provided a vital support network that kept us going, including especially Bill Philips and John Bruhn in the School of Allied Health Sciences. Roberta Howell, Paula Levine and George Jakobi masterminded the final pulling together of editorial revisions, bibliographic entries and the like.

And lastly, and on a more personal note, the two senior authors would like to acknowledge their families: Courtney James Catron, Court Catron, Jr., Margaret Catron, Maggie Cooper, June Rowson Squarebrigs, Barbara Wai Kinn Yee, Carlos Daniel Chiriboga and David Anthony Chiriboga II. It is truly a miracle they did not disown us during the many stolen hours it took to complete this volume!

DAVID A. CHIRIBOGA   LINDA S. CATRON
Galveston, Texas   *San Francisco, California*

1

INTRODUCTION

David A. Chiriboga

The social phenomenon we call divorce has gone from the unusual and suspect to the common and socially accepted in the United States in a space of less than thirty years. After a temporary surge in divorces immediately following World War II, when the soldiers returned home, there was a period of stability until the mid-1950s. From 1957 to 1977, the incidence of divorce in the United States among persons 44 years or younger more than doubled, while marriage rates began a slow decline (Glick 1984). For some social scientists the converging rates of marriage and divorce heralded the impending demise of the American family. Doom and gloom prophesying was enhanced by the fact that divorce was seen as being most prevalent among those potentially least protected from its impact: the young, minorities and the impoverished.

More recent U.S. figures reveal inconsistencies in demographic patterns. Marriage rates began to climb once again by the late 1970s but then resumed a gradual decline. The corresponding figures for divorce have vacillated back and forth. Most recently, from 1983 through 1990, the trend has been in the downward direction. During this period, the divorce rate per thousand population dropped from approximately 5.1 to 4.7 (National Center for Health Statistics 1990). Despite these fluctuations, the incidence of divorce remains high. Estimates are that 1,163,000 couples, or well over two million persons, divorced during 1989 (National Center for Health Statistics 1990). If one takes into consideration the children and the parents of divorcing persons, it is reasonable to assume that over six million persons were directly affected by divorce during that single year.

Today the future of marriage and the family looks modestly optimistic.

Using 1985 data from the U.S. Bureau of the Census, Arthur Norton and Jeanne Moorman (1987) report evidence that lifelong probabilities of divorce will reach their peak with the cohort currently in their thirties, and may have already begun to wane. Looking just at the figures for women in the last five years of each decade (e.g., 25–29, 35–39), Norton and Moorman report that of those in their thirties, approximately 56% will divorce at some point in their lives. In contrast, women in their twenties have a slightly—but encouragingly—lower 54% probability of divorce. Rates are also lower for those in middle and later ages: it is 36% for women in their forties and 24% for women in their fifties.

Regardless of whether there is reason to be more or less optimistic about the fate of the American family, the fact remains that many millions of lives are touched each year by divorce. Current estimates are that one out of every five families with children under age 18 is headed by a single parent (Taeuber and Valdisera 1986). Moreover, the fluctuations in the rate of marriage and divorce inform us that the social fabric of adult life is gradually changing, and that a variety of patterns may be emerging within American society. For example, notwithstanding the peaking of divorce rates, we are witnessing a steady increase in the overall number of adults who are divorced. In the long run, the prevalence of divorced persons may have social fallout such as greater numbers of older adults without social supports, or greater numbers of people who find it harder to play a care-giving role to both younger and older generations. There is, for example, evidence that divorce may interfere with the support provided by adult children to dependent parents (Cicirelli 1983).

ORIGINS OF OUR STUDY

A Social Condition of Need

In the late 1970s the social phenomenon of divorce was relatively understudied, although the research of Waller (1930), Goode (1956) and Hetherington, Cox and Cox (1976) had emphasized the significance of the area and the more clinically oriented work of Krantzler (1973) and Weiss (1975) had demonstrated the need for clinical intervention. It was rapidly becoming clear that divorce affected the lives of many people. In 1976 over three million persons, or roughly 1.5% of the population, were directly involved in dissolution of a marriage (Bloom, Asher and White 1978); 14% of the adult population had at one time been divorced (Norton and Glick 1979). Divorce emerged from these statistical descriptions as an increasingly accepted alternative to an unhappy marriage. The total number of Americans contending with the effects of marital dissolution, including spouses, children and those relatives and friends indirectly affected (Hetherington, Cox and Cox 1976), was projected to run into the millions.

THE LONGITUDINAL STUDY OF DIVORCE

In 1977, a multidisciplinary team of researchers began the first wave of interviews for what was to become known as the Longitudinal Study of Divorce. Data were collected on 333 persons who had recently filed for divorce in San Francisco and Alameda counties, California. The main thesis outlined by our study was that during the period immediately following separation, an individual could undergo either or both psychological growth and psychological dysfunction. Of particular interest were the personal and social characteristics associated with adjustment and maladjustment to separation.

One very important decision we had to make at the very beginning was at what points in the divorce process respondents should be interviewed. Prior research (Chiriboga 1972; Lazarus 1966) had suggested that psychological disruption during the months immediately following a stressful event such as marital separation, while important, might not correspond directly to how individuals function in the long run. Therefore, the study design called for interviews to be conducted during the period immediately after separation (up to eight months) and in the long run (defined for convenience as between three and four years following separation).

By 1980 the research team was ready to begin a follow-up of the original participants. In this follow-up, conducted approximately three and a half years after the initial interviews, two lines of inquiry were emphasized: (1) identification of persons standing at long-term risk and (2) clarification of the stressors, mediators and responses to the divorce process. We were interested in determining where people ended up after they had gone through an experience like divorce.

Sample Selection Procedures

We drew a random sample of potential respondents from records of persons who had filed petitions for divorce at the county clerk offices in San Fran-

cisco and Alameda counties, California. An individual's eligibility for participation in the study was based on the following criteria:

1. Separated from spouse and engaged in the legal process of divorce.
2. Married for more than one year and over the age of 20.
3. Separated for a period no greater than eight months.
4. Spouse not a participant. Only one person of a divorcing couple could
   participate in the study; when both spouses were randomly drawn, one
   was selected by random assignment.

Although these inclusion criteria were followed in subject screening, due to
inaccuracies in court records, 23 persons with separations longer than eight
months were contacted and interviewed; these subjects were eliminated from
analyses focused on the initial stages of divorce.

Of those potentially available, 18% were unreachable by mail or phone,
18% either refused outright or were unable to participate when requested,
and 64% agreed to participate. In actual numbers, this amounted to 333
men and women.

Follow-up. Tracking people over three and a half years can be hard, especially when they are in the throes of a divorce. In spite of this, we were able
to find and interview approximately 85% of the original sample at follow-up.
Thus, 283 of the original 333 individuals comprised the sample at follow-up.
Of the remaining 15%, 9% refused and 6% could not be located.

Description of the Sample

The 199 women and 134 men we interviewed ranged in age from 20 to 79,
with 75% being under 40 years of age. It was the first marriage for three-
quarters of the sample; about half had been married between 5 and 19 years.
Approximately 40% had no children and 40% had one or two children. The
average length of separation was six months at the time of contact.

The sample was reasonably well-educated, with over half having attended
at least one year of college. Examination of sex differences showed that a
greater percentage of the men were highly educated. More men reported
incomes of $10,000 and over compared with the females in the sample.
These differences are similar to what one would expect in the U.S. population as a whole.

Follow-up. Three and a half years after the initial interviews, a 66% majority (188 people) had divorced but not remarried. Twenty-one percent were remarried and 4% (10 people) had reconciled. Some differences were found when this distribution was broken down into different age-groups. For example, a greater percent of men aged 50 and over had remarried compared to women of the same age: 20% versus 15%. In general, however, sex differences in marital status at follow-up were not marked.

Interviewing Procedure

Baseline data collection occurred between April 1, 1976 and May 31, 1977. Addresses and phone numbers of the respondents were obtained from records at the county clerk offices. Respondents were sent a letter about the Divorce Study, informing them that a staff member would contact them within a week. If the interviewer was unable to reach the respondent by telephone, a second letter was sent requesting that they fill out a card and return it to the Divorce staff. The interviews were held at a location chosen by the respondent; the majority were held at the respondent's home, place of work, or an office at the University of California. All interviewers were trained by the staff and evaluated prior to starting their job. The interview contact proceeded in two stages. During the first stage, the intent of the interview, and the areas covered, were explained. The respondents were then asked to read the Experimental Subject's Bill of Rights and Consent Form which they had to sign before the interview began. The second stage was the actual interviewing: each interview took approximately three hours and consisted of structured and unstructured questions. A few of the interviews were done by mail when there were no other options.

Follow-up. The follow-up procedure was very similar to that at baseline. The interview took approximately three hours and also consisted of structured and unstructured questions, many of which duplicated those from the first interview. Procedural standards were the same in every other respect as those at baseline.

Instruments

The items for the baseline interview were developed through consultations with the staff of the California Divorce Law Research Project (Dr. Weitzman), the Divorce Project (Drs. Wallerstein and Kelly), the Life Events and Adaptation in Adulthood Project (Drs. Pearlin and Lieberman), and the Divorce, Role, Health Status and Service Systems Project (Drs. Sussman and Kitson). Reviews of existing studies on divorce and stress also influenced the selection of items. Decisions on the content of the interview were based on a desire to enhance the potential for generalizing from the findings as well as to facilitate collaboration with other ongoing projects in the Human Development and Aging Program at the University of California, San Francisco.

The main topics covered in the interview were: demographic, life before separation, the divorce process, relationships, physical health, mental health, goals, activities, time perspectives, stress and coping, and emotional well-being. The instruments used in the interview included several that also were used in the companion study of normative transitions (Lowenthal et al. 1975; Fiske and Chiriboga 1990): the Adjective Rating Scale (adapted from Block 1961), the Goal Sort, the Life Events Questionnaire (developed in collaboration with Drs. Mardi Horowitz and Richard Rahe), the California Symptoms Checklist (developed in collaboration with Drs. Robert Butler and Alexander Simon), the Life Evaluation Chart (adapted from an instrument originally developed by Jean MacFarlane), the Leisure Query, Activities Checklist and Bradburn (1969) Morale Scales.

In addition to the instruments that overlapped with those in the companion study, we concluded a number of instruments drawn from other studies of divorce or similar life crises, such as the Social Supports Schedule (adapted from the work of Pearlin and Lieberman), and Kitson and Sussman's modification of Goode's (1956) Trauma Index.

Follow-up Interview. The follow-up interview was very similar to the first interview. Many of the additional questions and instruments were drawn from other studies in order to facilitate cross-study comparisons in the future. Materials were drawn from the following projects: the Cleveland Divorce Study (Case Western Reserve: Kitson and Sussman), the Separation and Divorce Study (Pennsylvania State University: Spanier), Stress and Coping Study (University of California, Berkeley: Lazarus), Divorced Family Systems (Northwestern University: Goldsmith and Ahrons), Divorced Mothers Project (Donahue and Colletta), and the Family Mediation Research Project (University of Georgia: Weber). In addition to specific questions, the following structured instruments were added to the follow-up interview: the Ways of Coping Inventory (Lazarus and Folkman 1984), Hassles Index (based on the work of Lazarus), and Self-Other Semantic Differential (based on the work of Osgood).

A COMPARISON GROUP: THE LONGITUDINAL STUDY OF TRANSITIONS

The Divorce Study originally began as a counterpart to another longitudinal study that focused on the impact of normative transitions. The Longitudinal Study of Transitions, led by Professor Marjorie Fiske, examined how people adapt to the normative crises and challenges that are associated with different stages of life. It included a sample of men and women aged 16 to 65 at their first interviews in 1969 and 1970.

The longitudinal study consisted of 216 subjects drawn from the San Francisco Bay Area, the same geographic locale as subjects in the Divorce Study. This was essentially a purposive sample, although it was grounded in a probability sampling approach (Fiske and Chiriboga 1990). Four groups were selected for study, each of which could be expected to undergo one or more normative transitions within three to four years: high school seniors facing challenges of entering the adult world, newlyweds facing issues revolving around parenthood, middle-aged parents whose youngest child was a high school senior who presumably would be leaving the home, and late middle-agers facing retirement. Gender and ages of participants were as follows:

- 25 high school males aged 16–18
- 27 high school females aged 17–18
- 25 newlywed males aged 21–38
- 25 newlywed females aged 20–34
- 27 empty nest males aged 44–61
- 27 empty nest females aged 39–57
- 30 pre-retirement males aged 53–65
- 30 pre-retirement females aged 45–67

Interviewing began in late 1968 and continued until late 1980, at which point the 168 remaining participants had each been interviewed at five points in time. The retention rate of about 78% over 12 years of study reflects a high level of commitment to the project on the part of the respondents. If we discount the 18 who died during the course of study, the retention rate was actually about 85%. There was little or no evidence of any bias in who did not complete the study; dropouts did not differ in mental health, sociodemographic characteristics, self-image or stress exposure (Fiske and Chiriboga 1990).

Transitions Study as a Comparison Group

From its very beginning, the Divorce Study was designed to build on the findings of the Transitions Study. This was because in many ways the transition of divorce presents itself as an appealing contrast to more normative transitions. Unlike normative transitions, divorce can occur at any age and is much less of an expected event. Perhaps more importantly, like normative transitions, divorce can also be viewed as a stress condition of major significance.

Over several years of study, the research team of the Transitions Study began to realize that no matter how major the changes involved in a normative transition, the more or less expectable nature of these changes acts as a buffering or protective factor (Lowenthal et al. 1975; Fiske and Chiriboga 1990). This realization was the inspiration for the second study, and the reason that a substantial overlap in instrumentation was built into the Divorce Study.

Whenever we compare Divorce and Transitions Study participants in this book, we use a subset of Transitions participants who were not themselves in the throes of marital separation or divorced. Comparison between the two samples on a variety of sociodemographic factors indicated little difference, save that the Divorce Study included more persons from minority groups, and women in the Divorce Study reported significantly lower family incomes than did women in the Transitions Study. However, income levels for life prior to the marital separation were comparable to those reported by Transitions Study women.

Since the Divorce Study began when the Transitions Study had already been in the data collection phase for about seven years, we had to decide at what two contact points the groups should be compared. After some deliberation, we selected the second- and five-year contact points from the Transitions Study, since the time interval approximated that for the Divorce Study, and because during this time interval most Transitions Study participants were themselves experiencing normative transitions.

IN ANTICIPATION

In the chapters that follow we shall address a series of issues and questions related to stress and adaptation that our research suggests may underlie much of what happens in marital separation and divorce. In each chapter we also try to identify risk factors and what might be called benefit factors: things that help and things that hinder working through the problems created by divorce. One common theme is that the risk and benefit factors associated with adaptation during the impact phase of divorce, immediately following marital separation, are often different from those associated with adaptation in the long run.

Most of our findings are based on statistical procedures such as regression analysis, discriminant analysis and multivariate analysis of variance. To make our results more accessible, we have minimized the intrusion of technical aspects of these analyses. One convention we followed was to avoid putting in information such as probability levels, F ratios and the like. Instead, we will generally say that something was significant or at a trend level. We also bring to each chapter two or three case histories to highlight some of the major points raised in the chapter. These cases were selected essentially by computer: we sorted out people on variables identified as critical and then took the cases that best fit the model.

I

STRESS AND ADAPTATION

2

CHILDHOOD STRESS AND ADAPTATION TO DIVORCE: A SHAPING CONDITION

Linda S. Catron and David A. Chiriboga

In this chapter we consider the first of the questions that form the focus of this book. This question concerns whether or not early childhood experiences affect how an adult functions during a divorce: there is evidence that early losses may set the stage for a heightened response to losses that are experienced later in life. In other words, childhood stress may represent a risk factor.

From a historical perspective, interest in the long-term influence of childhood experiences is relatively recent. Probably the earliest discussion can be found in Freud's ([1933] 1964) theory of psychosexual development, which called attention to the implications of earlier experiences for subsequent development. He later made the bold statement that "the child is psychologically father to the adult" (Freud [1938] (1969), 18) and went on to suggest that the first year of life is of most importance in later development. Following Freud's lead, the view emerged "that early experiences strongly influence the entire course of human development" (Kagan 1980, 12). The basic hypothesis is that stressful conditions experienced in childhood may lead people to overreact to losses experienced as an adult (e.g., Brown and Harris 1989; Lester and Beck 1979).

A thorough search of the literature failed to locate any study other than our own that dealt specifically with the relationship between childhood stress and adaptation to divorce. There is, however, a vast array of studies, primarily based on retrospective data, about the general influence of childhood stress. Given the importance of retrospective data, we will begin with a general presentation of problems related to its use. We next suggest some of the ways in which childhood stressors, especially losses, may affect the adult years. We also discuss measurement problems, and then describe how childhood stress was measured in our study and what we found. In addition to some rather clear-cut evidence in favor of the child's experiences shaping the adult, results also point to the utility and reliability of what turns out to be a rather short and simple information tool: the Childhood Stress Inventory.

RETROSPECTIVE ANALYSES: ISSUES AND PROBLEMS

Although a few prospective studies extend from childhood to adulthood, only one has considered the long-term influence of childhood exposure to stress. This study assessed the implications for adult functioning of going through the Great Depression of the late 1920s and early 1930s. Drawing upon data from the Berkeley longitudinal studies, the basic finding was that the Depression did indeed exert a long-term impact (Elder 1978).

Given how time-consuming a longitudinal study must be, the majority of researchers interested in the implications of childhood stress for adulthood have resorted to retrospective studies. These fall victim to a host of methodological problems related to the use of retrospective techniques, including principally the potential for biased recall (see Mechanic 1974; Dohrenwend 1973; Rabkin and Streuning 1976; Pearlin and Lieberman 1979). In spite of methodological problems, it sometimes may be necessary to employ retrospective studies. As Yarrow, Campbell and Burton (1970, 74) have pointed out:

New, sometimes unanticipated questions demand answers; and the information required for such answers is not always available in current knowledge. In such circumstances it is often expedient to turn to the retrospective method as a means for approximating quickly the data needed.

Support for the use of retrospective data comes from a host of reliability and validity studies. These studies compared retrospective reports with public documents, sought validating information from friends and relatives, used the test-retest method, and compared retrospective with prospective reports. From this empirical research has emerged one finding that is particularly striking: the reliability of retrospective data is more affected by errors of omission than commission. As applied to the case of childhood stress, the implication is that people would be more likely to forget to mention such experiences than they would be to invent them.

This tendency towards errors of omission suggests that what people do report is likely to be valid. For example, in an article titled "Life Changes—Do People Really Remember?" Jenkins, Hurst and Rose (1979) examined life changes reported on one occasion and then recalled nine months later. While 17% of the men added new life events during the second interview, 63% forgot previously reported life events. Similarly, on the basis of his clinical experience, Bowlby (personal communication 1983) also reports that adults tend to make errors of omission rather than commission in their retrospective accounts of childhood experiences. Without such errors of omission, the statistical relationship between childhood stress and adult outcome would be much stronger (Steele, Henderson and Duncan-Jones 1980).

THE LITERATURE ON CHILDHOOD STRESS AND ADULT ADAPTATION

An underlying premise of much research is that childhood stress may predispose an individual to overreact to subsequent loss experiences. The literature on the sensitizing influence of childhood stressors is vast and we will not attempt to cover it completely. Instead we will cover three topics relevant to our own work: the difference between presumed and perceived childhood stressors, the sensitizing influence of childhood stress on adult social relationships, and the possibility of a strengthening or "steeling" effect of childhood stress.

Presumed and Perceived Childhood Stress

Stressful conditions can be subdivided into those that the researcher presumes to be stressful, on the basis usually of face validity, and those that are perceived by respondents to be stressful. Much of the literature deals with presumed childhood stress. This by definition consists of events that are fairly easy to recognize and ones most people would agree are stressful, including parental death, divorce, desertion, and severe punishment.

Studies of presumed events may focus on a single major event or problem, such as death of a parent, or may consider the effects of multiple events. In one study of psychiatric disorder among ten-year-old children, six antecedent variables were identified: (1) marital conflict, (2) lower socioeconomic status, (3) large families and/or overcrowding, (4) father a criminal, (5) mother suffering from psychiatric disorder, and (6) appointment of a legal guardian. Children from families that had only one risk factor or an isolated stress were no more likely to develop childhood psychiatric disorders than were children from families with no risk factors. However, the presence of two or more risk factors caused the rate of psychiatric disorder to increase exponentially (Rutter 1977).

Perceived Childhood Stress. Studies of perceived childhood stress deal with the degree to which subjects retrospectively or prospectively perceive their childhoods as being stressful, regardless of the number of life events or chronic stressors reported. Such studies are extremely rare, despite the fact that research with adults has emphasized the importance of the individual's subjective appraisal of the stressfulness of events and experiences (e.g., Lazarus and Folkman 1984; Hobfoll 1988). About all that is known is that individuals vary in whether they evaluate the same kind of childhood events as benign, positive, threatening, or harmful (Rutter 1981).

Childhood Stress and Adult Attachments

Childhood stress may affect adult adaptation indirectly through disruption of attachments. It has been suggested that disruption of social bonds as a child influences relationships in later life. Bowlby (1977), for example, delineated three maladaptive patterns of social supports during adulthood that he believes are derived from disruptions of attachment in childhood. He calls these maladaptive patterns compulsive self-reliance, compulsive care giving, and compulsive support seeking.

The compulsively self-reliant consciously or unconsciously attempt to avoid attachments in adulthood because of parental rejection of earlier attempts to form a secure attachment. In addition, they may avoid attachments in order "to avoid being subjected to pressure to become someone else's caretaker" (Bowlby 1977, 207). Although the compulsively self-reliant have difficulties developing attachments in adulthood, they may be successful in science or business (Bowlby, personal communication 1983).

The compulsive care givers form many close relationships but are always in the role of providing rather than receiving care. As a child, compulsive care givers may have had a disabled or depressed mother who was unable to take care of the child, but instead demanded that she herself be cared for (Bowlby 1977). In some sense, people in this category may not know how to ask for, or receive, help.

Like compulsive care givers, *compulsive support seekers* also develop many relationships but they are in constant need of support. According to Bowlby (personal communication 1983), there may be an important sex difference, with compulsively self-reliant persons more likely to be male and compulsive support seekers and care givers more likely to be female.

Of particular relevance to these compulsive support seekers and care givers are their problems in relation to marital partners: "A person may exhibit anxious attachment and make constant demands for love and care; or else he or she may exhibit compulsive care giving to the other with latent resentment that it seems neither appreciated nor reciprocated" (Bowlby 1977, 208).

Other studies indicate that childhood stress may lead to emotional withdrawal, inability or lack of interest in forming close ties. Kitson (1982) reports evidence to this effect, adding that the impaired ability to become attached and to remain attached may be a major cause of marital disruption. On the other hand, in a 35-year prospective investigation of 95 men, Vaillant (1978) found that a poor childhood environment predicted poor object relations in adult life but not poor marital relationships. In fact, Vaillant (1978, 657) found that "in many men marriage served as a means of mastering unhappy childhoods."

Positive Consequences of Childhood Stress

While most studies have focused on the destructive rather than the strengthening potential of childhood stress, a few investigations have examined the positive potential. The literature suggests at least two positive consequences of stress: (1) increased competence and improved coping, and (2) a reduction in the perceived stressfulness of subsequent events.

Increased Competence and Coping. Although rare, studies do exist that suggest a possible growth-promoting effect of certain kinds of stress during childhood, especially with regard to mastering threatening events, developing a sense of competence and more effective use of social supports (e.g., Murphy and Associates 1962; White 1959, 1979). The outcome of a stress experience can also influence whether or not the child's competence and coping ability are improved or debilitated:

Presumably it matters whether the child emerges successfully from the first stress with improved coping mechanisms, enhanced self-esteem or a more effective physiological response. If he does, he may become more stress-resistant. On the other hand, if he is left distraught, unable to cope, or physiologically impaired by the first stress, he may instead become more vulnerable. (Rutter 1979, 810)

Among children, the overwhelming and the growth-promoting influences of parental divorce may coexist:

This persistent underlying sadness, combined with early self-reliance and early entry into the next developmental stage, seemed to have important implications for character development, including particularly self-concept and relationships with adults and peers. (Wallerstein 1978, 39)

Positive role models may also counteract childhood stress. There is evidence for an increased competence among girls, but not boys, from families that suffered major economic reverses during the Great Depression. Citing changes in family relations caused by the father's loss of earnings and a compensatory reliance on the mother's labor and earnings, Elder (1981, 19) notes that the mother provided a strong role model for her daughter. In consequence:

girls from deprived families displayed the competence that so many of their mothers exemplified in jobs and household management; these girls were more goal oriented, self-adequate, and assertive than those from nondeprived homes.

Decreased Stressfulness of Later Events. Under certain conditions childhood stress may lead an individual to perceive later stressors as less threatening. Persson (1980) gave an inventory of current life events questionnaire to older men and women and compared the responses of those who had lost a parent before the age of sixteen due to death versus those who had grown up with both parents. There were no significant differences in the evaluations of women. However, compared to the nonbereaved, men who had lost a parent in early life provided significantly lower evaluations of distress related to current life events. These results suggest a strengthening or steeling effect of certain childhood stressors. Similarly, Bornstein et al. (1973) found that prior experience with death of a family member was related to decreased vulnerability to depression in widowhood.

A METHODOLOGY TO STUDY CHILDHOOD STRESS AND ADAPTATION TO DIVORCE

The virtual absence of studies dealing with childhood stress and adaptation to divorce left us more or less in the role of explorers. We questioned participants concerning early life events, with the underlying hypothesis that childhood stress predicts psychological functioning during both short- and long-term phases of divorce. Our rationale was that sensitizing effects might be operating during the impact phase of the divorce process. However, we also suspected that the more enduring relationship with impaired psychological functioning might become evident during the long-term follow-up, when individuals would be operating on a more "normal" level.

Baseline Measures of Childhood Stress

Our analyses included two measures of childhood stress, one dealing with presumed and the other with perceived stress. These measures were drawn from a Childhood Stress Inventory and a Life Evaluation Chart, both of which take approximately 15 minutes to administer.

Perceived Childhood Stress. The measure of perceived childhood stress was drawn from the Life Evaluation Chart originally developed by Jean Mac-Farlane and modified by Lowenthal et al. (1975). In the Divorce Study, the Life Evaluation Chart consists of respondents' ratings of satisfaction with each year of their life and their projections for future years on a scale from 0 ("rock bottom") to 9 ("top of the world"). The measure of perceived childhood stress consists of an average of each respondent's ratings for years 1 through 13. The measure of perceived childhood stress was computed to the thirteenth year in order to be in keeping with the years covered by the instrument assessing presumed childhood stress (see below). The three-year test-retest correlation of the measure was .41 for women and .53 for men. Although these correlations are highly significant, the reliability must be judged as moderate rather than high.

Presumed Childhood Stress. Our measure of presumed childhood stress was created from a much longer instrument, the 138-item Life Events Questionnaire (Chiriboga 1989). The measure of presumed stress consists of the sum of the respondents' retrospective reports of the occurrence of the following 12 events: (1) a long separation from parents when under 13 years of age, (2) separation on bad terms from parents or brothers and sisters, (3) finding out that one was adopted, (4) intense arguments between one's parents, (5) intense arguments with one's parents, (6) severe or unusual punishment, (7) divorce of one's parents, (8) remarriage of one's father or mother, (9) separation from one's father or mother due to death or divorce, (10) the frequent absence of one's mother or father, (11) the death of one's father or mother, (12) the death of one's brother or sister.

The respondents checked off each of the events experienced. The range of reported events went from 0 to 9, with 34.9% of the sample having experienced none of the individual childhood stresses. Most frequently reported were intense arguments with parents (29%) and between parents (29%), the frequent absence of a parent (18%) and parental divorce (17%). There are no significant age or sex differences on the summary measure. Internal (alpha) reliability of this measure was .70, a minimally acceptable level for exploratory research (Nunnally 1967). It was not possible to examine the test-retest reliability of the presumed childhood stress measure using Divorce Study data because the childhood section of the Life Events Questionnaire was inadvertently omitted from the follow-up interview. However, data for two points in time were available for seven of the same items in our companion study of normative transitions. Computed over a two-and-a-half-year period of time, test-retest correlations were significant: .54 for men and .79 for women. Like similar correlations for the perceived stress measure, these results indicate a moderate stability over time.

Interplay of Perceived and Presumed Childhood Stress. Of particular interest to this study was the interplay between perceived and presumed childhood stress. The correlation between perceived and presumed childhood stress was .29 ($p < .00$) for women, and .14 ($p < .10$) for men, indicating that persons, especially women, who reported more presumed childhood stresses are more likely to evaluate their childhood years negatively. While the association reached significant levels for women, the magnitude of both correlations is not particularly high, indicating that the two measures are only minimally related for men and women.

To examine presumed and perceived stress a bit further, we used interactive terms in the regression analyses. Effectively this produces what can be thought of as fourfold table which we labeled as follows: the Overwhelmed (high presumed, high perceived), the Challenged (high presumed, low perceived), the Self-Defeated (low presumed, high perceived), and the Lucky (low presumed, low perceived). No significant differences were found by age and gender for this interaction term. By way of preview, the interaction term did not predict symptoms and will not be discussed any further in this chapter. However, the interaction predicted one aspect of transitional status for men, as will be discussed in chapter 4.

CHILDHOOD STRESSORS: EMPIRICAL FINDINGS FROM THE STUDY

The keystone of our statistical approach was a type of statistic called hierarchical set multiple regression analyses. This allowed us to look at how well each of several sets of measures helped in prediction of the number of psychological symptoms reported by participants at each of the two contacts. The following sets of measures were put into the analysis, one after the other: (1) the two measures of perceived and presumed childhood stress, (2) the interaction of presumed and perceived childhood stress, and (3) demographic variables, including age, income, education, whether participants were working or not, number of children, religiosity, and whether participants belonged to any ethnic or national group.

In a third analysis focusing solely on the prediction of change in adaptation, we added a fourth predictive set. This set consisted of baseline psychological symptoms, and actually was included before any other measures in order to control for the influence of initial status upon subsequent psychological functioning. By removing the effect of initial status, what was left in the measure of symptoms at follow-up was the change from the first interview in the number of symptoms.

The Prediction of Baseline Adaptation

For Men. The analysis for men predicted an overall 10% of the variance in symptoms. In other words we were able to better understand a part, but only a relatively small part, of symptom expression. The set of childhood measures made the only significant contribution, explaining 5% of the variance. Of the two childhood measures, perceived childhood stress was the only one with a significant association. Results indicated that men who evaluated their childhood years negatively reported significantly more psychological symptoms at baseline.

For Women. The overall amount of variance predicted for women, at 9%, was roughly equal to that found in the results for men. In contrast to the results for the men, however, the childhood measures did not predict psychological symptoms. The only finding of any consequence was a tendency for more educated women to report fewer symptoms.

The Prediction of Adaptation at Follow-up

The intent of follow-up analyses was to discern whether baseline measures of presumed and perceived childhood stress predict adaptation approximately three and a half years later.

For Men. The three steps of the multiple regression analysis for men at follow-up predicted 14% of the variance. As was the case for the prediction of symptoms count during the impact phase of divorce, only the childhood measures significantly predicted follow-up symptoms for men. The childhood stress measures as a set explained 7% of the variance. Although the simple correlations with symptoms were significant for both measures of stress, only the presumed childhood stress variable significantly contributed to the set's prediction of symptoms. Results indicated that men who reported more childhood life events when interviewed at baseline were more likely to have numerous psychological symptoms at follow-up. Note that at baseline it was *perceived* childhood stress that predicted symptoms for men, while at follow-up the predictor was *presumed* childhood stresses.

For Women. The regression analysis for the women at follow-up predicted 10% of the variance. Paralleling results for baseline symptoms, neither the set of childhood measures nor their interaction significantly predicted adaptation for women. However, education was not associated with long-term symptomatology. Instead, women who reported themselves to belong to some ethnic or national group, and women with lower incomes, reported more symptoms.

The Prediction of Change in Adaptive Status from Baseline to Follow-up

When we looked at what predicted follow-up adaptive status in the last section we were primarily concerned with whether the same variables were important at both the impact and long-term phases of divorce. However, the analyses did not really cover change in adaptive status from baseline to follow-up. In order to measure change, we entered baseline symptoms status into the prediction equation first. What this did was basically remove the influence of baseline psychological symptoms; what remained of the follow-up symptoms data was change from time one to time two.

For Men. Not surprisingly, the predictive equation was strengthened by the addition of baseline status on symptoms. The overall equation accounted for 38% of the variance in follow-up symptoms, of which 28% could be attributed to initial symptom level. After entering symptoms as expressed at the impact phase of divorce, the measures of childhood stresses continued to make an independent and significant prediction of psychological symptoms at follow-up. These measures explained 5% of the variance. Both presumed childhood stress and perceived childhood stress made independent contributions to the sets' prediction of symptoms. What these results tell us is that, even with the effect of baseline psychological symptoms controlled, the childhood measures as a set remain predictive of difficulties in long-term adaptation to divorce. Thus, presumed and perceived childhood stress has an enduring and chronic influence on men's adaptation. None of the other sets significantly predicted follow-up adaptation.

For Women. Fifty percent of the variance was accounted for by the three sets, with 45% attributable to initial symptom level. After entering symptoms level from baseline, neither childhood measures nor their interaction significantly predicted follow-up psychological symptoms for women. This finding further confirms the sex difference in the influence of childhood stresses on adaptation to divorce. Income and ethnic identity continued to make a significant contribution.

Some Alternative Combinations of Presumed Stress Items

In the main analyses we used a summary measure of presumed stress, but we also considered alternative groupings of the 12 individual items that made up the measure of presumed stress. Several of these alternatives provided additional insights into the possible role of childhood stressors, but here we will discuss what happened with just one. For this one alternative we grouped the 12 items according to how strongly they correlated with each other. Three subscales were obtained. The first dealt with separations and divorce: it included parental divorce, and separations from parents due to divorce or death, or a parent's remarriage or absent father or mother. The second dealt with family discord and consisted of arguments with parents, arguments between parents, severe and unusual punishment and separations on bad terms from parents or siblings. The third dealt with deaths and was composed of parent's death and death of a sibling.

When we substituted these new variables in place of the summary measure of presumed stress, we found as before that the measures did not predict symptoms for women. For men the new set accounted for 6% of the variance in baseline symptoms and a surprising 13% of the variance in symptoms at follow-up. For the baseline analysis, perceived stress continued to play a role but now we find an interesting twist: men experiencing the death of a parent and/or a sibling in childhood are reporting significantly *fewer* symptoms. At follow-up the results are even more interesting. All three subscales contribute significantly, with family discord and separations and divorce being associated with greater symptomatology. However, once again, the deaths subscale is associated with less symptomatology.

These results deserve attention, especially because the use of subscales led to an increase from 7% to 13% in the amount of explained variance at follow-up. One explanation is that different kinds of childhood stress may result in different consequences, some leading to a sensitizing effect and some to a "steeling" or hardiness factor. Combining these divergent types into a single summary score weakens the strength of association, since the individual items pull in opposite directions.

CASE STUDIES

The results of this childhood stress chapter will be highlighted by cases of people with varying degrees of presumed and perceived childhood stress. The first two cases, both men, illustrate the sensitizing and the strengthening influence of childhood stress on adaptation to divorce as measured by baseline and follow-up psychological symptoms. Maladaptive patterns of attachment evident in these men will also be discussed. In the third case we consider the relationship between a woman's exposure to childhood stress and subsequent maladaptive patterns of adult attachment.

Nate Cole: The Sensitizing Influence of Childhood Stress

Nate is an extremely attractive man of medium height, trim and tanned. He resembles Robert Redford, with his headful of blond hair and thick reddish mustache. A 46-year-old manager for a large discount department store, Nate has just ended his third marriage, a marriage that lasted 12 years. His first marriage lasted eight years and they had three children, his next marriage lasted for about a year. Nate's past reveals a troubled childhood; he reports six presumed childhood stresses, including long separations from parents when under 13, parental divorce and remarriage, and the frequent absence of mother or father. He also has perceived childhood stress since his Life Evaluation Chart plummets from absolute tops to very low during his first 13 years.

For Nate, childhood was the loneliest period of his life. "As a young boy growing up, my mother and father were separated," he explains, "my mother was working hard and having to support me, and I was left with various aunts and only saw my mother occasionally. My brother got to live with my father." Loneliness for Nate means "being very alone . . . *nobody* cares."

As we move to the present, we find that not only does Nate report considerable childhood stress but he does not seem to be handling the challenges of divorce all that well: he is far above the average on symptoms during both the impact and long-term contact points. He also seems to have a long-standing inability to form lasting commitments to people, a factor that induces loneliness.

Nate believes that the "only way to combat that is to get out and meet people and then it [loneliness] doesn't exist anymore." "As long as I'm alone . . . I don't know how to entertain myself (or I didn't at that time—as a boy) —and it's still true today. I couldn't come home and cook dinner for myself. I don't care to do too many things alone except read a book." When asked if he has ever lived alone, Nate replied, "only for very short periods of time. Actually, I've never really lived alone for any period of time. I couldn't handle it. That's the reason for so many marriages and broken relationships."

Nate seems to have certain maladaptive patterns of attachment. With his third and last wife, he portrays himself as being a compulsive support giver. On the other hand, his obsession with dating, his multiple marriages, divorces and advice seeking all suggest a compulsive support seeker. Evidence of his compulsive support giving is in Nate's description of his wife: "She's in crisis all the time . . . I married her out of obligation, I felt sorry for her . . . she needed somebody, but it's over now . . . the more I help her, the less she can help herself . . . I have to let her go . . . it feels like dealing with a child." When asked how often he thinks about his spouse, Nate provided additional information: "Only when she calls . . . I feel sorry for her . . . have nothing but pity for her . . . I have to fight taking her back . . . but she has to handle it on her own."

Nate's compulsive support seeking can be seen in his relentless search for women. Next to playing golf, "Finding and conquering a woman" is his second most favorite thing to do. When the interviewer probed about this, Nate said: "That it works—satisfaction—as my psychiatrist used to say, the Don Juan complex has been accomplished." The interviewer noted this: "Nate mentioned several times during the interview that he really likes pursuing women and that it is a problem because he always wants to marry them, and that at first everything is perfect but then he starts looking for faults."

Relevant to this description of his dating patterns is what Nate confided about sex: "I want to satisfy the person I'm with . . . hopefully I can be satisfied with them. In new relationships, it's no problem, but as they [the relationships] linger, it becomes a problem." With sex being satisfying during the initial phases of a relationship, this further propels Nate's search for women.

When asked if he was currently dating anyone, Nate said: "I first started going with 9–10 women with varied personalities. I've narrowed it down. Now I'm seeing one woman four days a week and I spend the other three days a week seeing what's available, what I am missing." About a woman he has been dating for six months he said: "I like the warmth. I like the way I have no problems with her. I like that she cooks for me without me asking her to. I like to play golf all day and that suits her fine. I like the way she caters to me. I feel guilty, too. I'm afraid it's too good, and I'll give up looking for other women. I am too controlled already without even realizing it."

By follow-up, Nate has married the woman he described in most detail at the first interview and is involved in playing golf and in spending time with his wife. Asked how this marriage differs from his previous one, he said: "There is love and understanding and communication." In fact, he said that his most important goal is to "improve on the relationship with my wife and grow closer together."

Certainly the abandonment and losses from childhood have had a lasting influence on Nate. His psychological symptoms are still high at follow-up, but down to 8 from the 12 at baseline. His scores on perceived childhood stress still plummet at follow-up but not quite as sharply. We hope this fourth marriage will last and will not dissolve, propelling him into another relentless search for the absent mother—and father—in his childhood. Hopefully this new marriage will ameliorate some of the feelings of loss and abandonment he still has from his childhood, but we have our doubts.

Ben Bennett: Childhood Stress as a Strengthening Influence

Ben Bennett, a 45-year-old architect, is in the process of divorcing his second wife. "We were living separate lives and both wanted more privacy," he says as an explanation for the breakup of a marriage that had lasted 20 years. "We had been going our own way for four years."

Ben is an aristocratic-looking, silver-haired man; when we first meet he is wearing glasses and a light blue, short-sleeved shirt open to reveal a healthy suntan. The interview took place in the kitchen overlooking the garden. He was friendly and introduced the interviewer to one of his dogs—an overstuffed dachshund.

Ben tells the interviewer that he experienced seven out of the 12 presumed childhood stresses, including: intense arguments between parents, long separations from parents, parental divorce, remarriage, death of father or mother, severe and unusual punishment, and having to go to work to support the family. Paralleling these presumed stresses, Ben's baseline perceived stress score plummeted to 2.5, "very low" satisfaction with life, following his tenth birthday. This perceived childhood stress in combination with seven presumed childhood stresses has resulted in Ben having one of the highest levels of childhood stress in the entire sample.

Despite his extensive childhood stresses, however, Ben's psychological symptoms are reasonably moderate: only five at baseline and seven at follow-up, about average for both the follow-up divorce study as well as the companion study of transitions. Why did childhood stress seem to have a strengthening rather than a sensitizing influence in Ben's adaptation to the stress of divorce? Some possible explanations include: (1) the presence of parental death, which has been previously shown in this study and others to have a steeling influence on later adaptation; (2) the timing of the childhood stresses; and (3) the moderating influence of Ben's new (third) marriage on his retrospective accounts of perceived childhood stresses and, perhaps, on his follow-up psychological symptoms, which could have been even greater without the influence of a new wife.

Taking another look at information concerning the perception of childhood stress, we see that between the ages of 10 to 15, Ben's Life Evaluation Chart rating drops to nearly 2.5 or between "very low" and "dissatisfactions clearly outweigh satisfactions." This suggests that many or all of the seven presumed childhood stresses may have occurred after his tenth birthday when the influence on long-term psychological functioning may not be as great (Freud [1938] (1969)). These early years seem to be the most critical for establishing a secure base for managing subsequent stresses and for forming subsequent attachment bonds.

There are at least two reasons why the death of a parent may have had a strengthening influence on Ben's management of subsequent stress. First, Ben's subsequent stresses may pale by comparison to the enormous loss and readjustment required after the death of his parent. Second, parental death may have resulted in Ben's having developed greater coping abilities and an increased sense of competence, which has caused him not to be particularly alarmed at such stresses as divorce in adulthood.

At first contact Ben seems quite socially isolated. Perhaps the childhood stresses have damaged his ability to become emotionally attached and, instead, Ben has become compulsively self-reliant. He reports that he is fairly often without anyone with whom he can share experiences and feelings; once in a while he has no one to talk to about himself; he avoids situations such as going to a restaurant or show because he is alone; he fairly often feels like he isn't having the sex life he would like. He states that he feels distant from other people.

Ben's primary attachment currently is with his two dogs. When asked who he lives with, he responds by saying "My dogs." Ben's most stressful event recently concerned the health of one of the animals. When asked what he tends to think of or daydream about, he replied, "My dogs . . . losing them. They're getting old." At the same time, Ben dreams "about going places and meeting people" and expresses hope of "finding a more compatible mate."

He has not been dating before or during the separation and says that he wants to wait until the divorce is final before starting to date. When asked about his plans for the next years, Ben said he wants "to meet a woman and get along well."

By the second interview, Ben's reliance on his dogs has been replaced by a new wife, a 45-year-old dental hygienist with two daughters. When asked how this marriage differs from his last, Ben notes the presence of younger children, more common interests and a better sex life. He relies on his new wife very much for companionship.

About the importance of sex for him, he now said, "It's number two, the second most important thing next to being together. It gives me pleasure." He credits "a good healthy sexual relationship" as having helped him the most since his separation. He said, "It made me more relaxed and allows me to think about something else besides sex." It seems that this closeness and sharing with his third wife has helped Ben to emerge from social isolation and compulsive self-reliance.

Ben now believes that the divorce has given him freedom. "I have felt relieved and free, much more responsible to myself. I regained freedom, and most importantly, being able to find a more compatible mate." Ben states that he now feels "more confident. During my marriage, I relied on my ex-spouse a great deal. Now I rely on myself." He and his ex are more distant, but still get together weekly.

Ben's response to questions dealing with social isolation indicated that he is less dependent, more in control of his life, less disappointed, and more responsible. When asked which of his goals are most important, Ben says "Maintaining a happy relationship with my spouse and paying off my house." He doesn't mention his two dogs at all.

Mary Ruffin: Childhood Stress and Divorce

"My mom and dad got divorced when I was five, and I turned out O.K.," exclaims 29-year-old Mary, "So I guess my kids will be O.K., too." Mary seems only partially correct in her self-perception; she does not report having a large number of psychological symptoms at the first interview (with 9 symptoms she actually falls below average for women) but at follow-up her 11 reported symptoms put her significantly above average. It is, therefore, not entirely surprising to find that parental divorce was not the only childhood stressor in Mary's life: she also reports that her father deserted the family and remarriage of both parents, as well as long separations from parents and intense arguments with parents. These stresses may help to explain some maladaptive patterns of adult attachments, including compulsive support seeking. As Mary's story unfolds we see continued attachment to a violent and abusive husband, social isolation, and compulsive support seeking first from her children and then, later, from men.

Mary wears her black hair short but styled, and could be extremely attractive if she tried for that effect. A medium-sized white female, she is lightly built and dressed in blue jeans and a casual top when she greets the interviewer. Her story unfolds at the kitchen table where she and the interviewer take refuge from Mary's three daughters, ages three, five and eight, and six other preschool children for whom she is baby-sitting.

Mary tells the interviewer that her husband drank and was violent. They fought all the time, and he was unfaithful. Finally, she had kicked him out and started seeing another man. "I needed a man so I called the only man who'd ever made a pass at me in all my married life. He was so good to me that night. He talked to me—squeezed my hand, gave me $20 to pay for the babysitter since we had gone out . . . and money just for myself too. Well, Jony [her ex-husband] found out that I had gone out and he came roaring in and said: 'If you file those divorce papers you're a dead woman.' Then, Jony slept in his car in front of the house every night. So I told him that was crazy, and we got back together. But, a few weeks later, we got into a fight, and Jony said he didn't know who he wanted, me or her [the other woman], so I told him to split and make up his mind. He said he had no place to go. I offered to share the house, but different bedrooms. My husband said 'No,' we'd share the same bedroom. It all got crazy."

A sense of social isolation hit "right after we first separated. I felt the world was down on me." Mary has few confidants or people she can rely on. She doesn't visit relatives as she explained: "I've alienated them because all they want to do is talk bad about my husband. I want to keep my problems to myself. They are too biased." This attempt to protect her husband from the criticism of her family suggests a continuing attachment to him at this first interview.

Her continued attachment to spouse is suggested by the fact that they have separated three times since April. The first of October was the last separation. At the interview, they are still seeing each other nearly every day and are seeking reconciliation counseling, although Mary is continuing to have sex with another man. When asked the last time she had seen her spouse, she said: "This morning. We chatted over a cup of coffee. I was just getting up and didn't say too much. He slept over last night but we didn't have sex or nothing. We talked about everyday things—general conversation. These days we don't go out or anything. I cook for him sometimes but that's all we share."

When asked who was the most helpful, Mary responds that "the kids have been my mainstay. Without them I would have fallen apart." She mentions at several points that she relies heavily on her children. From a clinical perspective, this may be creating inverted and damaging role reversal where the child is required to meet the parent's needs, to parent the parent. This pattern is often seen in depressed or physically ill mothers and can result in children becoming either compulsive support givers in an attempt to have their own needs for support met or becoming compulsively self-reliant, so they are not recruited to meet someone else's needs.

The separation and pending divorce has changed the way Mary feels about herself. "At first when my husband started running around I almost died. I always considered myself a homemaker and a mother but now I feel almost cheap, you know what I mean. I depend on my boyfriend for that little bit of affection and tenderness and my husband is the provider but I don't love either."

By follow-up, she is divorced. Asked what kinds of things influenced the decision to actually divorce, she says "I don't how how to say it. I tried on and off for the last three years. We lived together, and I just got tired of being beat up. I got beat up one too many times, so I went and got my final decree and when I told him, I got beat up again."

By now Mary has resolved her feelings of isolation, lack of self-worth and attachment to former spouse. One favored strategy seems to be compulsive support seeking, particularly from men. At follow-up, when asked if her separation/divorce has changed the way she feels about herself, she says, "I have this thing about having to have a lot of men around me, I guess proving to myself that I'm attractive to men."

Asked "What about sex? What is the importance of sex for you?" Mary says: "Well, right now I think that my problems all started around needing a man, but sex has been very helpful, the idea of having sex with somebody else—that somebody else desires me. I am not totally lost." She confided that she will consent to sex even when she doesn't want it because she doesn't want to hurt anybody's feelings and doesn't know how to say no. Sex for her is a source of acceptance and makes her feel "wanted, loved, beautiful."

Mary now wants less sex than she's getting. She has sex several times a week and explained that she is currently seeing three men, one of whom supports her. When asked whether she is currently working or looking for work, she replies "I've got somebody that keeps me." The interviewer notes that "she laughed, but meant it."

Thus, we can see that her support seeking has financial as well as emotional overtones. When asked what sort of things she tends to think or daydream about, she said: "I don't want a lasting relationship with anyone. I want to make money. I want to become self-sufficient. I want to be involved with someone because I like them not because I need them." Asked her goal, she said: "I want to become financially independent—that's all. I really don't want to be possessed now." When asked how she thinks her life will change, Mary replies "God, I hope I'm more secure, more stable emotionally."

During the process of separation and divorce, Mary became increasingly more ambivalent about her care-giving responsibilities to her children. At first, her children provided a form of support, propping up her low self-esteem. At first contact, the interviewer notes that: "With nine kids in the house (three her own) you can just imagine that there were interruptions, but the amazing thing about it was that the respondent never let the kids' trials or traumas get to her. She was very accommodating and sympathetic. She changed dirty diapers, kissed wounds and settled arguments, all in the course of being interviewed. The interruptions never seemed to upset her or distract her. She is really, in my estimation, a perfect mother—calm, totally in touch with her kids at all times no matter what else she might happen to be doing."

By follow-up, however, Mary's excellent care giving has shifted into ambivalence and neglect. When asked what sort of things she tends to think or daydream about, she says "What I think about most of the time—this sounds horrible—I dream about the day I won't have to take care of the kids anymore." Later, when talking about how her life has changed since the decision to initiate the divorce, she says: "I feel less secure and more restricted. I have children and they dictate to me whether I can go out or not. They pull their sick thing and I feel I have to stay home with them." In response to the interviewer's question about changes in relationships with children, Mary says: "I don't think I'm as close to them as I was before, not as sensitive to their feelings and stuff, basically, because I don't take time for them anymore. I'm working or going out. The men get off scot-free—all men do."

SOME CONCLUDING THOUGHTS ABOUT CHILDHOOD STRESSORS

The question guiding this chapter was whether or not childhood stress is related to greater difficulties in adult adaptation to the transition of divorce in adult life. We hypothesized that those who reported higher levels of presumed and/or perceived childhood stresses should have significantly more psychological symptoms at both baseline and follow-up. The hypothesis was partially supported, since childhood stress did significantly predict the number of symptoms reported at both the impact and long-term contacts, but only for men. Even when the effects of baseline psychological symptoms were removed, childhood stress continued to significantly predict follow-up psychological symptoms for men. In addition, when we combined the items related to presumed stress in different subscales we were able to predict follow-up psychological symptoms more strongly than when we used the cumulative measure of presumed stress.

Our findings naturally raise several more questions than they answer. For example, why did childhood stress significantly predict adaptation for men, but not women? Why did perceived stress significantly predict baseline psychological symptoms, while presumed stress predicted follow-up psychological symptoms? And third, why did combinations of presumed stresses more significantly predict follow-up symptoms than cumulative presumed childhood stress? Here we will provide some further thoughts on the relationships we uncovered.

Childhood Stress Predicted Psychological Symptoms for Men, but not Women

There are several possible explanations for the greater long-term vulnerability of men than women to the influence of childhood stress. To begin with, the literature (e.g., Rutter 1981) on the short-term influence of childhood stress indicates that boys are more vulnerable than girls to a broad array of stresses, including family discord, parental divorce, and separations. Adult male vulnerability to the sensitizing influences of childhood stress may simply be a continuation of this initial vulnerability of boys.

Another explanation concerns gender differences in access to social supports. For many men, wives serve as the sole source of social support. In other analyses we also found that men were more likely than women to report that their former spouse could have been the most helpful person during the process of marital separation (Chiriboga et al. 1979). The loss of one's only confidant and one's spouse simultaneously could be described as a "double whammy," in that it leaves the men without anyone to turn to.

An interesting question concerns what the marriages of these men were like prior to separation. One of our colleagues, Margaret Clark, suggested that we examine the nature of the marital relationship prior to separation; she thought that men who reported more presumed childhood stresses might be considerably more dependent than those who did not. This conjecture was confirmed: men who reported greater presumed childhood stress were more likely to rely on their wives prior to separation.

For a variety of reasons, then, without the moderating influence of friends or a spouse men may be considerably more vulnerable to the pervasive influence of earlier experience. In the broader context, these findings suggest a model of continuity rather than of change for human development. From an applied perspective, our findings suggest that men who report perceived and presumed childhood stresses should be identified as possibly being at risk during the divorcing process. Since these men may have difficulty in attracting informal sources of social support, such as friends, relatives, and new partners, it may be advisable to organize counseling around the provision of social support during stressful transitions such as marital separation.

Perceived and Presumed Stress Predict at Different Points in the Divorce Process

Another question is why perceived stress predicted psychological symptoms at baseline and presumed stress predicted them at follow-up? Perceived childhood stress was measured by averaging each respondent's rating of the first 13 years of his or her life on a scale from 0, or "rock bottom," to 9, or "top of the world." Some investigators (e.g., Finlay-Jones et al. 1981) have found that subjective evaluations are often less reliable than more objective reports of childhood stress. In fact, the test-retest reliability scores on the measure of perceived childhood stress used in the Divorce Study were lower than the test-retest reliability scores of presumed childhood stress from the Transitions Study. It may be that perceptions of childhood stress are more subject to being influenced by the respondent's current psychological situation. It is possible, therefore, that respondents' retrospective evaluation of their childhood years was more consonant with current psychological condition during the initial interview, when the measure was obtained.

In contrast, the cumulative measure of presumed childhood stress, a sum of twelve stressful childhood events reported in the first interview, predicted follow-up adaptation to divorce. Why, then, did presumed childhood stresses fail to predict symptoms levels at the first contact point? One possibility is that marital separation brings with it a host of stressors that may affect all aspects of life. Exposure to these multiple stressors may have obscured the short-term influence of presumed childhood stress upon general functioning level. With the quelling of the "noise" and chaos of the impact phase of divorce, the influence of earlier events begins to reemerge at follow-up, in a fashion akin to the "sleeper" effect described by Peskin and Livson (1981). Cumulative presumed childhood stress, we conclude, has a moderate but enduring influence on men's adaptation.

Evidence for a Steeling Effect

When we used the summary measures, the evidence generally went against the notion that childhood exposure to stress might have a growth-promoting or steeling effect. In other analyses we explored the implications of combining the individual stress items in different ways, and found that some combinations generated better predictions of outcome. As we looked at the individual items that made the greatest contributions, we found that most of the childhood stress measures had a sensitizing influence, but one, combining parental death and/or sibling death, had a steeling influence. This was especially true for men. When stress items with both sensitizing and steeling influences were combined together in a single summary measure, this acted to reduce the overall amount of variance predicted.

Why were those men who reported parental and/or sibling deaths less likely to report psychological symptoms following divorce? Bornstein et al. (1973) and Persson (1980) report similar findings about the steeling influence of certain childhood stresses. Bornstein et al. (1973), for example, found that prior experience with death of a family member was related to decreased vulnerability to depression in widowhood. He concluded that the experience of earlier and major loss led to the decreased perception of the stressfulness of subsequent stress. This is a kind of "relative deprivation" hypothesis. Mainstream stress research has also suggested that prior exposure to a particular class of stress may lead individuals to feel less threatened when the stress is repeated (e.g., Horowitz and Wilner 1980).

A similar explanation was offered by Persson (1980) after he found that older men, but not women, who reported the death of a parent in childhood were significantly more likely to evaluate subsequent life events as being less stressful than men who had not experienced such events. Alternatively, it may be that early bereavement leads to an avoidance of further emotional involvement with others as a means of avoiding the pain associated with loss. Further work is needed to see which of these explanations is most relevant to these steeling influences of parental and/or sibling death.

Does Childhood Stress Lead to Divorce?

Another intriguing question is whether persons who report numerous childhood stressors are more likely to manifest relational difficulties in adulthood. Several researchers speculated that divorce begets divorce: that children of divorced parents are significantly more likely to get divorced themselves. While it was not possible in the Divorce Study to investigate the relationship between childhood stress and adult divorce, it was possible to do preliminary analyses by turning to the Study of Transitions. We looked at the divorced and never divorced members of our companion study of people going through normative transitions such as parenthood, the empty nest and retirement.

The divorced and nondivorced participants in this companion study were compared in terms of their retrospective reports of the sum of childhood stresses. The 32 divorced subjects (12 men, 20 women) had significantly more childhood stresses than the 147 nondivorced subjects, but there were no specific types of childhood stress that seemed more important than any other. These results provide at least partial confirmation of the idea that exposure to numerous childhood stresses may enhance the likelihood of divorce during the adult years. A possible mechanism may be a relationship between childhood stress and problems with adult attachments.

On the Use of Retrospective Data

At present there is a paucity of prospective studies extending from childhood to adulthood that focus on the long-term influence of childhood stress. The present study, like most other research on the long-term influence of childhood stress, relied on self-reports of events that occurred in the distant past.

Assessments of the reliability of retrospective accounts of childhood stress therefore became a critical central.

Using the test-retest method, it was possible to assess the correlation over time for both measures, although for presumed stress we were forced to use data from our companion study. Given the very different circumstances that obtained for participants in both studies at the two interview points, the fact that the correlations were moderate in strength is encouraging but certainly not definitive.

Finally, it should be reemphasized that because our measures of childhood stress are based on self-reported conditions of the past, many would view such an approach as a fatal flaw. It seems almost axiomatic that researchers discount the use of retrospective data, citing in particular the bias in reporting that may result from present experiences. In other words, like nations, we as individuals are seen to rewrite our pasts to fit our present and expected future. At the same time, given the impossibility in most situations of revisiting the past or of conducting lifelong prospective studies of respondents, the use of retrospective measures has appeal. Here we have attempted to show that this type of measure may have reasonable psychometric properties and provide valuable information about the risk factors and possible steeling or beneficial factors for persons in the throes of divorce.

3

DIVORCE STRESS AND ADAPTATION

David A. Chiriboga and Linda S. Catron

In this chapter we continue to explore the many ways in which the stress process affects the experiences and well-being of men and women, some of the ways in which respondents attempted to cope with divorce, and what seems to set apart those who have more or less stress.

BACKGROUND

Divorce and Health

The prevalence of divorce assumes particular importance when viewed in the context of its association with numerous health problems. For example, the separated and divorced manifest a higher rate of suicide (Trovato 1987; Zeiss, Zeiss and Johnston 1980; Stack 1989), mortality (United Nations 1987), and morbidity (Holmes and Masuda 1974; Nystrom 1980). Divorced or separated individuals have proportionately higher rates of alcoholism (Hallberg and Mattsson 1989), hypertension (Lindgarde, Furu and Ljung 1987) and a wide variety of other health problems (Carter and Glick 1976; Huntington 1986). Finally, there is a long-established association between divorce and problems in psychological adjustment (Waller 1930; Goode 1956; Tschann, Johnston and Wallerstein 1989).

The Issue of Causality. In our study we do not consider whether our participants may be divorcing because of preexisting mental health problems, primarily because we had no solid information on such problems. It is extremely rare, in fact, to encounter studies that do follow people from a point prior to marital separation. This is unfortunate, since without such studies it is nearly impossible to learn whether the physical and mental health risks associated with marital disruption represent consequences or themselves may have led to divorce in the first place. Most probably, mental health in the aftermath of separation results from a combination of factors.

Even the large, epidemiological projects provide inconclusive results concerning whether divorce might lead to mental health problems. In a study that followed nearly seven thousand persons over a 10-year-period, marital separation and divorce were not associated with a greater prevalence of depression (Kaplan, Roberts, Camacho and Coyne 1987). However, the very long period of time between contacts, reliance on necessarily brief and highly structured questions, selective dropout of sample members and a host of other factors make the results of this study difficult to interpret.

Although there is no clear link between health and the breakup of marriages, separation and divorce have consistently been shown to affect health. The descriptive work on marital separation portrays it as a time of tension and turmoil for most participants, including those who initiate the separation (Weiss 1975). The complex ramifications of this major transition pervade an individual's life, regardless of whether the change was desired or not (Hunt 1966; Wallerstein and Blakeslee 1989). It is often noted, for example, that Holmes and Rahe (1967), in their well-known Schedule of Recent Events, found only bereavement to rank higher than divorce and separation as a potential stressor.

Divorce can also provide an opportunity for personal growth, in spite of the pain and confusion attendant on the process (Ambert 1989; Cauhape 1983; Hunt 1966; Krantzler 1973). Growth, when it occurs, may be related to feelings of mastery that arise from having dealt with a major stress, and may also be related to the challenges that arise as a result of a new lifestyle. The bottom line is that both growth and distress can occur, with the actual experience of divorce seeming to depend on the individual context. While nearly all participants in research studies appear to experience stress and turmoil, for some this condition is relatively brief and minimally disruptive, with substantial relief possible even within the first year (Weiss 1975). For others, the strain of separation and divorce may be more profound, with recovery taking years or never becoming fully complete (Wallerstein and Blakeslee 1989).

Divorce and Bereavement. It is not uncommon for people to equate divorce and bereavement, and to portray both situations as involving similar processes of "grief work." At the same time, a number of clinicians and researchers have emphasized the differences between the two types of loss; their general conclusion is that divorce and bereavement have very little in common (e.g., Goode 1956; Weiss 1975). As Jacobson (1983) points out, the fact that the spouse is alive, and the degree of anger usually experienced, highlight the differences between divorce and bereavement. Another difference lies in the generally greater ambivalence faced by divorcing persons as compared to the bereaved. At least in the early stages of the divorce process, there often is little certainty concerning whether or not the divorce will actually take place.

As a further example of differences between the two types of loss, the senior author recalls a period when he led several seminars for divorced persons and for the recently bereaved. The differences were striking. For example, among participants in the divorce seminars, putting down their former spouses was a source of amusement as well as a means of affirming their common sources of distress. Most participants desired to rid themselves of any remaining bonds with their ex, and to establish new relationships. Among the bereaved, idealization of the former spouse was common, and the subject of dating was treated with considerable ambivalence. Many participants expressed the fear of desecrating memories of a beautiful relationship by dating, having sex, or marrying another. In contrast to divorce seminar groups, members of the bereavement group had difficulties in seeing anything bad or problematic in their former spouse.

OF STRESSORS AND MENTAL HEALTH

We have noted that marital separation and divorce have been linked with a variety of indicators of dysfunction. Many experts believe that psychological disturbances characterize the immediate response to the situation. What Krantzler (1973) referred to as a period of temporary insanity, Jacobson (1983, 27) calls "a state of acute, time-limited disorganization" that evolves out of ineffective attempts at coping with marital separation.

A Stress Process Model

In most of what is discussed in this and the following chapters, we have followed a model of stress that draws on the works of Lazarus and Folkman (1984), Pearlin (e.g., Pearlin et al. 1981), Hobfoll (1988) and many others.

Our model builds on the idea that the basic components of the stress paradigm consist of stressors (the condition creating the distress), mediators and stress responses.

Stressors are most often defined as so-called "life events," and in this study we included an instrument designed to capture a broad range of positive and negative life events. Called the Life Events Questionnaire, it is a 138-item instrument that covers a multitude of life events and provides the respondent's own evaluation of whether each reported event should be classified as positive or negative (Chiriboga 1984; Chiriboga 1989). An important point to make is that we did not assume separation or divorce to be single and distinct life events. Rather, we assumed that both can bring with them a host of other life events. There is, in other words, a ripple or chaining effect since a disturbance in the marital relationship has implications for relationships with family, friends, work colleagues and many other spheres of life.

Mediators are those conditions that modulate or perhaps even prevent a stress condition. Cognitive appraisals, coping strategies, self-concept, social supports and general sense of control are among the most common mediators studied. Finally, when we speak of stress responses we must differentiate between the short-term response and what happens to people in the long run. One emerging finding in stress research is that the way people initially respond to a stress condition may bear little relationship to how they end up (Chiriboga 1972; Fiske and Chiriboga 1990).

In addition to these basic components, antecedent factors such as childhood stress may play a role, as can general contextual factors such as age, gender, income, number of children, ethnicity and the like. Finally, in a stress condition approaching the magnitude of divorce or bereavement, we must consider event-specific factors such as length of marriage, who was in control of the decision-making process leading to divorce and timing factors such as how long it has been since critical markers of the stress process were reached (see figure 1).

Figure 1
A Provisional Model of the Stress Process

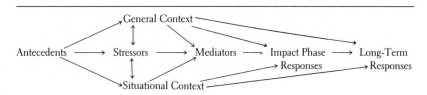

Measures of Mental Health

In studying psychological well-being, we have relied on one particular measure, a measure of psychological symptoms. On occasion we also report findings from two measures that were less clinically focused: measures of positive and negative affect.

Psychological Symptoms. We used the California Symptoms Checklist-42, a measure derived from the Cornell Medical Index that asks the respondent to check off each of 42 symptoms he or she has experienced (Chiriboga and Krystal 1985). Each respondent's score on the Symptoms Checklist consists of the total number of symptoms that he or she reported having experienced. These 42 items were selected by a team of psychiatrists for their clinical relevance to psychological dysfunction; the measure was given at both contact points in the study, as were all the measures of adaptation and life events included in this chapter.

Bradburn Positive and Negative Emotions. The Bradburn Positive and Negative Emotions requires one to check off a short list of emotions experienced in the past week and report on the frequency of those emotions (often, several times, once or not at all). The Bradburn Positive Emotions score consists of the sum of each of these emotions: on top of the world, excited, pleased and proud; while the Bradburn Negative Emotions score consists of the sum of these emotions: lonely, depressed, bored and restless. In addition, we asked another question from the Bradburn Scale: "In general how happy are you these days: Very happy, pretty happy or not too happy?"

The Psychological Well-being of Participants

When we looked at how participants fared on the summary measure of psychological symptoms, we found that women consistently reported more symptoms than men. At first contact, women averaged slightly over 11 symptoms while men averaged about 9; by the second interview, several years later, women on the average had dropped to 9 while men averaged about 7. The greater symptomatology of women, in evidence both during the impact phase of divorce and in the long run, was not a surprising finding. Using the same instrument, we have found women in the companion Study of Transitions to also score consistently higher than men.

More important perhaps is that, other than the sex difference, the only difference we found was that symptom levels dropped significantly for nearly everyone between the impact and long-term phases. This finding suggests that by the time people have been separated for four years or more, there has been a general subsiding of psychological duress, whether it had been the cause or the result of divorce. Some support for this position comes from the companion study of transitions: whereas symptom levels for Divorce Study participants were universally higher during the impact stage, at follow-up there were no differences between the two samples. For example, the average number of symptoms reported by Transitions subjects aged 50 and over was 6.28; this comes quite close to the 6.67 overall average for Divorce subjects.

Additional support for the idea that by the long term follow-up things had more or less returned to their normal state, for most people, comes from the Bradburn (1969) measure of Negative Emotions. The only significant difference found for this measure was an overall drop in negative affect by the time of the long-term follow-up. Men and women at every age-group reported, on the average, a drop in experiencing negative emotions.

Morale: A Slightly Different Story. When we turn from measures focused on problems to measures more oriented to wellness, the story shifts somewhat. During the impact phase, for example, there are very distinct gender differences in reports of happiness. During the impact phase men are significantly more likely to feel "not too happy": 30% feel this way, compared to 15% of the women. These gender differences are especially impressive when we compare them with results from national probability studies, where men and women generally do not differ and from 8% to 14% report feeling not too happy (Bradburn 1969).

Age differences were dramatic at the first interview, with the older participants less likely to report feeling happy. For example, among the men, 23% of those under age 40 felt not too happy, as compared with 38% of those in their forties and 53% of those aged 50 and over. The situation was the same for women, among whom only 11% of those under 40 felt not too happy, 24% of those in their forties and 45% of those aged 50 and over. Looking at these results from another perspective, older adults were especially likely to depart from national levels of reporting happiness.

By the time of our follow-up, the situation had changed. Data collected at the second interview now conformed much more closely to those in our companion Study of Transitions: men and women did not differ, and only about 10% reported feeling not too happy. In fact, an impressive 52% of men in their forties felt "very happy," although only 10% of men aged 50 and over felt the same way. Women in their forties were also doing well: 36 percent reported feeling very happy, and 22% of women aged 50 and over felt equally happy.

Curiously, when we look at the Bradburn measure of Positive Emotions, no change in overall level is found from first to second interview but there were some interesting age differences. Men and women aged 50 and over began by reporting fewer positive emotions during the impact phase; by follow-up the oldest group of men had increased in their level of reporting but older women had slipped even further behind. Perhaps the most interesting group is the men in their forties: they show the greatest overall increase in the amount of positive experiences reported, paralleling in this case the findings for the global question on happiness. Overall, the results from both indices of positive and negative functioning strongly suggest that problems had diminished, and life was generally more satisfying, some four years after the participants had separated from their spouse.

THE IMPACT STAGE OF DIVORCE: A TIME OF MULTIPLE LIFE EVENTS

While marital separation and divorce are cast as important but single "life events" in many of the more popular stress inventories, our pilot studies produced the hypothesis that separation, at least, can generate a host of associated events, some good and some bad. In this section we will consider evidence supporting this hypothesis, and also evaluate age and gender differences in the stress context of marital separation.

Our Approach to Measuring Stressors

We have already mentioned that our life event instrument included 138 items, each of which could be rated as positive or negative. Positive life events, or positive stressors, might seem like a contradiction in terms. Stress research, however, has indicated that positive changes can create their own set of demands and challenges, and therefore deserve consideration (Chiriboga 1984). From the life event instrument we developed subscales for positive and negative events on each of 11 different dimensions of stress:

1. marital/dating (arguments with spouse, dating, etc.)
2. family (more arguments than usual with children, children have problems at school, etc.)
3. work (arguments with co-workers, promotion or demotion, etc.)
4. legal (jail, lawsuits other than divorce, minor law violations, etc.)
5. habits (change in routine: eating, sleeping, smoking, drinking, etc.)
6. internal events (not achieving an important goal, etc.)
7. nonfamily relationships (arguments with friends, etc.)
8. personal (e.g., discrimination, changes in religious beliefs, etc.)
9. financial (major or minor loans, etc.)
10. home (move to new city or within city, problems finding new home, etc.)
11. school (bad grades, etc.).

Summary scores for total positive and negative stress were also computed.

Overall Levels of Stress Exposure

Just to give an overview on what was happening to participants during the impact stage, we will look at summary scores for negative life events and positive life events. For negative life events, there were no age differences, but women reported more negative stress exposure than did men. There was also a tendency for the men aged 40 and over to report the fewest negative events, but for women in the same age-group to report the most. On the other hand, men aged 40 and over, and women aged 50 and over were also lowest in the overall reporting of positive events. Men and women in their twenties reported the highest levels of positive events.

What these findings tell us is that gender and age do play a role in levels of stress exposure during the impact phase of divorce. In order to really understand the findings, however, we must look at the specific areas of stress being reported.

Areas of Negative Stress Exposure

We looked at age and gender differences on the 11 negative event measures derived from the same 138-item Life Events Questionnaire (Chiriboga and Dean 1978) that provided the overall events scores. There were no age differences, across all 11 dimensions, in experiences with negative stressors.

This similarity, consistent with findings for the summary measure of life events, is surprising, since most studies that include young adults, and middle-aged and older adults have found significant declines in stress exposure after young adulthood (e.g., Chiriboga 1984; Holmes and Masuda 1974; Horowitz and Wilner 1980).

One possible reason for the lack of age differences is that marital separation increases the levels of stress reported by middle-aged respondents over and above the increase found in young adults, to the point where the usual exposure gap is closed. Not only were the younger and older respondents the same, but all scored highest in the same two negative dimensions: marital and dating, and internal. Since these two dimensions contain items applicable to the divorce process, this concentration of events was not entirely unexpected. It may simply denote that, at the point of marital separation, the most turmoil is still experienced in the broken relationship.

There were three other findings of interest. The first dealt with negative experiences in the "personal" dimension, which includes more abstract experiences such as having to make plans for the future, experiencing discrimination, and so forth. Compared to everyone under 40, older men in the sample were the least involved in this type of stress experience, while women over 40 were the most caught up with personal stressors. Findings of this sort suggest that for middle-aged women, marital separation has a tremendous effect on future planning, and how other people view you. For men, on the other hand, at least during the early stages, marital separation had little influence on future planning or the way they were viewed by others.

For men and women at any stage of life, other basic differences in negative stress experiences had to do with stresses related to money and the home. In both areas, women encountered more negative stress than did men. Again, the implication is that women are harder hit by marital separation.

Areas of Positive Stress Exposure

Age differences were more pronounced when attention turned to the 11 measures of positive life events. In general, men and women aged 40 and over experienced fewer positive events at work, in marital and dating activities, in nonfamily relationships and in the personal dimension. Here again is evidence for an unequal involvement of stressors, with the older participants being hardest hit. The results suggest that young adults can benefit more than older adults from the separation stage of divorce. For example, men and women aged 40 and over reported experiencing a higher proportion of negative to positive events than did younger respondents. One overall conclusion that can be reached is that the breadth of impact is indeed so extensive that it is more appropriate to think of the divorce experience as a "transition" than as a "stressor" or life event. We will consider this idea in more detail in the next chapter.

Comparing Divorce to Normative Transitions

As a means of placing in context the uniqueness of the stress exposure faced by participants during the impact phase of divorce, we compared them with participants in our companion Study of Normative Transitions. To equate for stage of the transition, data for the Transitions subjects were drawn from the third contact point, when all subjects were also fully engaged in one of the normative transitions under study. Transitions respondents who had been or were going through separation or divorce were eliminated from all analyses.

Negative Events. Analyses of variance for the 11 negative stress measures revealed that divorcing subjects were consistently exposed to more stressors than those undergoing normative transitions. For example, among the men, separated respondents of all ages reported significantly higher levels of negative stress in areas related to habits, internal events and marital or dating relationships, and had higher summary scores than did men in the normative study of transitions.

Of particular interest is that separated men aged 40 and over showed the greatest differences from their age peers undergoing normative transitions. These older men scored higher on 8 of the 11 stress dimensions: habits, work, internal, marital/dating, nonfamily, personal, financial and home. Not surprisingly, they also scored higher on the overall score. These findings expand upon the impression, gleaned from age comparisons within the divorce sample, that during the separation stage, the middle-aged men were more at risk than younger men.

Differences between women undergoing normative and nonnormative transitions were not as distinct. Only in areas related to internal stressors (thoughts and feelings of a distressing nature) and in marital/dating issues were the separated women as a group experiencing greater stress. Moreover, separated women in the middle years of life were not very different from middle-aged women in the other study. Instead, it was the separated women aged 30–39 who reported the most stressors. In fact, they were significantly higher on all but nonfamily events when contrasted with their age peers in the normative Transitions Study.

Positive Events. Our comparisons to this point suggest that the transition of divorce is generally associated with more negative events than are more normative transitions, especially for middle-aged men and women in their thirties. However, while the divorce transition is associated with more negative events, it is also associated with more positive events.

Among both men and women, separated respondents reported significantly more positive events than did adults experiencing normative transitions. For example, separated men of all ages reported more positive events having to do with marriage/dating and nonfamily relationships; the divorced men over 40 also reported more positive changes in habits, at work and in the overall measure of positive events. Similarly, divorcing women aged 40 and over differed most from their age peers undergoing normative transitions. They were more likely to report positive changes in work-related issues, in nonfamily relationships, in habits, internal events and the marital/dating area. Moreover, the ratio of positive to negative stressors was significantly more positive for these middle-aged women. Coupled to the fact that they were not so different from the normative transitions women on negative stress exposure, these middle-aged women seem to be doing quite well during the early stages of divorce.

One implication of these findings is that individuals in the process of divorcing at any age can expect a substantial amount of change in their lives. Not all of these changes are negative: the separated men and women generally scored higher on positive as well as negative stressors when compared to age peers who were in the midst of normative transitions. Moreover, the context of divorce for men at midlife was somewhat different than that for women. At least in the early stages of marital dissolution, middle-aged men reported a greater array of negative experiences than did men at earlier stages of life. For middle-aged women, on the other hand, there was a greater sense of challenge and opportunity posed by the separation. The impression one gets is that many of these women had broken out of rather boring and stultifying lives established when they were quite young. In the midst of often horrendous difficulties, many were experiencing for the first time a sense of accomplishment and discovery. A number of the middle-aged women, for example, were completely overwhelmed by the idea that someone would actually pay them for their labors.

Stress Exposure: Winners and Losers

Up to now we have considered positive and negative stressors separately, and yet of course each person going through a divorce experiences both, in varying proportions. To conform to the reality of the divorce experience, we decided to divide up our recently separated participants into those who scored high or low on both overall positive, and overall negative stress exposure. We then placed them into four categories:

1. The Bland. These people, numbering 77, scored lowest in both negative and positive events;
2. The Winners. These people, numbering 67, scored lowest on negative events but highest on positive;
3. The Losers. These people, numbering 75, scored highest in exposure to negative events and lowest on positive;
4. The Challenged. These people, numbering 75, scored among the highest in both negative and positive events.

Naturally, grouping people into the above categories makes no sense unless the kinds of experiences represented by these categories do in fact seem to make a difference in their lives. To find out whether the categories are in fact meaningful we used a statistical procedure called discriminant analysis. What this procedure does is allow us to consider both what factors seem to distinguish between the four groups, and whether in fact the groups are different from each other.

Our first step was to look at some of the contextual or background factors in divorce. Age was the most important factor: the Losers were on the average the oldest, followed closely by the Bland; the Challenged were the youngest, but the Winners were also more likely to be young. Education also made a big difference, and one that was strong after its relationship with age was removed: the Bland and the Winners reported the highest education, the Losers and the Challenged reported the lowest. Having an ethnic identity also seemed important, with those identifying themselves with an ethnic group more likely to fall into the Losers' category, and Winners being least likely to maintain an ethnic identity. Finally, men and women who reported more childhood stressors were also more likely to be classified as Losers, and Winners were least likely to report childhood stressors. Curiously, several factors that might be thought to differentiate between groups did not; these included gender, income, number of children and number of months separated.

Next we considered the role of various ways of viewing the self. Described in greater detail in chapter 7, the measures were derived from a factor analysis of a 70-item Adjective Rating List. The most important contributor was a measure reflecting an overall negative self-image. Consisting of a count of self-ascribed negative attributes, this measure reflected a trend indicated by the first set of measures: a trend for the Losers in fact to be people who might be expected to suffer more from divorce. We found the Losers to be highest on negative self-image and the Winners to be lowest.

Four other self-concept measures made independent contributions. Losers were more likely to maintain self-images marked by hostility and aggression, while Winners were lowest in this category. Losers were lowest in desirable self, while the Challenged were highest. Losers were highest in self-images reflecting vulnerability, while the Bland were lowest. We found the Bland and Losers to be lowest in self-orientation, by which is meant a concern about one's needs and wants; the Challenged were highest. Generally, then, we find that the self-image of the people we classified as Losers in the stress arena to be quite distinct, with the distinction being that each difference reflects a possible vulnerability or deficit. Winners did not emerge in quite so clear-cut a fashion.

Following the self-image measures, we included two summary measures that dealt with whether individuals felt more or less in control of their lives in general, and specifically with regard to the separation and divorce. Both made a significant difference: as we now might expect, Losers were least likely to feel in control either of their lives in general or of the divorce; Winners were most likely to feel in control of both.

Finally we looked at whether the divorce stress category seemed to differentiate the psychological well-being of people. Negative Affect made the greatest difference, but Positive Affect and Symptoms also played a role. Again the results are consistent. Losers reported greater negative affect, the least positive affect and the most symptoms. Winners reported the least negative affect and shared with the Challenged the distinction of reporting the most positive affect. The Bland reported the fewest symptoms, with the Winners being a close second.

The consistency with which our classifying system differentiated between key components of the stress model was somewhat unexpected. The results underscore the importance of considering not simply the degree of negative stress exposure but also the presence of positive experiences. One message underlying the findings seems to be that where one falls in the stress categories only partly depends on the social context: to a considerable degree it is affected by factors that are not very changeable: exposure to childhood stress, age, ethnicity and education. Characteristics of the personality, as reflected in the self-image data, were also important. Studies using the same measure indicate that the subscales of the Adjective Rating List are among the most stable components of individuals for periods as long as 12 years (Fiske and Chiriboga 1990).

The success rate for correctly classifying people into their actual categories was 57% (by chance this should be about 25%). Losers were most likely to be classified correctly: about 63%. At 54%, Winners were least likely to be classified correctly. About 25% of the Winners were classified by the computer as Bland. Interestingly, of the incorrect placements, none were into the Winner category.

While the results are encouraging, a limitation of the findings not only for the stress categories but for all analyses of the impact phase is that they are basically cross-sectional in nature. That is, we are looking at associations between measures collected at the same time from the same person. As discussed extensively in chapter 2, issues of retrospective bias and the lack of prospective data potentially detract from the generalizability of findings. However, these limitations were not as influential when we turned to the prospective study of long-term impact.

STRESSORS IN THE LONG TERM

Change in Exposure to Negative Events

As was the case for psychological symptoms, there was a significant decline in the overall level of negative life events reported by follow-up. Moreover, whereas initially there were no age differences in overall level of exposure to negative events, by follow-up we find that those aged 50 and over were reporting significantly fewer events. The greater likelihood of women reporting negative life events, found for the impact phase, continues at follow up.

While decline in exposure to negative events was the rule, Divorce Study participants were generally reporting significantly more negative events than persons in the Transitions Study. The only people for whom this was not true were Divorce Study men and women in their twenties: while their averages were higher than those reported for the comparison group, the differences were not significant. Moreover, at both points of comparison, men and women in the Transitions Study did not differ from one another in levels of reported stress, whereas in the Divorce Study women consistently reported more negative events than did men.

Change in Exposure to Positive Events

The situation was slightly different for change in the summary score for positive life events. During the impact phase, as you may recall, we found that men and women in their twenties and thirties reported more positive events. In the long run, the younger participants dropped slightly in exposure to positive events but the older participants reported significant increases in such events.

When we compare our results with those for Transitions Study participants, we find that by follow-up the levels of positive events are roughly the same across the two studies. Two groups in the Divorce Study do stand out as being significantly higher than their counterparts in the Transitions Study: men aged 50 and over, and women in their forties. Reading the actual cases provides a sense, for these two groups, that there are some very positive long-term implications stemming from the rather negative transitions they have just undergone.

Winners and Losers in the Long Run

When we were considering the factors that best "predicted" and helped explain differences on the Divorce Stress Typology for the impact phase, we were limited in our interpretations by a key point. That point was that data on antecedent and contextual factors were of necessity based on information collected at the same time as we collected data on stress exposure and current functioning. As we turn to a consideration of Winners and Losers in the long run, we actually have prospective data at hand.

Comparison Between Impact and Long-Term Phases. Our first task was to determine whether people changed very much in stress categories. In other words, is one's stress type something that is relatively stable over time, or is it something that changes with life circumstances? Overall, there was slightly more evidence of change than there was of stability. The most stable were the Bland, with 53 percent remaining in that category over the three and a half years of study; another 20% of the Bland became Winners at follow-up and 20% became Losers.

Approximately 35% of those classified as Winners at impact remained Winners throughout the Study. Twenty five percent ended up as Losers. On the other hand, while 32% of the Losers were consistent, 20% ended up as Winners and 26% ended up in the Challenged category, reporting high degrees of both negative and positive events. The Challenged were relatively stable, with 47% remaining in this category. As might be expected from people with so much going on at the first interview, only 9% of the Challenged ended up in the Bland category; the remainder were equally distributed among Winners and Losers.

Predicting Stress Category from Impact Phase. Given that evidence of both stability and change existed in the Divorce Stress Typology, our next question concerned the dynamics of change. What factors seemed to make a difference? Our analysis of the Divorce Stress Typology at follow-up paralleled that done for the impact-phase Typology: we used the same discriminant analysis procedure, and we included the same set of predictors, each of which represented some characteristic of the individual or the situation as assessed during the impact phase. As before, the first set of variables allowed to enter the equation represented contextual factors. Once again age of the participant is most important but we find a subtle difference: while both the Losers and Bland are likely to be older at impact, only the Bland continue to be older at follow-up. The Challenged continue to be youngest. Unlike analyses for the impact phase, gender becomes important by follow-up. The Challenged are more likely to be women, as are Losers. The Bland and Winners are more likely to be men. Like impact, education enters next and the same pattern is evident: the most educated are likely to be Bland or Winners, the least educated are likely to be Losers. Unlike impact, income now plays a role; the primary group difference is that the Challenged are lowest in income. We also find that in the long run the number of children seems to make a difference: Winners on the average had the fewest children (less than one), while the Bland had the most children.

One way of assessing the value of measures contributing to the discriminant analysis is to consider how successful they are in predicting which group individuals should be placed within. When just the contextual variables discussed in the last paragraph were included, little more than 37% of the participants were correctly placed. Naturally, accuracy varied by group. More of the Challenged were placed accurately (56%) than any other group, but only 15% of the Winners.

The number of childhood stressors continued to figure in the equation for follow-up categories: those now classified as Challenged report the highest incidence (over two) of childhood stressors. The Bland report the fewest childhood stressors. Overall success of the classification procedure reached 41% with the addition of childhood stress.

Turning to self-image, we found group differences in how negatively the self was viewed: the Bland were lowest in overall negative self-image, the Losers were highest. On what we called Masterful Self-Image, Winners scored highest and Losers the lowest. The more self-oriented are Winners and the Challenged, while the Bland are lowest. The Challenged maintain self-images marked by greatest vulnerability, while Winners are lowest in perceived vulnerability of self. With the addition of self-image variables to the equation, the success rate for classification reached 47%. Of particular interest is a marked jump in the accuracy of predicting the Bland category: 72% were correctly placed, as opposed to 51% when demographic and childhood stress measures were included.

The sense of control again played a role in differentiating stress categories, but in the long run what becomes important is not one's general sense of control over life but the amount of control over the situation one felt. In contrast to what made a difference for stress categories at impact, Winners in the long run turn out to be those who felt least in control over the divorce situation during the impact phase. The Losers and Challenged were most likely to feel strongly in control of the situation at the impact phase. Success at classification reached 48% with the addition of situational control to the prediction equation.

Our measures of adaptation as reported during the impact phase also help in distinguishing stress categories. For example, those who later were classified as the Challenged and Losers showed the most negative affect when interviewed for the first time. The Bland and Winners, in contrast, reported the least negative affect. Initial symptom levels were not involved but happiness did make a difference: Losers were significantly less happy. It is interesting, however, that even though negative affect and happiness contributed significantly, the overall successfulness in classification actually dropped when they were included in the prediction equation: from 49% to 48%.

At this point in the prediction process, our accuracy of classification at follow-up was down slightly from what we found at the same point for the impact stress Typology, being 48% accurate as compared to 57%. The Bland were predicted at a surprisingly high 71% accuracy rate, and the Challenged at a respectable 58%. Winners were predicted with 23% accuracy, less than expected by chance. Losers were predicted at 37% accuracy. Overall, these results suggest that one can predict reasonably well who will not be very stressed in the long run, and who will experience lots of both positive and negative events.

Since we now were predicting follow-up categories of stress, it made sense to include measures of stress exposure obtained during the impact phase three and a half years in the past. The statistical procedure added 11 of the possible 22 subscales for positive and negative events, while accuracy of placement went from 48% to 58%. Five negative events scales were included. During the impact phase, those who ended up as Challenged reported the most negative stress at work, followed by the Losers. The Bland and Winners were equally low. Concerning negative stress in the areas of marriage and dating, again the Challenged were highest, followed by the Losers, the Winners and finally the Bland. At our first contact the people who would later be classified as Challenged reported the most negative stress in the family realm, and the Bland reported the least. Curiously, both Winners and Losers had reported equal degrees of family stress at the first interview. For negative events in the home, Losers again were the highest, the Challenged next, while Winners and the Bland were equally low. When we look at negative events in the legal arena there is a clear distinction: the Losers had experienced far more legal stress than any other group.

Six positive events scales also figured into the prediction equation. The Challenged not only reported the most negative work stress at our first contacts, but also the most positive. Winners were a distant second, followed by the Losers and finally by the Bland. Losers and the Challenged, curiously, reported more positive inner events at baseline. Winners and the Bland report essentially no experiences of this type, suggesting that their inner lives may not be as intense. Winners reported the most positive family events during the impact phase, while the Bland reported the least. Regarding positive events in what we called the personal arena, the Challenged once again emerge as highest and the Bland as lowest, the Winners being moderately high—higher at least than the Losers but not nearly as high as the Challenged. Once again, the Losers were the only ones to report events in the legal area, and so this distinguishes them from everyone else. Finally, the Challenged reported more positive school events, followed by the Bland; the Winners and Losers fell in between.

The Role of Children

One factor that made a difference in who ended up a Winner or Loser in the long run was the number of children. People who ended up as Winners were least likely to have children. This finding matches a general theme in the literature: the presence of children is a barrier to recovery from divorce-related stress. Although the matter has not been considered in detail, children and their multiple needs for parenting are generally portrayed as a handicap for divorcing women (e.g., Weiss 1979). For example, in discussing why they focused on divorcing women who had children, Maury and Brandwein (1984, 193) state that "her childless counterpart can slip back with relatively little difficulty into the status of the never-married woman." Similarly, Jacobs (1986) argues that many divorced fathers develop a syndrome marked by fears that they will lose the love and companionship of their children. We next look at whether the presence of children acts to exacerbate or reduce specific types of stressors, for mothers and fathers.

Impact Stages Events of Father. Fathers were more likely to report negative events related to family, and this was especially true of fathers in their twenties, who scored higher in this category than all other fathers and nonfathers. Fathers also tended ($P = .09$) to report more negative events related to home life. On the positive side of things, fathers were also more likely to report positive events related to their family.

On the other hand, fathers scored lower than childless men on overall happiness. Thirty-five percent of the fathers were "not too happy" and less than 15% were very happy during the impact phase of the investigation. This compares with 21% in the lowest category and nearly 25% "very happy" among the childless. There were no differences on positive and negative emotions but we found younger fathers to have fewer symptoms than the childless while fathers aged 40 and over manifest more symptoms.

Impact Stage Events of Mothers. As might be expected, mothers reported more negative events related to family and finances. For two other areas, results were less expectable. Mothers in their forties reported more health-related negative events than other mothers, but the group reporting the most health-related negative events were childless women aged 50 and over. There was a tendency (P = .09) for mothers in their fifties to report the fewest negative events related to internal thoughts and feelings, while childless women reported the most.

Possibly because they lived with a family, mothers also reported more positive events related to family life. The remaining findings suggested that having children imposes constraints against the possibility of positive changes: mothers reported fewer positive events related to personal life and finances, and tended (P = .09) to report fewer positive nonfamily events.

Like fathers, mothers were significantly less happy than the childless. Slightly over 20% were not too happy, compared to less than 8% of the childless. Mothers tended (P = .09) to report fewer positive emotions but were not different from the childless on the experiencing of either negative emotions or symptomatology.

Fathers in the Long Run. By the second interview, fathers tended to report fewer negative events in the personal sphere than did childless men, but fathers in their forties reported more than childless men of the same age. Fathers in their twenties and forties reported more reported negative events in the legal area, but fathers in their 30s and aged 50 and over reported fewer. Fathers reported more negative events in the financial area and tended (P = .10) to report more negative home events.

With regard to positive experiences, fathers reported more events related to marriage and dating, even though (as we shall see in the next chapter) having children seems to slow down the progress through divorce to postdivorce life. Fathers also reported more positive events related to home. On our measures of morale and symptomatology, there was little difference between the fathers and the childless at follow-up. If anything, fathers were in better shape. For example, over 38% of the fathers were "very happy" at follow-up, as compared to 28% of the childless.

Mothers in the Long Run. By the second interview, mothers were reporting more negative life events related to family and tending to report more financial stressors (P = .06). Again demonstrating what might be called a barrier effect, mothers reported fewer positive events related to nonfamily and personal life. Although mothers were not significantly lower on overall happiness, 43% of the childless reported being very happy, as compared to 33% of mothers. Mothers also reported significantly fewer positive emotions and tended (P = .06) to report more negative emotions.

A TEST OF THE STRESS PROCESS MODEL

In the analyses described thus far we have focused primarily on the distribution of stress events and factors associated with their distribution. Next we will examine the utility of the general stress process model as a means of predicting psychological symptomatology. Hierarchical set multiple regression analysis was chosen as the statistical approach because it allowed us to consider the contribution of different types of measures. Following an order suggested by the stress model, we first looked at social background characteristics, then childhood stress (the total count of presumed stressors), then the 11 individual subscales for negative events, followed by the 11 positive event subscales. In separate analyses we also looked at what happened when summary scores for all negative and all positive life events were substituted for the individual subscales. Incidentally, there were no major differences between men and women in the relationships we found, so in the following analyses the sexes are combined.

Stress as a Predictor of Symptoms at Impact

After an initial analysis identified which of the measures actually were related to symptom levels during the impact phase of divorce, we deleted the noncontributing measures in order to minimize any artificial inflation of results. Of the sociodemographic characteristics, we found that being a member of a minority group, being a woman and having less education were all independently related to greater symptomatology. The overall relationship was significant but explained only about 4% of the variability in symptoms. In other words, these social characteristics were indicated to be minimal risk factors. They may also be general risk factors for greater symptomatology, regardless of whether one is going through a divorce or not: being a woman and having less education were associated with greater symptomatology in our companion Transitions Study, as well as in the Divorce Study (e.g., Chiriboga 1984). Since the companion study had relatively few minority group members, no analyses were made of this possible risk factor.

Childhood stressors as defined in this chapter did not predict very well and the measure was not included in the secondary analysis; (more detailed analyses, as described in chapter 2, are necessary to really evaluate the contribution of childhood stress). We next entered seven of the negative events subscales; together they boosted the explained variance from 4% to nearly 30%. The relationships were consistent: greater symptomatology was associated with more negative stressors related to health, inner thoughts and feelings, family life, social relations, personal activities, home activities and school. As a matter of interest, these subscales outperformed the summary measure of total negative events: the latter brought the total explained variance to 18%, as opposed to the 30% made possible by the subscales.

Finally we entered the single positive events subscale indicated to make a contribution to symptoms: positive events related to family life. Although family events were significantly related to symptoms, the inclusion of this measure boosted explained variance from nearly 30% to just over 31%—not a great deal. Paralleling what we found in the negative stress arena, the individual subscale tapping positive family events actually outperformed the total positive event score. Such results emphasize the importance of a positive family environment, although in fact this "beneficial" factor does not exert a strong influence.

Overall, we found that the life event subscales, especially those focused on negative events, are strongly related to the expression of symptoms during the turmoil surrounding the impact phase. Stress exposure, in short, proves to be a risk factor, but particular areas are more important than others. The fact that the individual subscales provided more information about symptoms than did the more global and inclusive summary scores suggests the presence of areas of particular risk, as well as potential benefit.

Stressors as Predictors of Symptoms in the Long Run

When our attention turned to long-term problems, we once again relied solely on potential risk factors assessed at our first contact with participants. The reason is not only that this allows us to use a prospective model but it also allows us to use information that could readily be available to health professionals who are interested in identifying persons who stand at long-term risk. In these analyses the information on men and women has been combined, due to the similarity of their separate analyses.

Predicting the long-term risk of psychological symptoms from information obtained during the period of marital separation can be accomplished in several ways. In this chapter we looked first at how well initial symptom levels predicted subsequent levels. Given that symptoms exhibit moderate to strong stability over long periods of time (Fiske and Chiriboga 1990), it seemed reasonable to expect that early expressions of symptomatology might be related to later expressions. In point of fact this was true with a vengeance: when we looked at how much of long-term symptomatology was predicted by initial level, we found it to be 41% (the multiple regression coefficient was .64 and highly significant).

Three social context measures were next entered, each being indicated in preliminary analyses to make a relatively strong contribution to prediction. With their inclusion, we now accounted for an additional 3% of the variability in long-term symptoms. People with more children, lower incomes and an ethnic identity were more likely to have symptoms, with lower income being especially important.

Since the total score for childhood deprivation once again contributed relatively little to prediction, we dropped that measure and in fact the majority of other stress measures. After controlling for initial levels of symptoms and social characteristics, only one negative life event made a strong showing: we found that persons with higher levels on negative events related to the home were more symptomatic several years later, regardless of how symptomatic they were at the first interview. Adding this measure increased our understanding of variability in symptoms to 46%.

Finally we included two positive stressors; their presence brought the total explained variability to over 49%. What we found was curious: persons who at first contact reported more positive events related to home and legal issues were more symptomatic later on. In other words, while in the short run positive events acted as buffers against mental health problems, in the long run those positive events that count did so in a direction opposite to expectations. Looking at individual cases provides some explanations. For example, men and women who reported positive legal events at first interview were generally those who seemed to be using the law as a means of getting back at their spouses. The pleasure of this experience, it would appear, is short-lived: people who use this strategy may be at some risk down the road.

As a footnote to the prediction of long-term symptoms we tried substituting the total negative and total positive event scores for the individual subscales. Here we found exactly what was indicated at baseline: the summary score did not do as well as as the individual subscales.

CASE STUDIES

Overall, the stressor component of our stress process model proved to be a justifiable way of approaching the complex phenomenon of adaptation to divorce, whether considered in terms of a stress typology or in terms of regression statistics. The cases we will use to illustrate key points in this chapter represent people who were stable in their Divorce Stress Category at both measurement points.

Cal Havens: Bland in Stress, Superficial in Ties

Cal Havens, a 30-year-old endodontist, greeted the interviewer in an angry, demanding mood, and kept her constantly on the defensive with critical comments like "That's a stupid question" or "That's poorly written." Cal's rather intense exterior demonstrates that membership in the Bland category of the Stress Typology is not necessarily related to having a bland personality. As we shall see, Cal's life suggests that people in this category may create some distance between themselves and others, and this distance may act as a buffer against certain life stresses.

Cal is not one of the least stressed members of the entire sample but he is consistently this way, being categorized as Bland during both the short- and long-term interview contacts. Cal also fits the profile of the Bland group because he is a highly educated male with a positive self-image, few psychological symptoms and few childhood stresses. As we examine Cal's life, we see a man tremendously wrapped up in the world of work, and who seems to view relations with others as interesting diversions that should not be too demanding of time. Cal says his marital relationship was permeated with "continuous arguments and poor communication." One major source of arguments involved the parenting role. Cal wanted more time away from their daughter than his wife thought proper, in order to pursue his interests in work, as well as sailboat racing, wine tasting and racquetball.

Although his somewhat superficial style of interpersonal relations seems to be his own choice, Cal feels he is a lonely man. He felt "lonely during his marriage, and often there was no reason to go home." These feelings of loneliness caused him to "have difficulties concentrating and participating in things." Cal's many divorced friends offer "encouragement and support to do what seems best for [him]." With the exception of a quickly enjoined legal battle with his wife over financial settlement, visitation rights and his daughter's need for psychiatric treatment, Cal speaks in glowing terms of his postmarital life. He said: "I'm having more fun, I have more interests, I am more social, I have a new companion, and I have a better relationship with my daughter."

Continuing on this positive theme about the changes in the four months since the couple separated, Cal said he now feels less dependent, less disappointed in life, and less distant from other people. He feels more responsible and more in control of his life. The divorce had changed the way he felt about himself: "I found it much easier to be alone than I originally thought."

In fact, Cal does not seem to have spent much time alone. He tells the interviewer that he had met a woman at his racquetball club and had been dating her. He "enjoys the companionship and doing activities together. She has taught me how to be more socially at ease." When asked how long he thinks the relationship will last, he said: "I may marry her." When asked about sex, Cal said that with his new girlfriend it is "better and it's more satisfying." While he reports having sexual difficulties with his wife, sex is now like "a fine bottle of wine, [it] can be enjoyed, discussed, but doesn't have to be every day."

Cal certainly does not function like a person undergoing major social upheaval. He reports only one psychological symptom: he misplaces things fairly often. Overall he feels himself to be "pretty happy," and in terms of specific emotions he reports feeling excited, on top of the world and pleased at least once. Life of course is not perfect: Cal also reports feeling angry and that he couldn't get going once during the week prior to the interview.

It may help to consider also the specific areas in which Cal reported positive and negative life events. Positive changes include getting involved in a new specialty area at work, falling in love, beginning to live with someone, giving up a spouse, more social contacts than before, a new close friendship, becoming more involved in hobbies and sports, a major decision regarding his immediate future, and a vacation. It is interesting that Cal views the loss of his spouse in relatively positive terms; as we have discussed earlier in this chapter, how one perceives a stressor can make all the difference in the world.

Cal also reports several negative events: he realized he would never attain an important goal, fell out of love, experienced sexual difficulties, separation from his spouse due to marital problems, began the legal process of divorce and experienced the loss of a pet that his wife took with her. It is perhaps a reflection of Cal's orientation that he notes the loss of pet but says nothing concerning his daughter.

Nearly three and a half years later, Cal is doing even better than before. Cal is still misplacing things and also sometimes has difficulties sleeping. Still feeling "pretty happy," positive emotional experiences have increased: he felt excited, proud, pleased and on top of the world at least once during the week prior to being interviewed. Similar to what he was feeling at the first interview, he reports feeling angry once during the past week and also that several times he felt he had more things to do than he could get done.

Negative events have decreased; Cal is now reporting only one negative stressor: the more chronic condition of being along. Even more than during the impact period, he perceives some events as positive that most people would consider negative: falling out of love, breaking up with a steady girlfriend, and breaking up an engagement. Other events which Cal rated as positive include spending more time at work, more responsibilities at work, a salary increase, fewer family responsibilities than usual, fewer problems with friends, more social contacts than before, a new close friendship, a purchase of more than $10,000 (a new house), and having to make a major decision regarding his immediate future.

Cal is quite comfortable with life. He never feels out of place, or without anyone to whom he can talk to share experiences and feelings, and he never avoids restaurants or shows because he'd be alone. He very often does have a chance to have fun, but once in a while does wonder if he is an interesting person, and feels like he's not having the kind of sex life he would like. He has become perhaps more discriminating about sex, which he says is "only important if I like the person."

About six weeks prior to the second interview, Cal began dating someone he had known for about a year and a half, a receptionist who works with him. Asked "what is your favorite thing to do." Cal provides this cryptic but comprehensive answer: "Good wine, good woman, good food, and a good racquetball game." For Cal, these are the ingredients for "a great social experience that is totally enjoyable and makes you forget other pressures." In retrospect, the decision to separate has changed his life in many positive ways: "Now I am more satisfied with myself, I have a better social life and a better lifestyle. I have a house, a new car, and a wine cellar."

In his rather materialistic wrap-up of his life, Cal is if anything making an understatement. He now lives in a very nice, large home with a spectacular view of the San Francisco Bay. While his beautiful, new girlfriend prepares dinner in the kitchen, Cal confides to the interviewer that he had gone through some "heavy duty" psychiatric problems and therapy. He believes that these problems caused the breakup of his marriage, but that he now thinks that he has come to grips with them. We find it curious that Cal rarely sees his daughter and mentions her only when directly asked. On the whole, Cal's rather superficial and use-oriented approach to social relations seems to have smoothed the transitional pathway leading from separation to reabsorption in a new life.

Maria Martinez: Challenged

Maria Martinez fits the profile of a Challenged person: she is young, highly educated, feels in control of her life and experiences more than her share of negative and positive events. Maria, an energetic and emotional 27-year-old Chicana with long dark hair, is in her second year in a school of veterinary medicine.

Maria is distraught that her marriage of only one year's duration is breaking up. Her husband, also a student in veterinary medicine, initiated the breakup and has been consistently most in favor of getting divorced. The reasons that Maria offers for the separation are rather vague: "We had arguments off and on and then we had a terrible spring semester and were separated during the summer because my preceptorship was in another city. We had a big argument over a movie at the end of summer and that finished it [the marriage] and he then asked for a divorce." Later in the interview she adds as additional problems his drinking, smoking and tendency to be a party-animal, and her overall lack of trust in him.

Maria reported a broad variety of emotions on the Bradburn Scale, including being lonely, restless, depressed and unable to get going. As might be expected of someone in the Challenged category, she also felt excited, pleased, proud and on top of the world at least once during the past week. She generally feels "pretty happy," and we can see from other parts of the interview that all is not entirely bad in Maria's life. In fact she reports some benefits of getting a divorce, saying "I can get to know other people," and "I know myself better and rely on myself."

Maria still sees her husband every day at school. The day before the first interview they studied together and then made love. Because of this pattern of seeing each other, Maria thinks there is a chance that they could still reconcile. She says "We are both more understanding of each other's thoughts and needs and that he is trying not to be so one-sided." She misses her husband's companionship, suffers from extreme loneliness and dreams about getting back together with him.

By follow-up, it has become clear that these dreams have been dashed forever. In fact, Maria says that the single most stressful event of getting divorced was seeing her husband with other women. This made her feel jealous and angry. At the same time she now feels she has grown as a person: "I have become more confident, independent, able to speak openly about almost anything to anyone—more vocal."

Maria hopes to develop independence and self-confidence, feel good about living alone and eventually establish a lasting, comfortable relationship with someone. She daydreams about the good times with her family, goes over stresses during the day and thinks about present relationships and past romantic involvements including her spouse. She now feels "very happy" and reports an even broader range of emotions that she experiences more frequently. This rather positive image is somewhat mitigated by the fact that she also now reports 16 psychological symptoms, as opposed to the 11 reported at first contact.

This increase in symptoms may be related to the high levels of negative as well as positive events she has sustained over the course of the study. Without providing an interminable list of positive and negative stressors, we will organize these stressors according to the major events in Maria's work, personal life and family, as reported in our second interview. By follow-up she has gradated from veterinary school and made major decisions concerning her immediate future, such as the choice of her speciality area and the location of her further training. She has moved to a new city and experienced an improvement in her living conditions. Her new work, a specialized training program regarding animal trauma cases, involves more responsibilities, spending more time at work, having trouble with other workers, feeling overwhelmed by difficult situations and having reoccurring unpleasant thoughts or images.

Concerning her personal life, she has fallen out of love within the past year, experienced sexual difficulties, had feelings of loneliness and experienced feelings of intense dislike for someone she deals with often. Events that Maria felt were positive included: developing a new close friendship, falling in love, a change in physical appearance, a change in drinking habits, home improvement, a purchase of less than 10,000 dollars, experimenting with drugs other than marijuana, a vacation and a long trip.

There are additional negative stressors concerning Maria's family. She reports the health problem of a family member, fewer family responsibilities, and fewer family get-togethers. These events are particularly sad for Maria who comes from a large, Catholic family of five sisters and two brothers. Being with her family is her absolute favorite thing to do, especially "finding our how they are; talking and sharing things; doing things together." All in all she is managing quite well, despite the many changes, both for good and for bad, going on in her life.

Tina Tighter: A Loser

At the first interview, Tina Tighter is asked what sort of things she tends to think about these days. She replies: "I think about the bad things that happened in the past and the bad things that may happen in the future." Asked about how her life compares to that of other divorced people, she says: "I don't think anybody is worse than me." These two responses seem to sum up the life and times not only of Tina, but of many of those we categorized as Losers in the Stress Category. Especially for those, like Tina, who remained in the Loser category, life is indeed tough.

As you may recall, on the Stress Typology, Losers are persons who score highest in negative events and lowest in the positive ones. These people are often from a minority background, older, have a vulnerable self-image, a low desirable self-score and have experienced childhood stress. Tina matches this profile reasonably well. She is an African American, a 40-year-old secretary who wears her hair in an Afro style. She is about 5'2" and 15 pounds overweight. The day of the interview she dressed in a garish, purple, sequined, sleeveless top and tight black slacks. Tina owns a bungalow with a sunny kitchen and garden in the flats of the East Oakland ghetto. The living room in furnished with expensive oak furniture, and the walls are covered with gold-veined mirrors and pictures of her children in gilded frames. Tina has two teenage daughters and one son, all of whom were fathered as the result of relationships prior to her marriage.

When asked what precipitated the decision to separate, Tina says: "When my husband beat my daughter and then she and I [Tina and her daughter] both jumped on him." Tina explained that her husband has a history of alcoholism and violence. In fact, Tina gave up hoping to reconcile with him when "he went to jail because he shot someone."

Tina is most concerned now with finding a new husband, especially one that will help her financially. When she was asked what kinds of things she thinks about, she replies: "Surviving. How I'm going to survive and when will I ever meet anybody who will think the same way I think. I think about the problems I might have the next day or that I had the day before. Most, will I ever meet anybody that I will be content with." What she wants is to "find somebody that understands me and maybe get married again. Have something with somebody. Share my life. But I just don't trust anybody."

Tina is not doing too well at this first visit. She reports 30 symptoms on our symptoms checklist, and reports herself to be "not too happy." Still, she sees some benefits to the separation: "I feel more free because when I was with him I felt tied down. He didn't want me going anywhere or doing anything. He didn't want me having any friends." She "enjoys going out— enjoying life—going to Reno. I enjoy gambling, being with people. I just like doing what I want to do." When she can do exactly as she pleases, she enjoys dancing because it helps her forget her problems. Her second most favorite thing to do is lying in bed watching TV—she feels not having to get up is very relaxing.

Consistent not only with membership in the Loser category, but also (as we shall see in chapter 11) with being a black American, Tina reports more than the usual number of childhood stressors. Five in total, these included the frequent absence of her mother or father, separation from her father or mother due to divorce or desertion, the divorce of her parents, the remarriage of her father or mother and having to go to work to help support her family. She still thinks a lot about these childhood experiences and is very unhappy about them. On the life history profile, which involves rating each year of life according to satisfaction or dissatisfaction, she hits rock bottom around the age of 30, 10 years ago, and continues at that level up to the present. Both now and at follow-up she is unable to project her level of satisfaction with life even one year into the future.

These childhood stressors may have contributed to her compulsive self-reliance, a characteristic that is revealed by her lack of trust in others and lack of confidants. At follow-up her self-reliance is even more prominent; she said she feels more distant from others "because I don't trust anybody now." She also feels more disappointed in life. She said she had lost friends since the separation. When asked what happened: "Well, because I stopped dealing with people, really, for a while." She said that there are no friends or relatives that she can tell everything to. She also said that she is without anyone to talk to about herself, she wonders if she may not be an interesting person and feels she is not having the kind of sex life she wants.

The three and a half years that had passed since the first interview did not make things any easier for Tina. She still finds it hard to meet men. She explains: "I feel, you know, like . . . it's kinda hard for me to find somebody I care about. When I was married I could find what I wanted but now . . . nothing." She later added: "I just feel like I'm too old now. I don't feel like I can find anybody." And when asked about sex, Tina said: "It isn't really important. I guess I've got a hang-up. I feel that's all men want. They don't want a lady they can take care of. They just want to take you to bed and then go on about their business. They don't want anything out of life."

Tina now reveals a history of sexual abuses that apparently had gone on without her knowledge: "My husband did things to my kids that I don't know anything about, and they tended to feel distant from me, thinking I knew. They just told me a few months ago. They don't want me to have any kind of man around. I feel less close to them now." Tina comments that since the separation the children have: "gotten closer to my mother. Because when I was with him, he didn't allow them to go over there. He was possessive and jealous, especially about my mother."

As she reviews her experiences from the vantage point of the second interview, she concludes that "Finances were the biggest problem. How was I going to survive? Financially, I thought it would be worse and it was. It's what I expected. That's why it took me so long to break it up because of the financial problems I'm having now. I knew it would be like this." She adds that the most stressful thing about the divorce was "the lack of funds. It really did me in. I almost lost my home. I couldn't make payments and had to borrow."

At follow-up there is little suggestion that Tina's psychological well-being has improved. She reports 29 symptoms and continues to report she is "not too happy" on the Bradburn Scale. During the past week she never experienced any of the Bradburn Scale positive emotions but she often experienced most of the negative ones, including feeling very lonely or remote from other people, depressed and unhappy, bored, restless, having more things to do than she could get done and vaguely uneasy without knowing why. In fact, she says that she feels most suicidal now: "But not because of the divorce—I always felt that way—before and after—partly because he was so terrible and now because I have no meaning in life—the kids are grown and away from home and I'm all by myself most of the time."

Ambrose Pierce: A Winner

Ambrose Pierce fits into the Winners category of the Stress Typology; in fact, he reports the lowest negative stress events and the highest positive ones both at the first and second interviews. In addition, we might also label him a Winner because he reported a relatively high level of symptoms, initially, but was extremely low at the second contact.

Ambrose is a tall, blond and handsome man with piercing looks. He wore faded denim jeans and a denim jacket with a red shirt open at the chest to reveal a medallion of a racing car on a gold chain. Ambrose easily develops rapport with the interviewer, in marked contrast to Cal Havens, and speaks in a sincere, relaxed style. Ambrose is 49 years old, and had training at a nationally recognized art school. Although he does not think of himself as belonging to an ethnic group, both a paternal and a maternal grandparent were Hispanic Americans. He is not working at present, but recently sold a moderately successful art gallery that also produced illustrations for professional publications and businesses. His wife is a radio personality who often makes the lecture circuit and the two often collaborated on the media aspects of her presentations.

Married at the age of 39, the couple now have a girl aged 9 and a boy aged 7. The couple were together a lot and had few problems on the surface; in fact they fought only 2 or 3 times in the whole 10 years of marriage. At the same time he feels that during the whole time he did not have a life of his own.

Asked what led up to the separation, Ambrose first focuses on economic issues: "My business wasn't doing well—no money was a big thing. Plus she had been out on speaking engagements for a number of weeks. When she came back she said she was tired of living on such a shoestring with so much insecurity—even though we always made ends meet." Gradually other problems emerge. For one thing, we learn that Ambrose maintained a whole network of friends that were his alone. "She didn't care for my friends—they were all Kooks to her." He also had many interests that his wife didn't share: spiritual interests (he is religious, she isn't), an interest in psychic phenomena and meditation, plays, (he liked the serious stuff, while she liked comedy and music), business, (she thought his own business was doomed), and art (she only liked the parts that helped her own work).

Initially his wife was most in favor of getting divorced and now they both are. He still sees her at least once a month. "Three days ago I went to see the kids and to get mail. We talked, went out to eat, talked about her work." Asked how he feels with his spouse he said: "Fine. She said the other day 'you know, you're my best friend.' We have resentments—annoyances more I guess you'd say, still. But we get along well." Asked when he gave up hope for the marriage, he replies "As soon as she said 'divorce.'"

Life in the five months that have passed since the separation has been pretty good for Ambrose. "I feel more free, more ambitious." Asked to predict changes that will occur within the next year, he replies "I think it'll be more structured. I have different friends and a new lifestyle now." The greatest benefit has been "I'm doing what I want to do." His goals for the next five years include creating "a more structured life, taking a job that is creative, that I really like, that's fun and pays a good salary. I want to do things to help people. I want to be a self-actualized person. I want a job or position with prestige. I'm up for jobs right now, both working in the media for good companies.

Evidence supporting this optimism comes from an instrument to be discussed in chapter 6, the Revised Trauma Scale that asks when people feel most and least of certain emotions. Ambrose reports that right now is the time he feels the least depressed, least anxious or worried, the most optimistic about the future, the most energetic and confident. He continues that he is "pretty happy" (and clarifies this with the word "peaceful"), and generally reports feeling all the positive and negative emotions on the Bradburn Affect Scales except for boredom. He reports 10 symptoms.

There is one episode where something akin to a breakdown may have occurred. When asked what was the loneliest period of his life he said: "The weekend everything flipped—two months after we separated." Ambrose was driving to see his kids and "the streets got wavy, everything was moving. Very disoriented time." When asked why that time was lonely he said "I don't know. I had sold the business. I went to a porno movie on Market Street and stayed there for three movies."

At this stage of the interview we suddenly learn something else about Ambrose: he is gay. Once this fact surfaces, Ambrose becomes more animated and he begins to discuss his dating life. He has been dating a man for the past two months, although he sees it as nothing serious. What he likes most about the relationship is: "Sex. It's like a bath—you need one every day." He thinks the separation has in fact led to an improvement in his sex life and it emerges that he is now living with his new love. One of the consequences of being able to freely live in his more preferred lifestyle is "I feel much much freer, stronger, and more whole."

Before turning to how Ambrose fares at our second contact, it should be noted that while he reports a host of positive experiences and few negative ones currently, Ambrose's childhood actually appears to have had more than its share of stress. Included are items dealing with separation on bad terms from parents or brothers and sisters, having to go to work to help support your family, the frequent absence of your mother and father and death of a brother or sister. On the measure of perceived stress based on the life evaluation chart he rated at 2 or "very low" until the age of 15, when his evaluation skyrockets to 8, or "very good."

As we visit with Ambrose at follow-up, we find that he has no regrets about the separation and subsequent divorce. "I didn't think about it before I left, then I moved into my office and for three months it was really hard. . . . I flipped, really, hallucinating and all, but after three months things were okay. . . . I really didn't think about it before, my lifestyle has really changed totally." Ambrose has been living with a boyfriend for two weeks now. He is a 26-year-old who works for the same large bank as Ambrose. They are a happy pair and Ambrose is pleased with the course his life has taken.

Ambrose now reports only six psychological symptoms and says he is "very happy" now. On the Bradburn items he often feels on top of the world, and several times during the past week felt particularly excited or interested in something, pleased about having accomplished something and proud because someone complimented him on something he had done. He only felt one negative emotion—anger at something that usually wouldn't bother him. At this stage of life he feels least depressed, least anxious or worried, most optimistic about the future, most energetic and confident, least suicidal, least angry with his former wife. He feels that he has become "a spiritual person . . . I'm very involved with metaphysics." As we listen to Ambrose, and review the two rather lengthy interviews we had with this man over a period covering nearly four years of his life, we are struck by the freedom he has obtained. In marriage he conformed to a lifestyle mismatched to his needs; the marital dissolution has allowed him to sculpt an entirely new life that is considerably more fulfilling than his old.

SUMMING UP: LIFE EVENTS AS RISK FACTORS IN ADAPTATION

Clearly life events are not the only issue that needs to be looked at in divorce, but they are just as clearly forces to be reckoned with. In this chapter we identified several risk factors. For example, the single best predictor of how well people will fare in the long run is how they are faring during the crisis of marital separation. There were also several social characteristics that were identified as risk factors. During the impact phase these included: being a woman, being a member of a minority group and being less educated. In the long run being a woman and a member of a minority group continued to operate as risk factors, and lower income as assessed during the impact phase also became important. We also explored the role that children have as both a potential stress enhancer and barrier against the opportunity to experience positive life events after separation and divorce.

One closing comment we would like to make concerns the predictability of event measures at follow-up. There is an axiom in psychology that the best predictor of something is usually the way that same thing was at an earlier point. In our companion study of transitions, we found both positive and negative life event subscales to be significantly correlated over relatively long periods of time. These correlations were not only for the same subscale at different points, but across subscales (Fiske and Chiriboga 1990). The implication is that exposure to stress is somewhat generalized: people who score high in one area are more likely to score high in several areas, and this holds true over time.

In contrast, the experience of life events at follow-up was not strongly related to the experiencing of events during the impact phase of divorce. The correlations were generally insignificant except when the same content area was being compared, and even here the magnitude of correlations never exceeded the mid-30s. What seems to be happening is that the events of the impact phase are interjects, phenomena whose presence has very little to do with the normal routine of day-to-day living. These events have a life and governing source that is different from what usually transpires, and therefore are not very predictive of levels of stress exposure some years later.

4

COPING STRATEGIES IN DIVORCE

David A. Chiriboga

In the preceding chapter we examined some of the stressors that may affect divorcing men and women. We found that while stressors were associated with greater symptomatology in both the long and short runs, they did not explain everything about symptom levels. One reason may be that people vary greatly in how they cope with the stressors of divorce.

SOME DEFINITIONAL ISSUES

Coping is a term we use to try to explain why some people thrive and others fail in response to the same basic conditions of life. Although the word is widely used, there is considerable disagreement, dating back to the time of Aristotle and Plato, about how to conceptualize and measure coping. One disagreement concerns whether coping refers to behavior directed towards alleviating a specific stressful situation, to general personality traits, to what used to be called defense mechanisms, or to some combination of all of these. At the most general level, the word "coping" can refer to any activity intended to reduce distress, or only to those behaviors and qualities associated with the actual alleviation of distress (Lazarus and Folkman 1984; Pearlin et al. 1981).

Another disagreement concerns whether there are few or many styles of coping. Many researchers have tried to identify multiple and distinct catego-ries of coping on the basis of factor analyses, but another tradition in stress research is to cast people into two camps: either as people who are vigilant and attentive to signs of a stress condition and who seek out information about stress conditions, or as people who act to avoid or minimize the stress condition (e.g., Janis 1974; Cohen and Lazarus 1973). Lazarus and Folkman (1984) divide coping behaviors into those that are problem focused and those that are emotion focused, while Miller (1989) speaks of Monitors who are vigilant and alert to signs of stress and Blunters who seek to avoid threatening situations by physical or cognitive means.

Despite the confusion over how the term should be defined, the meaning and nature of coping remain important topics. After all, we usually cannot avoid contact with stressors and so therefore the question most often becomes not one of avoidance per se but of reducing the stress response. And as far as the question of styles versus categories of coping is concerned, the two are actually not mutually exclusive positions: there may be multiple categories of coping, and these may be the "building blocks" from which coping styles are developed.

Three Categories of Coping

There is an emerging consistency in the kinds of behaviors covered by the term coping. Leonard Pearlin, formerly with the National Institutes of Mental Health and now associated with the Human Development and Aging Program, San Francisco, has outlined the basic categories of coping. For Pearlin (Pearlin and Schooler 1978; Pearlin et al. 1981) there are three basic categories. One involves taking direct action to resolve the problems being faced by the individual. Confronting the situation, studying for an exam and asking for help are examples of direct actions. The second category consists of indirect actions that involve redefining the situation or which help pave the way towards a solution but which in themselves do not resolve the stress. Reading about the situation, deciding that it's not so bad after all, and making friends with the right people are examples of behavior that can represent indirect attempts at coping with stressful conditions. Third and finally, there are palliative behaviors, which represent attempts to deal not with the stress condition but with the emotions generated by the stressor, which may threaten to overwhelm the individual.

Pearlin's coping model is clearly not the only way of specifying the concept of coping, but there actually is considerable overlap among competing models. For example, in the two-category model used by Lazarus and Folkman (1984), problem-focused coping would probably subsume both Pearlin's direct and indirect behaviors, and emotion-focused coping seems to overlap conceptually with Pearlin's palliative category. Lazarus and Folkman do, however, add another important ingredient: they emphasize that coping is not all overt behavior but involves cognitive assessments as well. Moreover, cognitive assessments of situations may change over time, as the individual reassesses the situation. Such reassessments they term "Cognitive reappraisal."

From the point of view of those interested in how people going through a divorce cope with stressors, two themes are salient. First, almost any kind of coping can help or hinder, depending on the context and the individual. Second, palliative or emotion-focused behavior has the potential of being the most disruptive, if continued long enough. Consider, for example, the individual who has been promoted to a position of leadership beyond his or her basic ability, but who feels unable or unwilling to admit this inability. Caught in a chronic stress context, one solution may be to resort to alcohol or cocaine. These drugs can, temporarily, make the individual feel masterful or more relaxed, and may be a reasonable expedient in the short run. However, they do not generate solutions and in the long run can exacerbate the problem.

HOW WE STUDIED COPING

Coping was assessed by the Lazarus and Folkman (1984) Ways of Coping Scale, which was administered at the second interview. Following the approach advocated by Lazarus and Folkman, we asked people to identify the most stressful experience of the past month and then asked them to check off which of 68 individual coping strategies (e.g., "Just concentrated on what you had to do," "Bargained or compromised to get something positive from the situation") they had used. Our first concern was to reduce the 68 individual items to a more manageable number. This was done by means of an oblique factor analysis. The analyses yielded eight factors, each of which can be considered as a "building block" for coping styles. *

The eight coping factors can be grouped according to Pearlin's conceptual framework. As mentioned earlier, Pearlin and his colleagues divided coping behaviors into those directed at altering the problem situation, those which

---

* For those interested in the technical details, the proportion of initial communality exhausted by the factors was .93, the mean squared residual correlation with the eight extracted factors was .00, and the average intercorrelation of factor scores was .20. The Cronbach alpha levels with one exception ranged from .62 to .80. With an alpha of .54, emotive action was the exception; it was retained since the analyses were intended to be exploratory.

seek to redefine or indirectly alter the situation, and those whose goal is stress management in the sense of managing the stress response. The factors that represented situation-altering behaviors include *Helpseeking* (e.g., "Talked to someone to find out more about the situation," and "Got professional help and did what they recommended") and *Active Mastery* (e.g., "Stood your ground and fought for what you wanted," and "Changed something so things would turn out all right").

Two coping factors represented situation-redefining and other indirect behaviors. One was *Growth* (e.g., "Changed or grew as a person in a good way," "Rediscovered what is important in life") and the other was *Wish-fulfilling Fantasy* ("had fantasies or wishes about how things might turn out" and "Daydreamed or imagined a better time or place than the one I was in").

The remaining four coping factors dealt with management of emotions. One factor suggested the use of cognitive strategies, and was labeled *Cognitive Control* ("Didn't let it get to you; refused to think too much about it," and "Made light of the situation; refused to get too serious about it"). The others dealt in one fashion or another with emotional-focused behaviors. *Emotive Action* ("Accepted sympathy and understanding from someone," "Let your feelings out somehow,") generally dealt with both accepting and releasing one's feelings. *Self-Blame* ("Blamed yourself," "Criticized or lectured yourself") was cast more negatively.

One factor, *Fatalism* ("Went along with fate; sometimes you just have bad luck," "Accepted it, since nothing could be done") seems to fall somewhere between redefinition of the situation and emotional control. For simplicity it was categorized at least initially under stress management because the theme of all five items included in this factor was to distance oneself and control distress, and to await a better day.

Life Course and Gender Differences in Coping Strategies

Having defined a set of coping strategies, our next goal was to determine whether younger and older respondents differed from each other. Previous work by Gutmann (1964, 1985) and others (Lowenthal et al. 1975), for example, suggested that middle-agers would stand out as being more masterful in their orientation to coping. Two-way analyses of variance indicated that the older divorcing men and women did not differ in any major and systematic way from the younger. Of the eight strategies, age was relevant only once: younger respondents, especially those in their twenties, were more likely to resort to Emotive Action, action, that is, which may indicate emotional discharge or ventilation rather than direct confrontation. For Fatalism, there was also an interesting interaction of age with gender: men in their forties were the least fatalistic of any group, while women in their forties were the most fatalistic.

Gender differences were also minimal, but suggest that, at least in the context of divorce, women tend to use more passive and emotion-oriented strategies. For example, they were significantly higher than men in Fatalism, and tended to score higher in Emotive Action and Wish-fulfilling Fantasy.

Coping Factors as Predictors of Adaptation among Men

The identification of factor-derived coping strategies led to a series of analyses in which we correlated coping strategies with the total number of symptoms reported at follow-up. We assessed the data for men and women separately, since there is evidence that men and women use very different strategies to cope with stress (e.g., Lazarus and Folkman 1984). Once again we used hierarchical regression analyses, which allowed us to order the entry of data in a manner consistent with the stress process model. More importantly, it allowed us to examine the contribution of each set of predictor variables, and compare how each set contributes to the prediction of symptoms. The predictive sets were entered in the following order: (1) social context variables (age, ethnicity, income and number of children); (2) the 11 negative life event subscales; (3) the 11 positive life event subscales; and (4) the 8 coping strategies. The event scales and coping scales assess data from the long-term contact, so here we are adding information that was not presented in chapter 3: we are looking at how life events for the year preceding the follow-up influenced symptoms, as well as looking at the relationship of coping to symptom expression.

Education was the only social context variable to be even slightly associated with the long-term symptomatology of men, and explained only 2% of the variance. The less educated were more symptomatic. Two negative event scales also figured. Contributing nearly 9% of explained variance, we found that the more symptomatic men reported more health-related events and more negative events related to home life. Slightly more than 2% of variance was explained by positive internal events (thoughts and feelings about things). With the addition of the final set of measures, the set that assessed coping strategies, a full 13% of variance in symptoms was explained. The more symptomatic men were more likely to use cognitive control and self blaming, and less likely to use active mastery strategies.

Coping Factors as Predictors of Adaptation among Women

An initial sweep to identify extraneous variables led to second regression analyses. Here we found that, as expected, measures associated with long-term symptomatology for women are quite different from those of men. For example, women with lower incomes and who belonged to some ethnic group were more symptomatic at follow-up. Together these two measures explained 10% of the variance in symptomatology at long-term follow-up. Three negative event subscales together contributed another 23% of the variance. More symptomatic women reported more inner events (for example, realizing they would never attain an important goal), more health-related events and to a lesser extent more work stress. Note that negative work events were also related to higher symptoms among the men. Three positive event scales contributed 5% to the variance. Those with more symptoms reported fewer positive events related to school and home life; curiously, they also reported more positive events related to marriage and dating.

As was the case for predicting symptoms for men, the coping set again played a significant role. Three coping strategies contributed 8.5% of the variance. More symptomatic women were more likely to use Cognitive control, Fantasy and Help Seeking as coping strategies. Intuitively it makes sense that persons who use strategies such as trying to control their emotional reactions by not thinking about problems, or by fantasizing a better life, might in the long run have problems. That Help Seeking is associated with greater symptomatology can be interpreted in two ways. First, persons who use higher levels of Help Seeking may be having a harder time finding someone to help them. Second, they may be more likely to seek help simply because they are in greater distress. We favor the second explanation, since other analyses (see chapter 9) indicate that people who favor Help Seeking as a strategy also have have more extensive social networks and therefore would probably not have a harder time finding help.

Reviewing the results, we find consistent differences by gender in the factors that predict long-term symptomatology. For example, it was the less educated men who demonstrated greater symptomatology, while among the women the more symptomatic were less affluent and more likely to belong to ethnic groups. The association of stress measures also varied by gender, although negative events related to health were found to associate with symptoms among both men and women.

As we expected, coping strategies did contribute to the prediction of symptoms, but again they generally did so in different ways for men and women. Attempts at cognitive control of the stressful situation were linked with greater symptomatology for both men and women. Men reporting greater symptomatology at follow-up (suggesting they had coped less adequately with divorce) were more likely to report using Self-Blame and less likely to use strategies employing attempts at Active Mastery. On the other hand, the more symptomatic women were higher in use of Fantasy and higher in Help Seeking.

In short, while coping strategies were associated with adaptation, at least as the latter is defined by the symptoms measure, the associations were often not what we predicted. One reason for these rather confusing results may be that regression analyses do not take into account the pattern of coping strategies. As an example, it may be that an individual benefits most from Help Seeking only when this behavior is associated with other coping strategies, such as Active Mastery or Emotive Action. To explore this possibility, we looked at profiles of coping.

PROFILES OF COPING

A pitfall in relying solely on factor analysis to study coping is that the technique generates what might be called independent "building blocks" of coping. Each of the eight coping strategies was independent of all others, and each could play a role in coping. Hence, since each individual could use one or more of the strategies, they coexist within the same individual, to varying degrees. One of our goals was to find out if the profile or pattern of coping strategies used by people made a difference, and also to find out whether any of our participants shared similar profiles or "styles" of coping. There is a type of statistical technique called "cluster" analysis that allows the user to compare profiles of scores across people. In our work we employed a cluster program developed by Tryon and Bailey (1970); both SPSS and SAS, the statistical packages most frequently used by social scientists, also include such programs, but the Tryon program is particularly robust since it makes fewer assumptions about how the data are distributed.

Seven coping types or styles were identified. The first type appear to be *Noncopers*. The 21 persons (12 men and 9 women) categorized as Noncopers were the lowest, or equal to the lowest, on seven of the coping strategies. They were intermediate only on Self-Blame.

Two coping styles were significantly higher than the rest on the situation-altering factors of Help Seeking and Active Mastery, but differed from each other on most of the remaining strategies. One style, labeled *Action Copers*, included 20 men and 17 women. High on Help Seeking and Active Mastery, they were generally low on the Situation Redefining and Stress Management coping strategies. The second style, labeled *Supercopers*, were not only high on Help Seeking and Active Mastery but on most of the other factors as well. Including 41 people, they were intermediate only on Self-Blame and Fantasy, two strategies that were reported in the previous section to be associated with greater symptomatology.

The 19 *Mystics* (6 men and 13 women) were highest in the perception of stress as a growth possibility. Like the Stoics described below, the Mystics were high on Fatalism and Emotive Action but low to intermediate on all other strategies.

The 32 *Stoics* (13 men and 19 women) shared with the Mystics the quality of being high in Fatalism and Emotive Action. But while the Mystics were also highly optimistic about the growth-promoting possibilities in their situation, the Stoics were the highest on a stress management strategy: Cognitive Control. That is, they were the most likely of all types to use selective ignoring as a coping strategy—a strategy that Pearlin and Schooler (1978) found to be the least effective mediator of stress.

The *Balanced* style consisted of 29 persons (8 men and 21 women) who generally fell in the intermediate region on all strategies. In essence they were "middle of the roaders" as far as coping is concerned. Finally, the 36 *Imaginative Escapers* (13 men and 23 women) were relatively high on the situation-altering and situation-redefining strategies but were extremely high on Self-Blame and Wish-fulfilling Fantasy.

The coping styles used by divorced men and women indicate a considerable spread in approaches used to handle stressful situations. The Action Copers, for example, were a relatively pure "situation-altering" group. In this, they stood in contrast to the Supercopers, who were high not only in situation-altering behaviors but on nearly all the others as well. The Noncopers, again in contrast, tended not to use any of the coping strategies included in the 68-item Ways of Coping Scale. Then there were the Imaginative Escapers, highest on the strategies of Self-Blame and Fantasy, that previous analyses with other samples (Chiriboga and Bailey 1989) have indicated as maladaptive. The Mystics and Stoics resembled each other closely on all strategies save that Mystics were higher on the Growth approach to redefining situations while Stoics were high in Cognitive Control, an emotion-focused strategy. And the Balanced stood out only as people who in fact did not stand out, but instead scored in the more or less average range for each strategy.

Towards a Specification of Style

To explore the significance of these different styles of coping, we first examined how people distributed on both coping and stress categories at the second interview (keep in mind that coping was assessed only at this second interview). Several of the coping styles had very distinct distributions. For example, 55% of the Noncopers fell into the Bland category, and 70% of the Active Mastery-style copers were either Bland or Winners at follow-up. On the other hand, 64% of the Imaginative Escapers were Losers or Challenged, in either case being high in exposure to negative events. The Stoics showed the highest proportion of Losers, at 34%, while the Active Mastery copers and Mystics were least likely to be Losers.

Another way of understanding the coping styles was to identify characteristics that predicted them. To do this, we examined the baseline characteristics of the people in each style. The reason for relying on baseline information was our interest in whether coping strategies reflect more or less enduring ways of approaching what life has to offer. We used once again a discriminant analysis model, in which several sets of variables were each examined for their ability to distinguish among the seven coping styles.

The first set of variables included age, gender, education, income, ethnicity (coded as no or yes) and number of children. Age and gender made contributions. The Noncopers were the oldest, with an average age of approximately 40. The Action Copers were next—they averaged 36 years—and the remaining groups were not significantly different. Noncopers, Action Copers and Stoics were more likely to be men; Supercopers, Mystics, Balanced Copers and Imaginative Escapers were more likely to be women. While the two variables made significant contributions, including them in the prediction equation resulted in only 23% percent of the cases being correctly classified. Forty-three percent of the Action Copers and 68% of the Supercopers were correctly placed, but practically no one was correctly placed in the other groups. The high accuracy of classifying Supercopers when only age and gender were included is surprising, especially since this level of accuracy actually fell when additional predictors were entered into the equation.

Since we were particularly interested in determining whether coping styles may reflect enduring predispositions, in these analyses we included the 13 individual items that assessed presumed childhood events. Four of these entered the equation, of which two were indicated in chapter 2 to have a potential "steeling" effect: separation on bad terms from parents, and parental death. Supercopers and Imaginative Escapers were most likely to report separation on bad terms from a parent, Action and Balanced Copers were least likely to do so. Death of a parent was most likely to be reported by Active Copers and Supercopers, least likely to be reported by Stoics. These findings suggest the possibility that Supercopers represent the "hardy" or stress-resilient profile identified by some stress researchers (e.g., Kobasa, Maddi and Covington 1981; Garmazy 1981). The remaining two childhood events had been associated with greater deficit in chapter 1, but their distribution across coping styles was not very revealing. For example, parental divorce was most likely to be reported by Active Copers and least likely to be reported by Mystics and Balanced Copers. Death of a sibling was most likely to be reported by Noncopers and Imaginative Escapers. Including childhood event measures brought the overall accuracy of prediction up to 28%.

Next we included Self-Esteem and several other measures of self-image derived from an Adjective Rating List (see chapter 7). Those manifesting self-images marked by hostility were most likely to be Balanced Copers and Stoics, while the lowest were Mystics. An image of oneself as vulnerable was most likely to be found among Stoics, and least likely among Noncopers and Imaginative Escapers. Those with an image of themselves as actively master-ful or forceful were most likely to be Active Copers and least likely to be Noncopers. Those with a socially skilled self-image were more likely to be Supercopers and least likely to be Noncopers. These results suggest the possibility that the Stoics maintain a rather negative self-image, while Active Copers and Supercopers are people who maintain relatively energized self-images. Despite the coherent picture afforded by the self-image measures, they increased correct classification by only 2%. Mystics were most poorly predicted, with none being placed correctly, while nearly 60% of the Action Copers were correctly placed.

Social support measures were then entered, including presence of a confidant, number of people talked to about the separation and possible divorce, number of friends, proximity to parents, proximity to other close relatives, how often relatives were visited and number of siblings. The results, while significant, are hard to interpret. Noncopers were definitely least likely to have a parent living nearby, probably because as a group they are the oldest. Imaginative Escapers were also less likely to live near a parent, while Action Copers and Stoics were most likely. Mystics and Imaginative Escapers talked to the most people about their separation and possible divorce, Stoics talked to the least. Noncopers had the most siblings while Action Copers and Mystics had the fewest. Having a confidant to talk to was most characteristic of the Balanced Copers and Mystics, with most of the remainder being indistinguishable. Overall, these results point to a possible isolation of the Stoics, but little else. Classification accuracy reached nearly 34% with the addition of characteristics reflecting social support.

Of two indicators of control obtained during the impact phase, one dealing with general perceptions of control and the other dealing with control over the divorce, only the general sense of control contributed to the predictive equation. Balanced Copers were most likely to feel themselves in control of their lives; this was least true of the Mystics, although Stoics and Supercopers also were low in overall sense of control. Introduction of the general control measure brought overall accuracy of prediction up to 37%. Not entered into the equation due to the technical aspects of the analysis, differences in perceived control over the divorce also deserve mention: Mystics were most likely to feel in control of the divorce, followed by the Supercopers and Balanced Copers; this was least true of the Stoics, who once again seem to be a group at risk.

Our next predictive set dealt with four measures of adaptation at first interview, all of which successfully entered the equation. Overall, these results suggested that Stoics may be people who generally exhibit the most disturbed psychological functioning, while the Action Copers come off best. Stoics, for example, averaged the most symptoms, followed closely by the Supercopers; Balanced Copers, Action Copers and Mystics were lowest. Imaginative Escapers and Supercopers averaged the most negative affect; Active Copers averaged fewest negative emotions. Noncopers and Stoics were lowest in overall happiness, Action Copers and Mystics were the happiest. On positive affect, Noncopers and Stoics reported the lowest scores; Imaginative Escapers reported the most positive affect.

Overall accuracy of prediction was definitely improved by the addition of the four measures of adaptation: 43% of the cases were predicted successfully, up 6% from the last set. Fifty percent of the Noncopers and 59% of the Action Copers were being placed accurately at this point; however, only one of the 36 Supercopers was placed in the right group. Since we are predicting follow-up coping styles from data collected over three years previously, this suggests that possibly the Supercoper category is a less stable one, and possibly one that is more dependent on the current context.

As a final way of predicting coping strategies, we added positive and negative life event scales from the impact period. Eight of the 22 subscales contributed to prediction. Imaginative Escapers reported the most negative personal events, followed by Supercopers; the Balanced Copers and Action Copers reported fewest negative personal events. Mystics and Stoics reported greater amounts of negative work events, while Balanced Copers, Supercopers and Action Copers reported the least work stress. Stoics reported the most negative financial events, Action Copers, Balanced Copers and Mystics reported the least. Stoics and Imaginative Escapers reported the most negative health events at first interview, Mystics reported the least. Generally, it would appear that Stoics and Imaginative Escapers were experiencing more than their share of negative events.

Turning to stressors that reflect positive changes, Noncopers and Mystics reported the fewest positive home events, Stoics reported the most. Noncopers and Balanced Copers reported the fewest positive personal events, Supercopers and Imaginative Escapers reported the most. Stoics and Noncopers reported the fewest positive health events, Balanced Copers and Imaginative Escapers reported the most. Stoics were essentially the only group to report positive legal events. Together these results are difficult to interpret, but again suggest a greater vulnerability of Stoics. Not only are they lowest in positive health events, but the two in which they are among the highest, home and legal events, were associated with greater symptomatology at the second interview.

Accuracy of classification reached 50% with addition of the life event measures from first contact, an improvement of 7%. Best predicted groups were Noncopers (65%) and Action Copers (60%), with accuracy for the remainder hovering around 50%. The one exception: only 21% of the Mystics were placed correctly.

Some Comments about Status at Follow-up

How persons within each coping style differed in adaptive status at follow-up also aids in our understanding. Here we will forego the more sophisticated statistics and look simply at correlations for a few measures of adaptive status. We will consider the total count of symptoms from the California Symptoms Checklist, response to the overall happiness question from the Bradburn Scales and the four positive and four negative emotions that were used to compute the Positive Affect and Negative Affect Scales (Bradburn and Caplovitz 1965; Lowenthal et al. 1975). For five of these ten measures of adaptation, significant differences were found, and it is noteworthy that now it is the Imaginative Escapers who seem most disturbed, and not so much the Stoics:

1. The least lonely were the Action Copers and the Supercopers, with the most lonely being the Imaginative Copers.
2. Action Copers and the Balanced were the least likely to report feeling they couldn't get going, while the Imaginative Escapers were the most likely.
3. The least depressed were the Action Copers, Supercopers and the Mystics, while those reporting feeling most depressed were the Imaginative Escapers.
4. The Noncopers, Action Copers and Balanced were the least likely to feel uneasy; the most likely to feel this way were the Imaginative Escapers.
5. The Action Copers had the fewest psychological symptoms while the Imaginative Copers and Stoics reported the most.

Finally, just to underscore these rather consistent findings, there was a trend ($p = .10$) for the Action Copers, Supercopers and Mystics to be the happiest at follow-up, and for the Noncopers and Imaginative Copers to be the least happy.

The various coping styles by and large were not linked to gender or to the life course. For example, although the research of Neugarten (1968) would suggest that middle-agers should be disproportionately represented among the Action Copers and Supercopers, this was not the case. In fact, if anything the middle-aged men and women were represented among the group in some ways furthest from what might be called active master: the Noncopers. The average age of the Noncopers was on the borderline between young adulthood and middle age, and close to half fell into the over-40 age range. This coping style was not necessarily associated with greater evidence of maladaptation, although there was a suggestion that Noncopers were less happy at follow-up.

CASE STUDIES: GOOD AND BAD COPERS

Karen Lai: Stoic

When we first meet her, Karen, a petite Chinese woman, is 32 years old. Her long flowing hair is somewhat disheveled, as a result of her habit of running her fingers repeatedly through it. Her house is bare, with each room having just the necessities: a table and two chairs in the dining room, two chairs in the living room. She seems dispirited and in fact it took quite a lot of convincing before she consented to the interview. On the Bradburn Morale Scales she says she is "not too happy" and says she feels very lonely or remote, and uneasy about things very often. Anger, depression, boredom and an inability to get going are other feelings she checks. Reporting 23 out of the possible 42 symptoms on our checklist, her comments are revealing. Responding yes to the item "has to be on guard even with friends," she adds "I've always kept my feelings to myself. I'm not a very spontaneous person but I was before I married. My husband kept telling me I was too honest and free with my thoughts." After saying no to an item regarding anger, she says "I cut down my expectations so I won't be upset." And after saying her feelings are easily hurt she continues "I try to avoid having feelings so they won't get hurt."

Karen's responses tell us something about the Stoic philosophy. Even here, over three years before she filled in the coping questionnaire, Karen is describing a way of life predicated on a deliberate attempt to minimize threat and her own reactions. Born in Los Angeles, Karen's family moved repeatedly before ending up in San Francisco when she was about 8 years old. She is currently completing a two-year program designed to make her a paralegal secretary. She is not working; she and her two small boys find it hard to make ends meet on welfare payments and what little her father can provide.

Before the separation Karen relied on the husband for almost everything, and "everything revolved around him." The marriage was almost a traditional arranged one, in that her stepmother introduced the two. "Joe comes from Taiwan, where they feel a woman is nothing—you know, walk two steps behind the man. We were together for almost four years. . . . I think the reason the marriage failed is because I let him walk all over me. He had strong opinions and always seems very logical and reasonable; all I had was feelings. Feelings didn't mean much to him. We didn't have any disagreements because I would give in to avoid hassles."

Karen's Stoic approach to life seems lifelong in nature. She describes herself as always having been a loner, and traces the origins back to her childhood. "I don't remember my childhood up to the age of 10. I've sort of blocked out my early childhood, when my parents got divorced. And when my father remarried it seemed like my stepmother resented us [Karen and her siblings]. Her son always came first, and that made me feel extremely lonely. I presume it was because of my childhood that I have these mental blocks against social life or people."

The separation happened quite suddenly. Her husband demanded that she stop going to school and they had a fight. Two weeks later they had another fight and he moved out. Somewhat uncharacteristically, Karen is resisting her husband's efforts to gain custody of the children and ownership of the house. The custody dispute in particular is the most stressful part of the whole separation. She worries about the children; her oldest boy is bitterly opposed to the divorce. On the other hand, Karen says the kids seem happier now that the fighting and shouting has stopped. Her social life is nil, she finds herself isolated from others and without a chance to enjoy life. Sex is a lost cause for Karen: "I try not to think about my sex life." In fact, when asked whether she has experienced any problems in meeting or dating people, she replies "I don't even know how to do it."

Karen has separated herself as much as possible from her husband. She sees him about three times a month, when he brings the children back from their weekend visits with him. On the last occasion they had a fight about bills, he threw all the papers on the floor and stomped out. When she is with him "I feel like I'm on trial, that I have to be on guard. I feel tense, I sometimes get a headache." Now separated for four months, she gave up hope of any reconciliation about a month prior to the interview. She has gone back to school as a means of preparing for a new way of life, but has made no effort at all to reintegrate herself back into society. On the stress typology at the impact phase, she is a Loser.

Three and a half years later, Karen remains a Loser on the stress typology, with many more negative than positive life events. Now 36 she is still trying to complete a degree in paralegal secretary work. She has worked intermittently as a secretary and her finances are in better shape than they were immediately after separation. She lives with her two boys in a small flat, and the divorce is still not final. A long and drawn-out legal battle continues over child support, alimony, custody and property. The events surrounding this battle continue to disturb her, and Karen vividly describes a courtroom scene in which her own children were brought in as witnesses to testify against her. Typically, she coped rather stoically: "I was under control outwardly. I tried to remain alert and wished I was someplace else."

Outside the courtroom Karen's husband has constantly harassed her, going to the extent of visiting her parents and "trying to belittle me and my children." Karen reports 16 psychological symptoms, down from 23 at first contact, and still reports herself to be "not too happy" on the Bradburn Scale. She does report more of a balance between positive and negative emotions. Her physical health has gotten worse since we last saw Karen, but she accepts her pain and discomfort and goes on with life as best she can.

Karen continues to feel somewhat isolated from friends, but in contrast to our first interview she now reports that she can talk to her parents and siblings about almost anything. During the separation phase, her family was some-what disapproving of the couple separating, but now is much more approving. Karen also reports that she and her children get along better than ever before. Curiously, she reports that the children have also become closer to both her parents and her husband's parents.

Karen is now dating on a regular basis, but is not particularly involved with anyone. She goes out once a week, but has sex much less frequently, partly because she is not very interested in it and partly because with the children it is difficult to arrange for privacy. All in all, life for Karen is gradually working towards a new routine. Her classes, numerous bouts with ill health and continuing hassles created by her soon-to-be ex-spouse all continue to create a burden. She puts up with the problems Stoically, if not philosophically. Her goals and dreams center on reestablishing a solid relationship with some man, but when asked about her plans she says "It seems like I don't have any control over my personal relationships." All she can do, she feels, is put up with her problems, and hope.

Lucy Daniels: Consistently Masterful

Lucy Daniels is an example of the new woman: at 39 she is a talented accountant working for the State of California. Separated for nearly seven months, she is poised and articulate as she describes her marriage of five years, her husband, her life. Her morale is high, she reports only 5 out of a possible 42 psychological symptoms, and she is making plans for the future.

While married, Lucy was willing to subordinate herself to her husband's needs and requirements. In this she was much like Karen Lai, because like Karen's, her husband was very demanding. But unlike Karen, Lucy maintained only the facade of dependence. When asked who was boss in the family she says "Hard to answer. I always knew in my heart of hearts that I was the stronger human being; therefore I could afford to give in. We played at his being the boss. But then, when it came to the divorce, I showed how intransigent and 'tough' I could be!"

Her first awareness of problems came over dinner one night: her husband suddenly announced that they had irreconcilable differences and he wanted out. She was, he declared, a bad housekeeper and too controlled. The couple continued living together for another three months, with Lucy doing her best to accommodate. The prospect of divorce was overwhelming; guilty about her own strong commitment to work, Lucy felt she had ignored the relationship. One night she called the bank where her husband was supposedly working late and found him absent. In the wee hours of the morning, they had a confrontation. He confessed to having an ongoing affair and the next day moved out.

"The initial shock numbed me. I was an emotional basket case, went through every possible emotion you could think of—all bad. Then I took hold of myself. What the hell: my pride was hurt. He'd been with this woman for over six months and I just thought he was working hard!"

At the point where we interviewed her Lucy is rapidly adjusting to singlehood. Asked what it is like, living alone, she replies "It's like I died and went to heaven! [laughter]. I can have a fire in the fireplace in the morning, read the paper; do everything I want to do and I don't have to give explanations for what and why I want to do it." Laughingly she continues "I'm back to the stage where my biggest problem is my hair doesn't grow fast enough. I'm back to a carefree existence, no more petty hassles!" Most helpful in her adjustment were friends, nine close ones, who "listened and made lots of suggestions and didn't try to take sides." When asked about future changes she says "I can't foresee any change, I'm in the process of rebuilding my associations with my girl friends . . . there are zero available men . . . if I want a social life, I'll have to make it myself; I expect to rebuild social ties to substitute for the one I lost."

At follow-up Lucy is now 42. As might be expected, she progressed rapidly through the transition of divorce. The final decree was handed down only four months after the first interview and by that time her life was reasonably settled. When asked what had been the greatest difficulty she experienced in the process of divorcing, she replied "I can't even remember . . . yes it was the sense of upheaval." When asked about the greatest benefit she replies "the sense of reestablishing control over the way I want to live life." Comparing herself to other divorced women she says she is "dammed lucky not to have kids!"

At the present time Lucy continues to enjoy her job, has received a major promotion since we last talked, and is financially better off than she has ever been in her life. She dates infrequently but is satisfied with her social and sexual life. In fact, she just broke off with a lawyer friend she had been seeing for three or four months: Lucy felt the relationship was interfering with her career. Clearly Lucy is calling the shots in her life, has taken charge and is doing the things she wants to do. Just as clearly, Lucy is in a rather privileged position: well-educated and with a job that is both financially and intellectually rewarding. How someone like Karen Lai might have reacted if given the same advantages is difficult to fathom.

SUMMING UP: TOWARDS A MORE STRESS-RESISTANT LIFESTYLE

We have seen that men and women going through divorce often experience difficulty in coping effectively with this transition. What strategies might be more adaptive than those they seem to use? Our coping typology has suggested several; the general literature on coping suggests several more. In what follows, we will not be considering specific relaxation techniques, such as developed by Jacobson and others, or biofeedback approaches or even hypnosis. Instead, the focus is on what the literature and research suggest as generally useful strategies that might help men and women cope with the stresses and strains of divorce.

One of the most important things to keep in mind, it appears, is that coping is a process and there is no single right or wrong way to cope. At the same time, there is some evidence that a balance should be maintained between the direct and indirect, as well as the palliative coping strategies. It appears that the most dysfunctional situation is one in which the individual remains locked into a palliative mode of coping.

In several studies of coping, especially those that deal with the so-called "stress-resistant personalities," people have been identified who, if they don't actually thrive on stress, do not seem particularly disturbed by it. In other words, they don't view the situation as stressful. The companion study of transitions, for example, included a group of individuals, designated as the "Challenged," who thrived on adversity (Fiske and Chiriboga 1990). Comparing characteristics of the Challenged subjects from the Transitions Study, the case histories of Action Copers and Super Copers from the Divorce Study, and the general literature on stress-resistant or "hardy" personalities (Kobasa, Maddi and Covington 1981), there seem to be several major ways in which they differ from other people.

First and foremost, stress-resilient individuals perceive themselves as exercising personal control over the situation. Control can be manifest in a variety of ways, and does not necessarily denote an aggressive and confrontational style. One means of achieving control may involve actively planning what to do next, organizing the situation or even participating in key decisions. In one study of older people being involuntarily relocated to a variety of community and institutional facilities, it was found that simple things like being asked what day or time they wanted to leave their residence could enhance a sense of personal control (Chiriboga 1972). In the Divorce Study, Mystics, Supercopers and the Balanced felt most in control over the decision to divorce; Stoics felt least in control. Reviewing cases, it became clear that certain groups, the Action and Balanced Copers in particular, tended to redefine the nature of the situation. Lucy Daniels for example simply reinstated her normal style of control and mastery, a style she had suppressed in order to accommodate the needs of her husband.

A second characteristic of the effective copers centers on being involved in meaningful and pleasurable activities. These individuals generally seem to have fulfilling and rich lives. In particular, they seem to develop a sense of commitment (e.g., Fiske and Chiriboga 1985) to some area of life, whether it be work or leisure or children, that provides a sense of meaning. In the divorce study, we found that a commitment to work, children, or to one's personal development seemed to make a difference. The group of copers designated as "Mystics," in particular, seemed to use their divorces as a challenge to personal development.

A third ingredient covers what is commonly referred to as "social supports." Social supports are generally recognized as a vital mediator in the relationship between stressor and response (e.g., Thoits 1982; Pearlin et al. 1981), and may be especially critical in the middle and later years (Cohler and Stott 1987). In our study, one of the best predictors of how many social supports were sought out was the respondent's perception of divorce-related stress (Chiriboga et al. 1979; see chapter 9). Yet the very importance of social supports can create its own problems. Friends are often lost through divorce, especially when they owed a primary allegiance to the former spouse (Weiss 1975). In addition, the person being divorced is very often the person generally turned to for social support. This is especially true for men, and men in fact were much more likely than women to view their spouse as their primary confidant in this and in the companion study (e.g., Lowenthal et al. 1975).

Divorcing persons in the more successful styles of coping were likely to be involved with social activities and exhibited a more developed social network than was apparent among the less successful styles. More important perhaps is that they seemed to know how to maintain social support systems. As we shall learn in chapter 9, at least one of the coping scales, Helpseeking, was quite strongly related to characteristics of social support.

II

PERSPECTIVES ON TRANSITIONS

5

PASSAGE THROUGH DIVORCE: A TRANSITIONS PERSPECTIVE

Linda S. Catron and David A. Chiriboga

Jim sits at the small kitchen table, staring intently at the interviewer. A tall and lanky 35-year-old white male, he has been separated for less than two months and is in the middle of his first interview with us. Spread before him lies a sheet of paper on which the interviewer has asked Jim to draw a life graph. "You know," he says, "I really don't think I can tell you what I think next year will be like. Or the year after that. Right now my life ends right here (he taps emphatically at a point representing the present year). Right now I can't project into the future—in fact, I really don't know what is happening to me right now."

In his uncertainty about the present, the future and life in general, Jim is not alone. The participants in our study were much more likely than people in our companion study of normative transitions to experience a complete inability to say anything about what their future lives might be like. As we studied these participants, we found one of the reasons underlying their inability was that they were going through a period of major and all-encompassing change. Torn from their predictable, if not comfortable, routine and day-to-day world, they suddenly were faced with decisions and issues that seemed mysterious and frightening and tedious, all at once. Every aspect of life, from what time to get up to what time to sleep, from what to eat to what kind of clothes to wear, had to be reexamined from a new perspective: the probably single adult. Many of them refused to accept this new role, or were experiencing major frustrations in terms of learning what was expected of them. An added frustration was that many were not even sure if they would go through with the divorce!

The situation these individuals faced has often been called a transition. The word transition is frequently used as a synonym for role change, but actually refers to a much broader condition of personal and social disruption that presents a challenge not only to the individual but to counselors faced with the task of providing help and guidance to those undergoing a transition (Golan 1986; Schlossberg 1984). In the next few pages we will take a closer look at transitions, attempting in the process to demonstrate why it makes sense to apply the concept to divorce. We also will present findings that deal with two issues. The first is how to predict transitional status, and the second is whether transitional status makes a difference in terms of the mental and social health of divorcing persons.

THE TRANSITION AS A REFLECTION OF CHANGE

Transitions have been defined both as major, lasting and relatively rapid forms of change (Parkes 1971, 1975), and as gradual developmental shifts (Chiriboga 1986; Levinson et al. 1978) that occur at predictable points in life. Since this book deals with divorce, we will be concerned primarily with those types of transitions that arise, often with little or no warning, at any point along the life course.

Transitions: Challenges to Our Assumptions

A recurrent theme in theories of transitions is that individuals experiencing major changes in their life must, for their continued well-being, relinquish one "assumptive world" in order to embrace another. An assumptive world is simply a certain perception of the way the world is, especially the part you yourself occupy. An entrenched socialist, for example, might see and interpret her country as either reflecting a socialistic and therefore good situation, or a capitalistic and therefore bad situation. Similarly, a very committed father may be totally wrapped up in his experience of being a parent and refuse to acknowledge the fact that his children are growing up and leaving home.

But assumptive worlds are not restricted to the fanatic: we all develop basic assumptions about ourselves and the world we live in. A number of scholars have indicated that relinquishing these assumptions (Parkes 1971; Gould

1978), illusions (Levinson et al. 1978) or commitments (Fiske 1980; Fiske and Chiriboga 1985) involves loss and, in many cases, mourning and grieving. Mourning and grieving may be particularly likely when the challenge to assumptions involves affectional bonds or attachments to persons, places, things and images of self (e.g., Parkes 1971; Marris 1975).

Jim, Revisited. In Jim's case, a very traditional perspective dominated his thinking about himself and others. Jim's idea of life was that people spent time growing up, having fun and going to school; then they got jobs (if they were men), married and had children, grew old and died. The keystone of his assumptive world involved his image of himself as a happily married man and father. He sincerely believed he and his wife would reconcile, despite her obvious anger and the dispatch with which she was hurdling the legal barriers to marital dissolution.

From Jim's way of thinking, divorce was just not something that good people did. A mistake had been made and all he wanted to do was get back together again. In the meantime he was really just holding on, waiting. His apartment was a dingy one-bedroom affair in a low-rent area, furnished with garage sale merchandise and furniture. Nothing in it looked or felt permanent: it was a stopping point along the way. Two months into it, he still had not told his friends about the separation; his parents knew, but seemed to believe Jim's pronouncement that it was just a temporary misunderstanding.

Smoothing Role Changes: The Importance of Transitions

The multiple challenges to Jim's assumptions about himself and the way life should be had proved overwhelming since his separation. On our symptoms checklist, he scored high on nearly every dimension. In spite of all the grief it was causing him, Jim still felt and acted like a married man, was convinced the marriage could be patched together and had not even thought of dating. The kind of abrupt role changes typical of divorce and other unexpected transitions often produce this kind of role confusion and denial, a confusion tied to the fact that the individual's assumptive world remains solidly based on the way things used to be (Chiriboga 1986).

Many of the so-called "less advanced" societies have developed effective techniques for smoothing the passage of their members through stressful transitions, and the study of these rites of passage helps to clarify the importance of socially shared meanings and activities surrounding personal crises.

Anthropological accounts of transitions in preindustrial society demonstrate how formal and socially recognized modes, such as rites of passage and ritual, can facilitate transitions. Rites of passage and ritual, unfortunately, do not characterize transitions in modern societies, perhaps because the circumstances and timing of role change in these societies may be less homogeneous.

Rites of Passage

The concept of rites of passage has been around since the turn of the century, when Dutch anthropologist van Gennep (1960) analyzed the order and content of the ceremonies facilitating birth, childhood, social puberty, betrothal, marriage, pregnancy, fatherhood, initiation into religious societies and funerals. The common theme found in the descriptions of these diverse events is that the ceremonies enabled individuals to move from one well-defined position to another. Van Gennep believed that this explained the prevalence of rites of passage, and he went on to delineate three stages of the rite of passage: separation, transition or liminality, and aggregation.

Another anthropologist, Victor Turner (1967, 94) has described these three stages in detail:

> [The first stage] of separation comprises symbolic behavior signifying the detachment of the individual or group either from an earlier fixed point in the social structure or a set of cultural conditions (a "state"); during the intervening liminal period the state of the ritual subject (the "passenger") is ambiguous; he passes through a realm that has few or none of the attributes of the past or coming state; in the third phase (aggregation), the passage is consummated. The ritual subject, individual or corporate, is in a stable state once more and, by virtue of this, has rights and obligations of a clearly defined and "structural" type, and is expected to behave in accordance with certain customary norms and ethical standards.

Each phase of the rite imposed a particular demand or transitional task upon the individual undergoing role change. During the separation phase, the task is to let go of the former way of life. Couples who continue to have dinner or sleep together, out of loneliness or continued affection, may not only be "postponing the inevitable" but delaying a task critical to the successful resolution of the entire transition.

During the liminal stage the task is to learn the skills and behaviors appropriate to a new way of life, which then must be implemented in the third and last stage. Going to school and attending Parents Without Partners meetings are examples of ways in which some individuals meet the challenge of the liminal period, while starting new careers or meeting new friends are ways in which people begin to reinvolve themselves back into society. In the remainder of this chapter we will be particularly concerned with the first two phases, separation and liminal, since the literature suggests that these may be the most critical phases of the transition.

Rites of Passage in an Agricultural Community. Turner (1967) has provided rich and heuristic description of the symbolic and structural aspects of the first two stages of a rite of passage to social maturity in one particular group: young Ndembu boys. First, the boys are separated from the larger society, since those in the liminal phase are considered to be contaminating and polluting to those who have not been inoculated against them. The important factor, from our perspective, is that the ability to physically separate people (in this case adolescent boys) from their normal life facilitates the transitional task of psychological separation. In the transition of divorce, one person (typically the woman if the couple have children) will usually remain in the residence and may, for this reason, face additional problems in letting go. But both those who remain and those who change residences often do not appear different to others. In fact, separated spouses not infrequently get back together again, during the early phases of divorce, to have dinner with people who still do not know about their marital problems. Hence it may take considerable time before friends and acquaintances begin to realize that the couple is in trouble.

During the liminal phase, Ndembu boys are in the ambiguous, dangerous and vulnerable state of being "betwixt and between" their past and their future roles and identities. They are given instructions about their future roles and status by an initiator who is already knowledgeable about that future status. Meanwhile, they are encouraged to develop close relationships with each other, relationships that have been known to last throughout the remainder of their lives. Turner coined a special word, "communitas," for this special closeness that develops among coliminals in the face of ambiguous and vulnerable circumstances. The bond might be likened to what happens among members of "self-help" groups for the divorced, who often become fast friends (Weiss 1975).

Once they have completed the liminal phase the boys are reincorporated into the larger society, this time with the rights and responsibilities of men. The larger social group recognizes and affirms the changes that have transpired in the initiates during the rite of passage. Overall, the social relations among the coliminals and between them and the larger society are supportive of the changes effected during the transition and facilitate meeting the tasks posed by each stage of the transition. This contrasts with the case of divorce in modern societies, where there is often a lack of public and even private awareness that a divorce has occurred and that new behaviors may be in order.

Rituals and Transitions

The rite of passage leading to social maturity represents the kind of normative transition that occurs more or less predictably at a certain age or time of life. Certain events in agrarian societies, however, represent unexpected or idiosyncratic transitions similar to divorce. Turner (1967) has described such an idiosyncratic transition. A Ndembu man had been having chronic problems in his social roles as son, son-in-law, husband, and tribesman. He suddenly experienced a number of health-related symptoms such as impotence, fatigue, heart palpitations, and delusions of persecution. A native healer was summoned and diagnosed the difficulties as stemming from ill wishes from the patient's wife, his mother-in-law, his deceased father, and the entire community. A ritual was staged that involved singing, dancing, the reciting of grudges by the community members as well as the patient and the exorcising of a tooth that symbolized the collective ill will.

As described, this ritual has many of the features of modern psychotherapy, such as the "making of the unconscious conscious by identifying a source of trouble and inducing the patient to share it with others" (Peacock 1976, 24). However, what distinguished this Ndembu ritual from modern psychotherapy is that it involves healing, not only the individual, but the entire community:

The Ndembu "doctor" sees his task less as curing an individual patient than as remedying the ills of the corporate group. . . . The patient will not get better until all the tensions and aggressions in the group's interrelations have been brought to light and exposed to ritual treatment. (Turner 1967, 392)

The healer is able to heal the community as well as the individual because Ndembu society, although in the process of modernizing, is typified by functionally diffuse social relations in which each person relates to others in the community in many different ways. This would be like having the postman be your brother-in-law, best friend of your uncle and spouse of your children's teacher, while the policeman at the corner is Aunt Mabel's husband and the pastor at your church, etc. Ndembu society is definitely a community in the old-fashioned sense, as opposed to the functionally specific social relations that characterize modern America. Because a disturbance in one set of relationships can affect many, the ritual brings all of these people, and their multiple relationships, together in a cleansing experience.

The relative scarcity of the diffuse social relationship pattern in modern societies may explain the scarcity of rituals in such societies. People are isolated by the specificity of their social relationships, especially in urban settings where next-door neighbors often remain ignorant of each other's names. Calling together all those who live on your block to participate in a ritual of separation for you and your spouse might cast you forever in the category of weird or bizarre. However, while researchers have concluded that there are few if any rituals of social relations that facilitate transitions in modern societies, Peacock (1976) has criticized this rigid delineation between primitive and modern societies. He suggests that a careful scrutiny of actual behavior in modern societies may reveal many instances of diffuse social relations.

There do appear to be instances of such social relations, but they may appear in unexpected settings. Fraternity houses and encounter groups for example, may lead to functionally diffuse social relationships. Similarly, halfway houses may stimulate these relations in order to facilitate the transition of socially marginal individuals (Catron 1976). There are other examples of diffuse social relationships and rituals in modern societies, as well as information concerning how rituals may facilitate the individual's ability and willingness to learn new behaviors (Kiefer and Cowan 1979). For the most part, however, individuals in developed nations must seek out meaning and a renewed sense of purpose and direction by themselves.

Transitions in Modern Society: The Case of Divorce

While many have referred to divorce as a transition, few have provided empirical evidence to substantiate the relevance of transitions to the actual process of divorce. From a more clinical perspective, several have reported the successful use of transitions models (e.g., Krystal, Chiriboga and Catron 1980; Golan 1986; Schlossberg 1984) as adjuncts to therapy, and others present findings that illustrate how key elements of transitional models may assist in crisis resolution (e.g., Maury and Brandwein 1984). In all the available literature, a central theme is the importance of feeling part of the social community.

The Role of the Initiator. In describing his seminars for the separated, Weiss (1976) identifies three major categories of helpers: the "expert" who presents lectures to seminar participants about the problems associated with the transition of divorce; the "veteran," discussion leaders and others who have already successfully negotiated the transition and provide an example that recovery is possible; and the "fellow participant" or member of the seminar who provides immediate and in-process understanding. Each of these kinds of helpers serves a different function. "Whereas experts can describe what is known, and veterans can report how they themselves responded to the situation, fellow participants can offer the immediate understanding that comes only from being in the same boat" (Weiss 1976, 226).

The experts and the veterans resemble those whom Turner (1967) has referred to as "initiators" people who serve to inform those in transition about the specific roles and behavior required once the transition is complete. Similarly, close and supportive relationships developed among the coliminals, and among Weiss's (1976) "fellow participants." In keeping with the social bonding reported by anthropologists studying transitions, Weiss reports that the members of his seminars for the separated sometimes continued to meet, both as a group and individually, after the seminar had been completed.

Divorce: An Unshared Experience? The transition of divorce in modern societies typically is not undergone as part of a group cohort that moves through time together and shares a common set of expectations and realities. Instead, divorce commonly is a solitary experience, unheralded, unannounced, and sometimes even undesired. The need for friends and a sense of kinship, however, remains. In Weiss's seminars, friendships often continued past the scheduled end, perhaps because participants had finally found people with whom the experience could be shared. Another reason may be the general loss of friends. Divorcing persons often experience a loss of those friendships in which the spouse was the essential link or those in which they feel like a "third wheel" in a couple-oriented society (Weiss 1975). In a book chapter titled "Alone, Alone, All, All Alone," Hunt (1966) reported that many divorcing persons are deserted by their friends for telling either too much or too little about the details of the divorce.

Those who are more psychoanalytically inclined may infer other reasons for the often hasty departure of friends in response to news of a contemplated or actual divorce. Friends for example may respond not only to the actual realities of the couple's relationship and the divorce, but also to the transference significance of divorce; that is, to their own feelings and fears transferred to that relationship. In this sense we see a link to what the anthropologists report: people involved in a transition are often seen as "unclean" and stigmatized until they complete the experience and reenter society.

Letting Go But Needing to Stay. Another major source of social support that is disrupted, or at least attenuated, during the divorcing process is spousal support. Empirical findings have illustrated the importance of spousal social support, even during marital separation and divorce. Chiriboga et al. (1979) employed a ranking system to identify not only who was the most helpful or supportive, but also, who could have been. Significantly more men than women reported that their spouse would have been the most helpful person, if she had been willing to provide help. For many of the men, the loss of this important source of social support was considered akin to a "double whammy —the loss of not only the person whom you are closest to, but also of the person who is most able to help you cope with the loss" (Chiriboga et al. 1979, 133).

Weiss (1975, 1979) also adds a comment relevant to the separation stage of the transitional process. He described postmarital attachment as the persistent longing for the previous spouse and the sense of bonding to that spouse. A central theme of Weiss's work is the persistence of attachment in the face of the erosion of love. According to Weiss, attachment is the cause of many of the separation-distress symptoms that Parkes (1971) also identifies. Continued attachment may be manifest in "attention to the image of the lost figure, an urge to make contact with the lost figure, anger toward the lost figure, guilt for having produced the loss, and the presence of an alarm reaction" (Weiss 1979, 205).

At least 75% of divorcing persons experience continued attachment to their spouse (Weiss 1975; Spanier and Castro 1979), a sobering statistic that suggests a general failure of the separation stage in divorce. Problems severing the ties might be greatly reduced if individuals rehearse and prepare themselves prior to the actual separation. On the basis of his observations of divorcing persons, Weiss indicated the salutary effects of engaging in anticipatory coping prior to actual separation. This conjecture was substantiated empirically by Brown et al. (1980; see also chapter 6), who found that the longer the individual reported he or she had considered separating, the less attachment and distress was reported subsequent to the separation.

Dating as a Means of Severing Ties. Social supports in general may act to modify and reduce separation distress due to postmarital attachment, but apparently cannot substitute for lost attachment (Brown and Felton 1978). On the other hand, having an ongoing or newly established intimate relationship may facilitate reestablishment of the normal social order. Dating prior to separation, for example, has consistently been found to associate with better adaptation to divorce (Goode 1956; Raschke 1974; Lachman 1977).

More recent work has indicated that having a new partner can be the most potent factor in diminishing the degree of emotional distress (Brown et al. 1980). Vernick (1979) also found that remarried persons were less attached to the former spouse. In the present study we find that those who had remarried by the time of our follow-up interview were significantly happier than those who were still separated or divorced but not remarried. The remarrieds also reported fewer symptoms at follow-up, while those who remained separated were second only to the reconciled in the number of symptoms reported.

SOME ASSUMPTIONS ABOUT TRANSITIONS

One purpose in writing this chapter was to evaluate divorce in terms of a transitional passage. Our foray into the existing literature underscores the relevance of transitions theory to the divorce process, especially those concepts related to the stages of a transition. In our analyses we decided to focus on ways of measuring how well individuals were meeting the demands of all three stages: those of separation, liminality and what we will here call reentry. Being dedicated social scientists, we naturally developed a series of basic research questions about these stages, and how transitional status relates to other concepts we were interested in.

The first question was whether childhood stress exposure would impede progress through the adult transition of divorce. More specifically, we anticipated that persons who report having experienced numerous presumed stressful events in childhood and/or who perceived greater childhood stress would experience greater problems in letting go of their former spouse, in negotiating the liminal period, and in reentering the normal social order. We based this question on the literature, cited in chapter 2, indicating that childhood stress can adversely affect such adult social contacts as access to social supports, capacity for intimacy and disengagement from the former spouse.

The second question concerned whether transitional status at baseline would be associated with symptomatology. Here we made the assumption that problems meeting the tasks posed by the transition would be reflected in the individual's well-being. However, for the third question we asked whether persons who had trouble meeting the demands of the three transitional stages during the first contact would show evidence of greater psychological symptomatology not only during the first wave of interviews but during the second as well. Would the problems in handling the tasks posed by the transition, early on, have any lasting consequences?

Measures of Transitional Status

As we considered the literature on transitions and on divorce, it became clear that to measure progress in dealing with the demands of the separation, liminal and reentry stages, we would have to assess a number of factors. These included ties to the spouse, feelings of anomie that would be associated with the liminal stage and the degree of connectedness to friends, family and new sexual/social partners. We also made a radical break with the more anthropological studies by hypothesizing that, in the transition of divorce, individuals experience and work through all three stages of a transition simultaneously.

Our assumption was that modern transitions are not packaged as neatly as they have been portrayed by anthropologists working with agrarian societies. Many of our subjects seemed to retain attachments, often quite strong, to their former spouse, while simultaneously pursuing new relationships and accepting their single status. In fact, during our pilot interviews we encountered individuals who had already remarried but who still kept belongings of their former spouse and expressed lingering doubts about whether they should have divorced (or accepted the divorce).

To assess transitional status we factor analyzed 25 structured questions concerning the presence or absence of respondents' social relationships with friends, family, the former spouse and new partners. All information was obtained from our first set of interviews with participants. The result was four scales. The first, called Spousal Contact, assesses how well individuals are dealing with issues of separation. The second and third, which we labeled Feeling Out of Place and Social Contact, dealt with the liminal period, while the fourth, Loneliness, considered how well the individual was reentering the social world.

Spousal Contact. The factor labeled "spousal contact" was determined by the individual's responses to these questions: (1) "About how often do you think about your spouse?" (every day = 9 to never = 0); (2) "How often do you ask your spouse for advice or help with something?" (every day = 9 to never = 0); (3) "How often does your spouse ask you for advice or help?" (every day = 9 to never = 0); (4) "Do you think there is any chance that the two of you will reconcile?" (yes = 3, doesn't know = 2, no = 1); (5) "When is the last time that you saw your spouse?" (same day as interview = 18 to more than 12 months = 01). A high score in spousal contact indicated that the respondent thought about the former spouse frequently, saw the spouse recently, thought that there was a chance for reconciliation, asked the spouse for advice and help, and received the spouse's requests for advice and help.

There were no age, sex or interaction differences in the distribution of spousal contact.

Feeling Out of Place. The factor labeled "feeling out of place" was measured by the subjects' responses to these questions: (1) "Do you feel out of place in a social situation because you are not married?" (never = 1, to very often = 4); (2) "How often do you avoid situations like going to a restaurant or a show because you would be alone?" (never = 1, to very often = 4); (3) "Do you wonder if you may not be an interesting person?" (never = 1, to very often = 4); (4) "Has your separation and pending divorce changed the way that you feel about yourself? (yes = 2, no = 1). People who felt more out of place were more likely to feel out of place in social situations, avoid social situations out of fear of being alone, feel they had changed as a person and wonder if they were an interesting person.

There were no significant age differences for reports of feeling out of place. However, there was a significant sex difference, with women being significantly more likely to feel out of place than men.

Social Contact. The factor labeled "social contact" was measured by four questions: (1) "Have there been any changes in your relationship with your relatives?" (no = 2, yes = 1); (2) "Have there been any changes in your relationship with friends and acquaintances since the separation?" (no = 2, yes = 1); (3) "Have you lost any friends?" (no = 2, yes = 1); (4) "Do you feel more or less distant from others as a result of the separation?" (more = 1, no effect = 2, less = 3). People who scored higher on social contact had lost fewer friends, did not feel more distant from others and had experienced fewer changes in relations with family and friends.

When we looked at the distribution of scores, no sex difference was found for social contacts. There was, however, a significant age difference, with respondents under 40 reporting less of a sense of change in social contacts than those over 40.

Loneliness. The factor labeled "loneliness" was measured by five questions: (1) "Are you without anyone to talk to about yourself?" (never = 1 to very often = 4); (2) "Do you have a chance to have fun?" (never = 1 to very often = 4); (3) "Are you currently dating anyone?" (no = 2, yes = 1); (4) "Are you without anyone you can share experiences and feelings with?" (never = 1 to very often = 4); (5) "Do you feel you are not having the kind of sex life you would like?" (never = 1 to very often = 4). Those who scored high on loneliness were often lacking anyone to share experiences with, were without anyone to talk to about themselves, had little chance to have fun, were not currently dating anyone and did not feel they were having the kind of sex life they wanted.

Significant sex and age differences were found for loneliness, but no age and sex interaction. Men reported higher levels of loneliness than women, and older persons reported more loneliness than younger ones.

Additional Measures Included in the Analyses

In addition to the measure that we were most concerned with, the analyses that follow included several others that served as either control variables, study variables or dependent variables. Control variables consisted of: Number of years married, Number of months separated (to control for the fact that we interviewed participants at varying times postseparation), Age, Gender, Income, Education, Whether working or not, Religiosity, Ethnic identity, and Number of children. We also included the same childhood stress measures described in chapter 2; our primary measure of adaptation was the total count of symptoms from the California Symptoms Checklist.

TRANSITIONAL STATUS: SOME FINDINGS

At this point, we will discuss the results of several analyses. The first analysis was concerned with the prediction of divorcing adults' transitional status, while the second and third invoked transitional status variables as predictors of both short- and long-term adaptation to divorce. Selection and ordering of measures in the analyses were guided by the stress process model.

The Prediction of Transitional Status

The possible influence of perceived and presumed childhood stress on divorcing adults' transitional status was of particular interest since the literature suggests that childhood stress may have a sensitizing influence on adult social relationships and attachments. Our own findings, as reported in chapter 2, have already indicated a relationship to overall adaptation may exist, but only among males. It was hypothesized that childhood stress would influence adults' transitional status since persons who had reported higher levels of perceived and/or presumed childhood stress might be more likely to experience continued attachment to the former spouse (high score on spousal contact) and to experience relative social isolation or lack of attachments to others (low score on social contact, high scores on feeling out of place and loneliness factors).

In addition to measures of childhood stress, we included measures tapping demographic as well as separation variables (e.g., the number of years married, the number of months separated and the number of times separated). A series of hierarchical multiple regression analyses were run, using the four transitional status measures as dependent variables.

Loneliness and Feeling Out of Place. Contrary to our expectations, loneliness and feeling out of place were not predicted by childhood stress measures. There was one finding at the trend ($P = .10$) level: men who perceived more stress during childhood were more likely to report feeling out of place in social situations (as measured by things like avoiding social situations out of fear of being alone, feeling that they had changed as a person, and wondering if they were interesting persons). This finding provides support, but only weak support, for the hypothesis that childhood stressors contribute to social isolation, or possibly to what Bowlby (1977) calls compulsive self-reliance.

Perhaps one reason why childhood stress did not significantly predict loneliness or feeling out of place is that these two measures are, at least partially, composed of questions that assess an individual's feelings about himself in relation to other people. As we will see next, childhood stress did significantly predict the two transitional status measures that reflected the actual frequency of contacts with friends, relatives and former spouse.

Spousal Contact. As mentioned before, spousal contact assesses the extent to which respondents think about their former spouse, see the spouse, believe in a chance for reconciliation, ask the former spouse for advice and help and receive the spouse's requests for advice and help. For women, childhood stress was the only set of variables associated with spousal contact, and the relationship was exactly as we had hypothesized. That is, women with higher levels of presumed childhood stress reported more spousal contact. We have, then, some support for Bowlby's (1977) thesis (see also Weiss 1975, Kitson, 1982) that those persons who experience separations and losses in childhood often have difficulty relinquishing a major attachment in adulthood.

For men the situation is more complex and definitely did not match our expectations. Among men the interaction of perceived and presumed child-hood stress, and not the individual stress measures, predicted spousal contact. To interpret the results we have to recall from chapter 2 the fourfold table created by this interaction: the Overwhelmed (high presumed childhood stress, high perceived), the Challenged (high presumed, low perceived), the Self-defeated (low presumed, high perceived), and the Lucky (low presumed, low perceived). Self defeated men were lowest in spousal contact, while the so-called Lucky men reported the highest levels of spousal contact.

The marked difference in results underscores how different the dynamics of divorce are for men and women. It is important to note that high levels of spousal contact within eight months of separation are not necessarily patho-logical. Baseline spousal contact may be a reflection of an individual's need to make sure that divorce is the correct resolution to marital problems. As will be discussed later in this chapter, higher levels of spousal contact during the impact phase of divorce was not associated with symptomatology for either men or women. However, the literature (Kitson 1982) suggests that high continued attachment to the former spouse three years after marital separation may be pathological.

Social Contact. Childhood stress was associated with a pattern of greater social isolation at baseline for women. Women who reported the occurrence of numerous stressful events were significantly more likely to have lower levels of social contact: to report that they felt more distant from others, had lost friends and had reduced their contacts with friends and relatives.

This pattern resembles the relationship between disruptions of attachments in childhood and difficulties in forming attachments in adulthood reported by Bowlby (1977) and others. Two examples from the literature are compulsive self-reliance (Bowlby 1977) and the inability to become attached to the spouse during marriage (Kitson 1982). Once again, then, we find the anticipated result among the women in our sample.

Among the men, once again, we find that only the interaction term seems to make a difference. Only at a trend probability level are the results reasonably consistent with our expectations. The "Overwhelmed" men, those scoring highest in presumed and perceived childhood stress, also averaged the lowest in social contact. In contrast, men reporting lower levels of both presumed and perceived stress, our "Lucky" participants, reported the highest levels of social contact. Given that this latter group also reported higher levels of spousal contact, we are left with the impression that they are more active in all spheres of social activity. In other words, having emerged from childhood relatively unscathed by attachment problems, they may have fewer inhibitions about attachments, even to their former partner.

The Prediction of Short-Term Adaptation

Although the prediction of transitional status was of major interest, since qualities of the passage through divorce hold implications for adaptation we also were directly interested in whether transitional status did, in fact, predict adaptation during both the impact and long-term phase of the divorce process. In this section, we will examine the role of several factors thought to influence adults' short-term adaptation to divorce. In addition to the transitional status variables, these factors include perceived and presumed childhood stress, interaction of perceived and presumed childhood stress, demographic variables, marital separation variables and variables reflecting the interaction of presumed childhood stress and transitional status.

Our basic hypothesis was that transitional status at the time of marital separation should influence both short- and long-term adaptation to divorce. Specifically, high levels of continued attachment to the former spouse (spousal contact) and low levels of social relationships and attachments to others (loneliness, feeling out of place and social contact) should be significantly associated with higher levels of psychological symptoms.

Previous correlational analyses (Catron, Chiriboga and Krystal 1980) had indicated the existence of a significant relationship between the transitional status variables and measures of short-term adaptation, at least for middle-aged subjects. Our current concern questions whether measures of divorcing adults' transitional status at the time of marital separation might not predict long- as well as short-term adaptation for all the respondents.

Hierarchical set multiple regression analyses were computed with the following six steps included to predict both baseline and follow-up adaptation: childhood variables of perceived childhood stress and presumed childhood stress (Set 1), the interaction of presumed and perceived childhood stress (Set 2), the demographic variables (Set 3), the separation variables (Set 4), the transitional status variables (Set 5), and the interaction of presumed childhood stress and transitional status variables (Set 6). Since the first three sets actually duplicate those reported in the prediction of symptoms for chapter 2, we will not dwell on the implications but will refresh your memory concerning what was found.

Results for Men. In a separate regression analysis for the men, the six steps predicted a significant 31% of the variance in symptoms. The childhood measures, as a set, explained a significant 5% of the variance. Of the two childhood measures, only perceived childhood stress was significantly associated, men who evaluated their childhood years more negatively being more likely to report psychological symptoms.

Even more significant than the childhood measures were the transitional status variables, which explained 18% of the variance. Men scoring lower in social contact, and higher in feeling out of place and loneliness were more likely to report psychological symptoms. These results provide support for the hypothesis that divorcing adults' transitional status would predict adaptation during the impact phase of marital dissolution. None of the other sets contributed significantly to the prediction of psychological symptoms for men.

Results for Women. For the women, the regression analysis predicted 27% of the variance (MR = .52, $p<.001$). As we reported in chapter 2, the childhood measures did not predict psychological symptoms. This finding represents a marked sex difference in the influence of the childhood measures on baseline psychological symptoms.

The demographic variables contributed 8% of the accounted variance. Education was the key variable: the less educated women were more likely to report numerous psychological symptoms. Duplicating the results for men, transitional status contributed significantly to the prediction, explaining 14% of the variance. Only two of the scales, feeling out of place and loneliness, were significantly associated. Providing some support for hypothesized relationships, women who felt more lonely and out of place were more likely to report greater symptoms at the first interview.

The Prediction of Adaptation at Follow-up

The intent of the follow-up analyses was to discern whether presumed and perceived variables continued to predict adaptation approximately three and a half years later. The analyses for the prediction of follow-up adaptation parallel those for the prediction of adaptation at baseline in both the use of hierarchical multiple regression analysis and in the order and composition of the sets entered. The following sets were entered: the childhood measures (Set 1), the interaction of perceived and presumed childhood stress (Set 2), the demographic variables (Set 3), the separation variables (Set 4), the transitional status variables (Set 5) and the interaction of presumed childhood stresses and the transitional status variables (Set 6). The measure of adaptation—psychological symptoms at follow-up—is also identical to that at baseline.

Results for Men. In the regression analysis for men, only two sets, those including childhood stress and transitional status, contributed. The childhood stress measures as a set explained 7% of the variance, with the presumed childhood stress variable contributing significantly: men who reported higher levels of childhood stresses were more likely to report psychological symptoms at follow-up. As we noted in chapter 2, this stands in contrast to the findings for the impact phase, where *perceived* childhood stress predicted symptoms for men.

The transitional status factors continued to be significant predictors of symptoms at follow-up, accounting for 11% of the variance. Two of the four factors, feeling out of place and loneliness, significantly contributed to the sets' prediction of symptoms. Men who scored high on loneliness and feeling out of place were more likely to report symptoms.

Results for Women. The regression analysis for the women at follow-up was not very effective. Neither childhood measures nor measures of transitional status were associated with adaptation for women. The only variables in fact that did contribute significantly to the prediction of adaptation were the same demographic variables whose contribution was already reported in chapter 3. Explaining 10% of the variance, having an ethnic identity and a lower income were associated with greater symptomatology.

Predicting Long-Term Adaptation: Revisited

In the analyses predicting symptoms during the impact and long-term phases, we focused on the qualities of the study variables. Another way of predicting symptoms at follow-up is to remove the influence of baseline symptoms. Doing this allows consideration of change in symptoms from one time to another. We therefore repeated the follow-up analyses, this time putting the symptom level measured at the first interview as the first set. Initial symptom levels predicted 28% of the variance in follow-up symptoms for men, and a very high 46% of the variance in symptoms for women. For men the contribution of the childhood stress measures was approximately the same after removal of the initial symptoms level. However, the contribution of the measures of transitional status was completely removed, for both men and women.

To review, then, we found that the set of four transitional status factors was significantly associated with symptom expression during the impact phase, and associated with long-term symptoms only if the initial symptom level was not controlled. The transitional status measures of feeling out of place, loneliness and social contact most consistently contributed to the prediction of psychological symptoms; spousal contact was not influential. When the effects of baseline psychological symptoms were removed in predicting follow-up psychological symptoms, however, the measures of transitional status were no longer associated with symptoms. This suggests that transitional status directly affects symptom levels only during the early stages of a transition. At the second interview, the effect may have been more indirect, and reflected primarily in initial symptom levels.

Children and Divorce: Revisited

In discussing factors that increased the likelihood of experiencing negative life events, and reduced the likelihood of experiencing more positive ones, we reported in chapter 3 that the presence of children seemed to play an important role. Here we will consider another possible effect of children: that of delaying the process of transiting from the marital role to the role of the single adult.

Marital Status at Follow-up. One way of looking at children as a delaying factor is to consider whether the presence or absence of children is related to marital status four years after separation. One impressive statistic: of the ten participants who reconciled with their spouse, nine had children. Further, a higher-than-expected number of fathers and mothers were still separated at the time we visited with them again. Of the 19 who had not completed the legal process of divorce, 16 (or 84%) had children. These distributions certainly suggest that children may delay progress.

Transitional Measures. We next looked at status on the four measures of transitional status. Spousal Contact furnished a rather expectable finding: men and women with children reported more thoughts and contact concerning their spouse. As Bohannan (1970) has noted, people with children may never be able to completely break their ties with the former spouse. One implication is that the complete break with the former way of life may never really be accomplished.

We also found men and women with children to report greater loneliness, one of the indicators of transitional passage. They experienced a greater sense of being socially isolated from others, a lack of opportunities to date and generally to enjoy the company of others. Here again is evidence that parents may find it more difficult to reintegrate themselves into the adult social world.

CASE STUDIES

We have reviewed the relevance of transitions to the process of divorce, and in the preceding sections have presented findings based on the way we actually measured transitional status. Our findings of course are based on numbers and here we will seek to flesh them out, as it were, with cases.

Bernice Bernard: Separated in Body, Not in Mind

An African American, Bernice Bernard is a stunning, tall 28-year-old who works as a clerk typist at the Office of Social Welfare. She has beautiful eyes, finely chiseled features, and hair neatly arranged in a short Afro. Bernice is well-dressed and somewhat formal. She is very shy, but has an open and easy-going manner. Her demeanor is somewhat at odds with other aspects of her life. At the time of the interview, garbage bags litter the kitchen of her apartment in a low-income project, and it is clear that Bernice does not spend much time housekeeping.

Married at the age of 18, Bernice has a 6-year-old son. She is having a great deal of difficulty with the process of marital separation and reports 37 psychological symptoms at the first interview—the most symptoms reported by anyone in the entire Divorce Study sample of 333 people. Her numerous psychological symptoms may be due, in part, to the sensitizing influence of a highly significant presumed childhood stress—the death of her mother. Bernice is unusual in that she not only checks off her parent's death, but spends considerable time telling the interviewer how traumatic life was at that distant time.

At our first interview, Bernice scores way above average on three of the four transitional status clusters—feeling out of place, loneliness and spousal contact. As far as feeling out of place is concerned, she views her life as much worse than other divorced people do and she was very troubled by the divorce. She often feels out of place and wonders if she is interesting. She often has no one to talk to or share experiences with and avoids going places alone.

Bernice's high scores on loneliness reflect the fact that she feels that she is fairly often without anyone to talk to, and she misses having her spouse to talk to. At baseline, she is not dating and she does not believe that dating would help her situation.

Bernice is unusual in that she not only scores high on spousal contact during the impact phase but also at follow-up, which emphasizes the point that she may have difficulties in relinquishing attachment to her former spouse. During the impact phase, Bernice repeatedly tells the interviewer that she really does not want to get divorced. She says that it was "a lack of understanding and arguments" which influenced the decision to separate. Although she initiated the actual separation, it was her spouse who had been most in favor of getting divorced. Asked what she misses most about the marriage, Bernice immediately says: "My husband. Someone to talk to."

At the first interview she sees her ex-spouse daily and, in fact, saw him on the day before the interview. "He came over for dinner" she says, then adds, "dinner and sex." When asked if this is typical, she responds, "Yes." Bernice hangs onto a hope for a reconciliation and when asked, "What is your second most favorite thing to do?", she said, "Spend time with my husband and son." When asked, "What is the most important thing about that to you?", she said, "Being with the two people I love the most."

She also says that the hardest part of getting divorced was: "Getting used to the idea of him going out and sleeping with someone else. I guess that sounds weird, but that was it." During the follow-up interview, she provides some additional information about this. When asked "What was the single most stressful thing that happened to you during your divorce," her response is "When I caught him sneaking with someone else." Although Bernice and her husband had already been separated at that time, she says "I acted like a madman. I mean mad-lady. I was angry and upset and got violent." When asked "Did you hit him?", Bernice said, "No, I hit her."

At the first contact Bernice tells the interviewer that she is very dissatisfied with how she handled the situation. "I really acted crazy, it was pitiful. See, it was his sister's friend. She sleeps around. One night she was supposed to come visit Jamie [their son] and me and didn't show up, so I went over there and banged on the door for hours until he opened it."

Asked "When you have the chance to think about yourself and your life would you say that you tend to think about the past or future?" she says the past, and when asked what sort of things you tend to think or daydream about, she responds: "What did I do to make him want to leave home. Why did I quit my job. That's about all."

Both first and second interviews contain ruminations and self-recriminations about her contributions to the dissolution of the marriage; for example, at the first contact she says that the marital separation has changed the way she feels about herself: "I see that I was—or am—a selfish person. I didn't take into account other people's feelings." She tells the interviewer at first contact that she daydreams about: "Where I made my mistakes in the past— being bossy, selfish, letting myself go, not valuing what I had." As might be expected, she falls into the Imaginative Escaper category of coping discussed in chapter 4.

At follow-up, Bernice is still daydreaming about her former husband and about the past rather than the present or the future. In addition to her ruminations about the breakup, she thinks of her ex-spouse every day and she still sees him several times a week. Although she does not think that there is a chance for a reconciliation, she does say that: "We're better friends now than we were during the last four years of our marriage. Our communication is better than it was." All this is rather curious since Bernice is not only dating a man who also works in the Social Welfare Office, she is engaged to him and they already have a 2-month-old daughter.

Bernice's level of psychological symptoms at follow-up is still substantially above average for the Divorce Study sample, but has been reduced from 37 to 22. She now says that she is "pretty happy" as opposed to the "not very happy" feeling she expressed at the first interview. She and her fiancé belong to the same rather traditional Baptist church and they enjoy going to services together. In fact, she has been transformed from a nonreligious, occasional churchgoer, to someone who considers herself to be religious and who attends church with her fiancé at least six times a week. Bernice tells the interviewer that her second most favorite thing to do is: "Going to service." When asked about that, she said, "Because I like worshipping God." In addition she said that going to service was the activity that helped her the most. She explained that "It makes you know that the only one you can count on is God Himself, anyway." In Bernice's cosmology, God has become the ultimate form of social support and guidance.

During the three and a half years since our first interview, Bernice has found new sources of strength. In response to a question about how she has changed since the decision to initiate the divorce process, she replies, "That's hard to think about because I messed up so much since. Well, I became more dependent on myself. I was never alone before, and I did that pretty good. I learned how to take care of myself. It was fun being on my own for a while." One of the greatest benefits that has resulted from the divorce is "Really finding out that I can make it on my own."

Woody Wilson: Betwixt and Between

Woody Wilson is a 5'9", handsome, 29-year-old business executive for a moderately large clothing manufacturer. Interviewed at his office, he was dressed for work in a crisp, white, Italian-cut shirt, with a tie and collar pin, and herringbone slim-cut trousers. His spacious, modern office had a view of downtown high-rise buildings. The walls were lined with signed graphics and a picture of a champion pedigreed dog. His desk was cluttered with papers and folders, and he apologized for the disarray, stating that he had hoped to clean up before the interview began. Woody was friendly, but somewhat nervous when he talked about his life and the fact that he's alone.

He was married at the age of 26 and now, only three years later, his wife is seeking a divorce. "We were both unhappy. Mainly she was unhappy so we decided to separate and each get our own apartments." At first he lays the blame for problems on philosophical issues unrelated to the relationship: "She was unhappy with her lifestyle and particularly with her job. She just couldn't take it anymore." Later in the interview he admitted that he might have been too domineering or too insensitive to her needs.

Woody has suffered losses all his life. He reports three presumed childhood stresses: intense arguments between his parents and with his parents, and having to go to work to help support his family. The intense arguments between and with his parents still cause unhappiness, and he thinks a lot about these early stressors.

At the first interview, Woody explains that his greatest difficulty with the separation process is, "Loneliness. No one to confide in. No one cares about you." Asked to define loneliness, he replies: "Not being able to share certain thoughts, ideas, wants, goals, ideals. Not being able to care for someone and have them care for you."

Woody's responses in the loneliness cluster are high. He has few confidants and states that loneliness strikes, "at night and lasts a few hours. Particularly all day on Sunday. Usually when I'm alone. In the mornings, in the evenings at dinner and later." He reports feeling that he is fairly often without anyone to talk to about himself. In fact, he sought psychiatric counseling seven times related to his feelings about the divorce. He frequently feels that he isn't having the kind of sex life that he would like.

When asked at baseline when the loneliest period in his life was, Woody said "now—because I've only lived in San Francisco for two years. My family and close friends are in the midwest." He has two friends nearby but he "hasn't seen them as much. We're more distant." He hesitates and then adds, "I have avoided them." Woody said that he feels "more distant from other people and more disappointed in life." At follow-up he explained that he had lost some friends since the separation—about six or seven of them because "they felt uncomfortable being friends with both of us—they had to make a choice."

Woody not only has avoided some of his friends, but he also feels out of place at the impact phase. Woody's responses are high in this cluster. He very often avoids going places alone and has changed the way he feels about himself. More specifically, he said: "I question how I acted sometimes during my marriage," he says. "My work priorities. The time I spent with my wife. Whether I should be more domineering. How strong I am as a person."

The separation was not Woody's idea. His spouse sought it and Woody says, "I still feel married." He daydreams about "what would have happened if I had never married or if the marriage hadn't failed." Woody still thinks about his spouse several times a week but never asks her for help. She, on the other hand, often asks him for advice and help, mostly financial, at least once a week. They saw each other the week before the interview to go over tax forms. When asked how he feels when with his spouse he says he "still care[s] very much for her, but we can't really talk about our personal lives. Don't go deeper than procedural matters. We try to keep it as least emotional as possible." He explains that this does represent a change since: "When we first separated we shared a lot together. We spent weekends together and I did not think we would go through with the divorce." He adds that he hasn't given up hope but about a month ago began to feel the chances for reconciliation were pretty remote.

Woody is not a happy person. When asked if he thought his life had changed since the decision to initiate the divorce process he replied, "I am less productive, feel empty, drink more, I feel like I am a failure and that I haven't accomplished that much." On the Bradburn Happiness Scale he is "not too happy" and also reports 18 symptoms. Further questions reveal additional problems, among them "not being to share a meaningful experience." And in response to the question what he missed most, he said "My wife and a strong relationship. The stability of a lover and the sharing of different goals."

The years do not bring great peace and resolution to Woody, but although he remains high on symptom expression he now reports feeling "pretty happy." When asked in what ways his life had changed since the decision to initiate the divorce process—he said "It's gotten better—I've become more independent. I take care of myself. I'm more of an individual than before. I look more deeply into relationships. I'm more understanding towards another person's feelings and wants." In the next few years he expects that "my standard of living will increase—that's about it. I have no plans for the next year." The greatest benefit of the divorce has been "less aggravation—financial problems that you have no control of—and the ability to do what you want to do. And you have more say in the direction of your life."

The greatest difficulty experienced in the process of divorcing, he now feels, is "the fact that I was alone. You miss having someone who cares about you, and whom you care about." He now feels that the single most stressful thing that happened to him during his divorce was: "Knowing that my wife was sleeping with someone else." He handled the situation by avoiding it: "I just kept to myself." He is now divorced and lives alone. When asked if he was dating—he answered yes but said "not currently, no one seriously, and no one steady." When the interviewer probes for more detail he says: "I'm dating a dog right now" and laughs. It turns out that he has bought a large and rather fanciful show dog that is the joy of his life and a major focal point of his leisure time.

At both baseline and follow-up, Woody mentions having problems with drinking. At our first meeting, however, he says that drinking has been the most helpful in coping. At follow-up, however, he now says that the activity that has been most helpful is "Working—the self-satisfaction that you're achieving something, doing something with your life—and attaining certain goals. That you are creating a lifestyle of your own—a new life, you might say."

Although his dating practices include meeting women at bars and taking them home for casual affairs, Woody does talk idealistically about a future marriage. He thinks that if he were to remarry it would be: "A happier marriage—more mature—share more things together and future goals. Ties would be stronger and we'd understand each other a lot more, there'd be a lot more love and understanding and I'd probably try to think more about the other person's feelings—I'd try to be more considerate and mature." Hopeful he is, but at the same time he gives the impression of a person who has retreated into the world of work and pet ownership as a means of escaping from his continuing problems with attachments.

SUMMING UP

Our goal for this chapter was to provide an overview of transitions, and investigate how the concepts that have evolved in this relatively new area might apply to divorce. The results have demonstrated the value of a transitions model, both from a quantitative standpoint and from the more qualitative perspective provided by our cases. We also found more support for the relevance of childhood stress measures as indicators of potential risk in divorce. In the remainder of this chapter we will touch on one last consideration: some thoughts on measurement issues in transitions.

Measuring Transitional Status

Showing the theoretical relevance of a concept like transitions to the divorce condition is one thing, actually trying to develop some operational criteria is another. Our approach was to identify a number of individual items that in terms of face validity seemed associated with the different stages and demands of a transition. The actual measures were the result of a factor analysis of 25 structured questions on the presence or absence of certain social relations or attachments with friends, relatives, the former spouse, and new partners. To a certain extent, these structured questions assess not only the respondents' social network, but also their perceptions of the availability and quality of these relationships with others.

The results strongly support the notion that a useful addition to the clinician's armamentarium of assessment tools would be some means of assessing transitional status. At present there appear to be few if any well-established and structured questions that accurately assess adults' current capacity for attachments or social relationships, or attachments to the past. Although more difficult to interpret, projective tests have been developed to assess attachments, both in children and in adults. For example, Hansburg (1980) has developed a projective test to examine the responses of adolescents, adults and the aged to separation from attachment figures. The test consists of showing respondents 12 pictures depicting various scenes of separation from the attachment figure and then scoring the responses according to whether the respondent imagined himself or herself moving towards the attachment figure, and the extent to which the respondent sought help and comfort from others.

As we conclude this chapter, one remaining point deserving of emphasis is that divorce in modern society is not a lockstep, ground phenomenon. Instead, we all proceed through divorce at our own rates, marching to the proverbial different drummers. The whole process is shrouded in mystery, with the beginning and ending difficult to ascertain because of the absence of clearly demarcated rites of passage and rituals. Most often, modern people must celebrate, mark and facilitate their own transition.

6

PASSAGE THROUGH DIVORCE: TIMING ISSUES

David A. Chiriboga and Linda S. Catron

In Chapter 5 we discussed a model of transitions appropriate for modern societies, and presented findings illustrating several basic concepts associated with transitions theory. Here we advance the basic transitions model one step further by adding an important but understudied dimension: the passage of time. We will be looking at two issues. First, what points along the pathway to divorce were reported to be most difficult, as well as least difficult, for respondents. Second, does the speed of passage through at least the early stages of divorce seem to make any difference in the mental health of people as assessed at the first interview.

DISTRESS AND THE MARKER POINTS OF DIVORCE

Our interest in time was sparked by William Goode's (1956) classic study of divorced mothers. Aged 20 to 38, Goode's sample all had been divorced from 2 to 26 months at the time of interview. One instrument they were given was a simple but telling one: each woman was asked when in the process of divorce they had smoked the most, felt in poorest health, had greatest difficulty in sleeping, drunk more than usual, had difficulty remembering things, felt most lonely and had the most problems at work. Their response choices ranged from "final decision" to "time of interview" and "never any increase" (Goode 1956, 186).

As these women recalled the different points in the divorce process, over a quarter pinpointed marital separation as the time of greatest trauma: it was during the period surrounding marital separation that 27% had most difficulty in sleeping, for example, 26% felt themselves to be in poorest health and 29% reported the greatest loneliness (Goode 1956). The point of final decision, and filing the petition for divorce, also were seen as having considerable trauma by up to 16% of the women. Perhaps even more interesting is that for each of the seven items, women were most likely to say that they had never noticed an increase in problems. Goode's (1956, 186) conclusion is that "there appears to be no one time period in which there is great personal disorganization for all divorces."

A Revision of Goode's Trauma Scale

Goode's research approach to the question of identifying points of major distress was a fascinating one, and demonstrates once again the utility of retrospective instruments. In our own research we also were interested in points of distress, and also were faced by a common problem in stress research: by the time the stressed subject is identified, he or she has usually already experienced the stress (bereavement, job loss, divorce, etc.). Hence, we too were faced with the need to rely at least partially on retrospective data, and seriously considered using Goode's original instrument.

Coincidentally, another team of researchers had made a similar decision, but had gone one step further. Gay Kitson and Marvin Sussman at Case Western Reserve University had modified the original Trauma Scale, expanding the content to include positive as well as negative items, and adding to the response choices. We adopted their instrument, but shortened it to include 23 items, of which 14 were trauma-related and 9 were positive. Examples of the 23 items are: "During which of these periods do you think your health was poorest?" "When did you have the most difficulty in doing your work efficiently?" and "During which of these periods do you think your health was the best?". Each of the 23 items was rated according to the point in the divorce sequence at which the problem or relief from problems was most evident: (1) before the decision to divorce, (2) at the time of the decision, (3) at the first separation, (4) at the final or only separation, (5) when first filing for divorce, (6) at final divorce decree, (7) now.

When we looked at what our respondents had to say, we found similarities and differences with Goode's (1956) findings. For one thing, the period prior to the decision to divorce emerged as the point most likely to be endorsed as most troublesome, although from 3% to 26% also reported this period as being the most positive (Chiriboga and Cutler 1977). Gender differences were dramatic. Women were significantly more likely than men to report the greatest trauma as occurring prior to the decision. Before the decision, women were more likely to report most difficulty with sleeping, being the most lonely, most depressed, most likely not to care about themselves (i.e., to be lowest in self-esteem) and least optimistic (Chiriboga and Cutler 1977). As an example, 44% of the women reported being most depressed during this early period, as contrasted with 21% of the men.

In contrast, men were more likely to view the period before the decision to divorce as being the most positive of all the periods they could rate (and this included the present time). Men were significantly more likely than women to view the period before decision as the time when they were least lonely and most energetic, and they tended to view it as the time when their health was the best, they were most optimistic and least depressed. As an example, 37% of the men and only 14% of the women reported being least lonely during the time prior to decision.

The period surrounding marital separation ranked second to the predecision period as being most traumatic, and the decision period ranked third. Pointing to the positive effect of taking some action to address problems, small but significant proportions saw positive effects occurring during the time of decision and separation. For example, 10% or more reported the period surrounding separation as being one where they were the least depressed, they were the least worried, most optimistic, most energetic, least angry with their spouse and their health was the best. However, the highest proportions of positive effects, from 41% to 56%, were rated as being present at the time of the first interview.

All in all, our results did indicate that the time prior to the decision was most troublesome for the women, while for men the troubles began at the time of the decision or later. Relief from problems begins to be indicated at the point of decision, but becomes most evident at the point most distant from the marriage: the time of the first interview. These findings substantiate but also expand upon Goode's conclusions, and add the dimension of gender differences in the significance of different stages of the divorce process.

DIVORCE AND THE SPEED OF PASSAGE

We have seen that progress along the pathway to divorce is associated with both positive and negative feelings, but up to this point our analyses have not considered how much time people actually took to go from one stage of the divorce process to another. We also have not considered whether being slower or faster in progress may be associated with well-being. To examine such questions in more detail, our strategy was to actually compute the number of days and months that passed, for each participant, as they encountered different stages of the divorce process. One stage that on theoretical grounds should prove important falls between the point when a decision is made to divorce, and marital separation. This might be called either the Anticipation Stage, the Rehearsal Stage, or the Deliberation Stage, since during this time the individual can indulge in role rehearsal, consider various options and make a last attempt to patch things together, etc., while still working from the base of an intact marriage.

Several researchers have hypothesized that people who take their time considering a divorce, during what we will call the Anticipation Stage, should fare better in the long run (e.g., Goode 1956; Despert 1953). Some supporting evidence is available: Goode (1956) reports that the more traumatized women in his sample were those who separated less than one month after a final decision to divorce had been made. His explanation for this finding, however, is that women who proceeded quickly from decision to separation were in fact those whose husbands had essentially presented them with a fait accompli. In other words, they had little or no say in the matter of divorce, and this lack of control, Goode suggests, is what really explains the relationship between quick passage and greater trauma.

A second critical stage may fall between the points of marital separation and filing a petition, and for the same theoretical reason: this period may also represent a time of contemplation and deliberation. As described in previous chapters, this in fact constitutes part of the "impact" stage of divorce, and it is a stage marked by considerable emotional turmoil. At the same time, those who suffer the agony in the interests of making the best decision may in the end suffer less.

The findings of Goode sparked our own interest in the issue of speed of passage. In several papers not designed for this book, an attempt was made to evaluate how long it took women in the sample to proceed between the two stages we have described: the stage falling between decision and separation, and between separation and the point at which a petition to divorce is filed. Since the project was also concerned with the idea, gleaned from the literature on bereavement, that the simple passage of time eventually produces its own healing effect, we also introduced a measure of how long the respondent had spent from separation to the point at which they were interviewed for the first time. By way of preview, the basic finding was that the speed with which women proceed from the point of realizing there is a real probability of divorce, to the point of separation, may lay the groundwork for how well they fare during the impact and long-term phases of the divorce process (Melichar and Chiriboga 1988).

Some Basic Procedures

Court records supplied information on dates of separation and the filing of a petition. This information was supplemented by interview questions that asked respondents for the approximate date when they realized they probably would be getting a divorce, as well as the date of final separation. The actual analyses differed from those that are generally being presented in this book since they only included data from women. The analyses were restricted to women in part because initial studies based on the Revised Trauma Scale suggested that men and women differed substantially in the significance of timing issues (Chiriboga and Cutler 1977), and in part because the process of cross-checking dates for each period was so laborious that the research staff revolted after completing the task for women!

Three Questions of Interest. The analyses focused on three questions. The first concerned whether it was possible to predict differences in the actual speed of passage from decision point, through the separation, to the point of filing a petition for divorce. Here the intent was to find out whether the speed of passage is based on chance factors, or is affected by characteristics of the women or of the marital situation. A total of 16 predictors were included: education, income, adequacy of income, number of children, age, woman's age at marriage, the number of years married, number of marriages, who was originally in favor of separation, who was in favor of separation at the time of the interview, who was to blame for the separation, who was boss in the family, reliance on spouse for companionship, reliance on spouse for guidance, reliance on spouse for practical matters and whether the respondent felt she had a life of own while living with her spouse.

The second question concerned whether length of passage through the first two stages of divorce was associated with adaptation. When addressing this question, those characteristics identified in the first question as being associated with timing were included as control variables. The reason for controlling for these measures is that some of them were themselves associated with adaptation; since the intent was to identify whether timing itself made a contribution, the effects of any predictor of timing had to be controlled. Goode (1956), for example, had explained an association of timing with adaptation as being due to the fact that people with less control had a shorter time interval.

The third question concerned the overall length of time through divorce. Here the focus shifted from a critical stage orientation to one dealing with the significance of time itself. The two periods of interest became time from decision to separation, and from separation to the point of being interviewed.

The Building Blocks of Timing

In Goode's (1956) study of timing, women were categorized into those who took up to a month, or more than a month, from point of decision to point of separation. The present study provided an opportunity to replicate, but also extend, Goode's work, since timing data were available not only for the Anticipation Stage but also for as much of the Impact Stage as experienced up to the point of the first interview. We also were employing data obtained much closer to the actual events being recalled, since the women in Goode's (1956) study were interviewed only after the legal act of divorce had been completed.

One of the first things we had to do was decide how to divide up each time period into smaller and more manageable units. We found that 42% of the women passed through the decision-to-separation period in one month or less, and another 7% took less than two months. In other words, for nearly half the women the amount of time spent from when they realized things really were over in their marriage, until the separation, was less than two months. Based on our frequency analysis we divided the subjects into three approximately equal groups: the Swift, who took one month or less; the Measured, who took over one month but less than six; and the Delayed, who took six months or longer (Melichar and Chiriboga 1985).

Once the separation occurs, the first legal step of filing a petition is generally not far behind. By the end of the sixth month postseparation, about 95% of the subjects had petitioned for divorce, and nearly 60% had actually petitioned by the end of the second month. For the period covering time spent between separation and petition, women were classified in two groups: the Swift, who took from 0 to 35 days; and the Delayed, who took more than 35 days (Melichar and Chiriboga 1985).

The third timing variable covered the period from separation to the first interview. This time period was divided into three categories: 0 to 140 days, 141 to 200 days and more than 200 days.

The Development of Timing Groups. On the basis of the three timing variables, women in the sample were grouped in two different ways: (1) according to how long it took for them to proceed from decision to separation, versus how long it took to progress to the filing of petition; and (2) how long it took to proceed from decision to separation versus how long it subsequently took before we interviewed them. These groupings were then used in a series of analyses which we looked at to determine how well we could predict timing (Melichar and Chiriboga 1985).

For the analyses covering the first two stages of divorce, six groups were created by juxtaposing the categories within each stage. The groups (and the numbers of women within each) were:

1. The Swift-Swift $(N = 28)$
2. The Measured-Swift $(N = 13)$
3. The Delayed-Swift $(N = 33)$
4. The Swift-Delayed $(N = 29)$
5. The Measured-Delayed $(N = 22)$
6. The Delayed-Delayed $(N = 16)$

It can be seen that there were several "polar opposite" groups. For example, the Swift-Swift took just about two months to proceed from decision point to the point of filing for divorce (note that they did not necessarily have control over this process, or the dispatch with which it was pursued). On the other hand, the Delayed-Delayed took at least seven months to proceed to the same point. Similarly, the Delayed-Swift took their time passing through the Anticipation Stage, but then went speedily through the next, in contrast to the Swift-Delayed, who expedited the first stage but then tarried in the second (Melichar and Chiriboga 1985).

Dependent Variables

The analyses examining timing issues used a broader spread of outcome or dependent variables than we have generally employed in this book, primarily because these were very exploratory analyses and we had no ideas concerning how strong or widespread would be the effect of timing characteristics. One group of dependent variables was drawn from the Revised Trauma Scale described in the first section of this chapter. Another set of dependent variables was drawn from individual items that together make up the Bradburn Scale (Bradburn 1969; Bradburn and Caplovitz 1965; see also chapter 3).

Several questions about health were asked, since the literature on both bereavement and divorce indicates that changes in health occur at various points along stressful transitions. The questions asked about health status since separation, health status prior to separation, number of visits to physician in past year and current health problems.

A final set of dependent variables came from the previously described California Symptoms Checklist (Lowenthal et al. 1975; Fiske and Chiriboga 1990). Instead of the more global summary score, we used six subscales derived by means of factor analysis: (1) ruminative depression, (2) agitated depression, (3) stress reaction, (4) somatization, (5) personal insecurity, and (6) interpersonal anxiety (Chiriboga et al. 1982). These subscales provide greater information about the specific kinds of problems people might be experiencing, but at the same time seem to be part of a more generalized symptoms factor.

Predicting Passage across the First Two Stages

As has been mentioned, the first goal in the analyses was to identify variables that might be influencing speed of passage through the first two stages of divorce. The approach used was discriminant analyses, a procedure that has already been described in previous chapters. In brief, we looked at how well the predictors helped to differentiate between six groups formed by contrasting timing categories for the Anticipation and Impact Stages: (1) the Swift-Swift, (2) the Measured-Swift, (3) the Delayed-Swift, (4) the Swift-Delayed, (5) the Measured-Delayed, and (6) the Delayed-Delayed.

The analysis identified four measures that seemed helpful in predicting the groups into which the women fell: the woman's age at marriage, number of years married, who was originally most in favor of divorce (self or spouse), and who was perceived by the respondent as the "boss in the family" prior to separation (self or spouse). Together, these four variables allowed the prediction equation to successfully place 40% of the women. However, accuracy of prediction varied by group: for example, only 8% of the Measured-Swift group were correctly placed, considerably worse than chance, while accurate prediction in the Delayed-Swift group reached 59% (Melichar and Chiriboga 1985).

Age-Related Predictors. Characteristics of the woman and her marriage do indeed appear to influence the subsequent transitional pathway. Of the four significant predictors of the timing, two dealt with characteristics associated with, but not identical to, chronological age: age at marriage and years married. It may in fact be no accident that correlates of age, but not age itself, were predictors. In studies of the life span, chronological age is generally recognized as being a misleading or "carrier variable." In other words, it is the correlates of age, such as length of marriage, that tell us most (e.g., Wohlwill 1978).

In terms of specifics, we found that women who married at a later age were more likely to move quickly, not only to separation, but also to petition for divorce. It may be that women who marry at an older age have had more premarital experiences to draw upon and, hence, are more mature and able to grapple with the question of divorce. An alternative, but not mutually exclusive, explanation may be that these older women tend to be better educated, informed, and socially and psychologically more independent (Melichar and Chiriboga 1985).

Years married, although correlated with age at marriage, made an independent contribution to the prediction of group placement. Those married longest were the Delayed-Swift; those married the shortest time were Swift-Delayed and Measured-Delayed. One interpretation of these findings is that people who have been married for longer periods of time think twice, figuratively speaking, before embarking on the realities of separation and filing for divorce. In contrast, those with "younger" marriages may act more precipitately, but then find themselves more unsure about the advisability of their actions.

Another way of considering the issues raised by the years married variable is to hypothesize, as have Payne and Pittard (1969), that divorce in midlife is more problematic because the married couple is more deeply embedded in a network of social relationships, shared experiences, and institutional ties. The greater these bonds, it can be assumed, the greater the emotional and social consequences of sundering them.

The Issue of Situational Control. Like the age-related variables, the measure that assessed who was originally in favor of separation possibly reflects a broader set of conditions (these will be discussed in chapter 10). Women originally most in favor of divorce were more likely to fall within the De-layed-Swift and Delayed-Delayed groups; as would be expected on the basis of Goode's (1956) interpretation, those least in favor were the Swift-Swift. Another way of viewing these results is that women who felt they were more in control over the divorce took the longest time to separate and to file a petition. In other words, women with more control over the situation may give themselves more time to work out the necessary psychological adjust-ments and objective problems prior to separation.

The Issue of General Control. The theme of control is also related to the woman's perception of who had been "boss" in the marriage prior to separa-tion, but here we are dealing with a variable that is tied not to the divorce but to a more generalized feeling of control. Women in the Delayed-Delayed group were most likely to report being boss in the family and women in the Measured-Swift group were the least likely. In other words, women who felt most in control were likely to take the most time, not only to separation, but also to petition. The women who felt least in control, in contrast, proceeded at a moderate pace to separation, but then went quickly to petition (Melichar and Chiriboga 1985).

Clearly, the two predictors related to control or independence reflect a host of other characteristics. Both kinds of control will become the topic of chapter 10. Here we will simply note that because these measures of control, and the two age-related measures, were associated with timing, they became control variables in the next set of analyses, where we looked at how well the timing variables predicted well-being.

ADAPTATION AND SPEED OF PASSAGE

There would seem to be an obvious relation between speed of passage through divorce, and how well people hold up in the process. In fact, of course, there are many things happening in the lives of people that may shape the trajectories they follow. Our next step was to focus on the possible implications of timing for adaptation, after controlling for the influence of the predictors of timing. The principal concern was whether the timing of major milestones does in fact influence adaptation. If there was an influence, we also wanted to know why.

In looking at speed of passage across the first two stages of divorce, we used a statistical method called analyses of covariance. Here we juxtaposed timing of the Anticipation Stage with how long it had taken to go from separation to the point of filing a petition, this time looking at them as two separate factors that could have independent effects, or could interact. In addition to the four antecedent variables identified in the last section, overall time spent from separation to interview served as a covariate.

We also computed a second set of analyses, where timing of the Anticipation Stage was contrasted with the amount of time that had passed between separation and interview. Here the covariates included the four antecedent conditions plus time spent from separation to petition. In preview, the results of all analyses strongly supported a conclusion that timing is relevant to adaptation and that the duration of each period in itself is important (Melichar and Chiriboga 1988). In what follows we will here just describe what was found about each of the three time periods.

Decision to Separation: The Importance of Deliberation

The results suggest that the decision to separate is a crucial marker point in the process of adapting to dissolution (Melichar and Chiriboga 1988). Women who took a longer time to go from the decision to the point of physical separation did significantly better on the average than other women. These "slow" women were less likely to feel they couldn't get going, more likely to feel excited and interested in things, more likely (with the swift) to feel proud, least likely (with the Measured) to report ruminative depression, and least likely to experience agitated depression. On the Trauma measures, which were scored according to when in the process of divorce a particular feeling occurred, the slower women were furthest from the points of not caring about themselves and (with the Measured) of greatest anger at the spouse, and felt closest to the point of maximum confidence and energy during the whole period of divorce. In short, for these women the rate of passage through an earlier period clearly bore a relationship to status at the time of the interview.

The Swift and the Measured groups showed somewhat inconsistent patterns (Melichar and Chiriboga 1988). Although the Measured group sometimes fared reasonably well, it generally vied with the Swift for the poorest outcome. Those in the Measured group were least excited and interested in things, least proud, highest in agitated depression, and furthest in time from feeling confident and energetic. Similarly, the Swift group of women were highest in ruminative depression and closest to the point of not caring for themselves and being angry with their spouses.

Separation to Petition: The Effect of Speed of Passage

In contrast to the adaptive significance of deliberation for the first time interval, it appears that after women separated a speedier passage was more adaptive (Melichar and Chiriboga 1988). Fewer dependent variables were involved, but the results indicated that women who progressed more rapidly from separation to petition felt less lonely, less likely to feel they couldn't get going, and were more excited by and interested in things. Only on the Trauma measure assessing when the respondent felt more confident was there a reversal of this pattern: those who slowly moved toward filing a petition for divorce reported being closer to feelings of greatest confidence.

The Interaction of Time to Separation and Time to Petition

The results, up to this point, suggest that women who progress slowly from decision to separation, but then speedily petition for divorce fare best. It is important to remember, however, that the two main effects must be interpreted in terms of the linear or additive model that underlines analysis of variance. While it may perhaps be "better" to proceed slowly in one time period and faster in the next, going at the presumably appropriate rate in one period should contribute to adaptation, regardless of rate in the other.

The possibility did exist that a temporal pathway characterized initially by a slow and then a fast passage would lead to a better outcome than could be predicted by the kind of analytic model we used. To find out if this might be the case, we looked at the interactions between the two timing periods (Melichar and Chiriboga 1988). Five significant interactions existed, and they indicated that the "slow then fast" scenario really was not necessarily the best strategy. The interactions were found for the Trauma variables "least anxious" and "most lonely," the Bradburn variables, "very lonely" and "depressed," and the ruminative depression factor from the Symptoms Checklist. In each case the same pattern was indicated; those women who proceeded slowly through both time periods fared best, and those who went quickly through the first and slowly through the second period fared worst. Here, then, we find that the slow but sure seem to do best. Perhaps more important, however, is that the opposite of the slow then fast, the fast then slow, is clearly associated with the most problems (Melichar and Chiriboga 1985).

From Separation to Interview: The Importance of Overall Duration

In turning to the last period to be considered, the focus shifts from how long it takes to reach a critical milestone in the process of divorce (for example, deciding to divorce or filing the petition) to the overall length of time that passed between decision and interview. The question became one of sheer length of time, since the respondents had relatively little to do with determining when the interview took place. In the following analyses, it should be kept in mind that one covariate was changed from the group included in the analyses for the first two stages of divorce. The one covariate that changed had to do with timing: instead of controlling for time to interview, the analyses controlled for the amount of time spent from separation to petition.

After controlling for the covariates, the relationship of this time interval to adaptation is far from clear (Melichar and Chiriboga 1988). What might be called the Brief Group, those interviewed within 140 days of separation, were the proudest (along with the Intermediate Group), and reported the highest positive score (along with the Intermediate Group). However, they were most likely to report feeling they couldn't get going, feeling vaguely uneasy without knowing why, had the highest overall tension score, the highest count of psychological symptoms, were furthest from feeling their healthiest and were closest to having memory problems.

Like the Brief Group, the Intermediate Group felt more pride and had the highest overall positive score; they also were the furthest from memory and alcoholic problems (Melichar and Chiriboga 1988). On the other hand, they were also the most bored, had the highest score on overall negative emotions and were similar to the Brief Group in being furthest from good health.

Those furthest from separation, the Distant Group, showed the most evidence of good adaptation (Melichar and Chiriboga 1988). They were least likely to feel they couldn't get going, least likely to feel bored, least likely to feel vaguely uneasy, were lowest on psychiatric symptoms, were lowest on overall negative emotions, lowest on overall tension emotions and were closest to feeling their health was at its best. On only two measures did they score worst: they were least likely to report feelings of pride and lowest on overall positive emotions.

It should be pointed out, however, that women in the Distant Group showed the best evidence of adaptation primarily by not reporting problems. That is, they were not high on positive psychological states, but rather were generally low on more negative states, such as the number of symptoms or the amount of negative emotions. It may be significant that they were not highest, but lowest on overall positive emotions. One interpretation is that positive and negative conditions and strains are dealt with at different times. The aversive strains may be dealt with first, and deficits in positive functioning may be attended to somewhat later.

A REVISION OF THE TRANSITION MODEL OF DIVORCE

In considering multiple periods or milestones, especially relative to the overall time of passage, it is useful to have an analytic model as a guide. As noted in chapter 4, one of the ways in which investigators have attempted to conceptualize the passage through divorce as a process and the timing of milestone events is by means of various models of transitions. These models are usually unspecified, in part because of the rather inchoate state of research on transitions (Chiriboga 1979a; Chiriboga 1986). As we have already mentioned, one of the more useful approaches to the study of transitions is the rites-of-passage model developed by van Gennep (1960) and Turner (1967). The usefulness of this approach stems from the attempt to go beyond noting how to tell when a transition is occurring and specify the phases of a transition.

The three phases of the rites-of-passage model could not be considered in toto in this study because the data pertained only to a period of time during which most respondents had not proceeded past the liminal phase. However, the results did have implications for the model, specifically suggesting that the rites-of-passage model, as traditionally formulated, may have to be revised to include an additional stage that would precede van Gennep's first phase.

This new stage, one covering the time between decision and physical separation, seems to be the place when the individual first really comes to grips with future events (Melichar and Chiriboga 1988). During this phase, the individual plays a much greater role in the initiation and outcome of the role transformation than is implied in the more traditional applications of the rites-of-passage model (Spencer 1965; Turner 1967). That model appears to operate best for the almost universal role changes that occur at predictable points in the life course, but less well for those changes that are unscheduled and unpredictable.

The results suggest a revision of the rites-of-passage model (van Gennep 1960) to include four phases: a phase of anticipation, a separation phase, a liminal phase, and an aggregation phase (Melichar and Chiriboga 1988). The four rites-of-passage phases could form the basis for defining components of the transition, but it is important to recognize that people do not proceed through each phase with the same dispatch, and indeed may find themselves involved in all four phases simultaneously. The reason is that modern phases of a transition are as likely to occur on a "psychological" or inner plane as they are to occur on an outer and more concrete level.

Adaptation and Relative Duration of Periods

In previous work we had found evidence that while men viewed the period immediately following separation as most difficult, women rated the predecision and preseparation periods as the most difficult (Chiriboga and Cutler 1977; see also Goode 1956). The period prior to separation, in other words, represented a time of high stress, but it also represented a period when efforts at adjustment were already beginning. These efforts appear to represent short-term transitional processes of coping and adaptation to the newly induced stress (e.g., Chiriboga 1979b; Horowitz 1976; Lazarus and Folkman 1984) and the creation of new social supports (Raschke 1977; Weintraub, Brooks and Lewis 1977; Cobb 1976).

The time taken to go from decision to separation had a relatively lasting effect on adaptation. The longer this period, the more likely the woman was to show improved levels of adaptation at the time of the interview. This implies that there had been more time to adjust to the impending dissolution. Both of the two faster groups (the Swift and the Measured) showed less adaptation; the Swift were more maladaptive on some variables, and the Measured on others.

Once women came to a deliberate decision, and subsequently separated, the quickest passage from separation to petition most often was associated with the best adaptation later (except for feelings of confidence, in respect to which the Delayed exhibited better adaptation). The reason for handling the post-separation phase with dispatch may be that it allows the woman to adjust concurrently to changes in all three systems.

Loneliness and depression were associated with interactions between the times from decision to separation and separation to petition (controlling for time from separation to interview and the antecedent conditions). Initial quickness (decision to separation), followed by slowness in filing the petition, was the most maladaptive condition. It seems best for the woman to have time to adjust to the decision before having to deal with the physical separation, and, after that, to move rapidly to the formal stage of legal petition.

It should be noted that the meaning of time between these two periods differs. In the decision-to-separation period, slowness is the basis for attaining improved adaptation and represents a time that is allowed for adjustment to the impending change. Time from separation to petition appears to be related to a totally different process having to do with the resolution of the formal aspects of dissolution. Time in these two situations has a different effect relative to ultimate adaptation.

CASE STUDIES

Joan Mikel, Martha Madigan and Emmy Lou Danford illustrate the relationship between timing and adaptation to divorce. Joan spent three very long years considering separation and then went through a fast, smooth actual separation and divorce. Also a slow starter but fast finisher, Martha Madigan had time to prepare emotionally for the divorce since her husband gave her a year's warning that he wanted a separation. Emmy Lou Danford, on the other hand, falls into the fast start, slow finish timing group because she separated precipitately from her husband upon discovering he had had an affair, but even at follow-up has failed to confront the realities of her life.

Joan Mikel: Making a Virtue of Delay

Twenty-nine-year-old Joan Mikel is an attractive, strawberry blonde sales person for a large corporation. Shapely and fit, she wore tight jeans and a sweater, just the right amount of jewelry and perfume and was barefooted. Joan greeted the interviewer at the door of her modern home in an exclusive residential neighborhood. She was just moving in; her modern glass and chrome furniture was ready to arrange. And, a brand new Porsche convertible preened itself in the driveway.

Joan and her husband, a banker, were both 21 when they were married, and had been married for eight years at the time of the first interview.

Childless, Joan feels she was the mainstay of the marriage. She reports she did all the household jobs except making household repairs. She depended on her husband somewhat for companionship and money, but very little for guidance and practical matters. She made the decisions about what house to live in, whether or not she should work and how much money to spend on food. As she explains, "taking a job in sales gave me the financial independence and confidence in myself and gave me the feeling that I could get along without my husband. I felt that there was something better than the relationship that I had."

Her financial and personal independence, in short, gave Joan a sense of personal freedom. Although she reports that both she and her husband shared equal power in the relationship, she was the only one who had been thinking about getting a divorce and she thought about it almost from the point she got her present job, over three years ago. The reason, she thinks, is that the marriage basically "was dull. I was bored and I found somebody else and I was also working and making enough money so I felt confident enough to leave."

Having prepared for the possible separation, Joan moved easily and expeditiously through the remaining phases of the transition of divorce. In fact, the interviewer at the second interview notes: "Joan didn't have that much to say about her divorce because, according to her, it just happened—no trauma, no difficulties, no nothing." From the vantage point of the nearly four years that had passed since the separation, Joan extols the virtues of her decision to divorce saying "I have experienced a lot of personal growth emotionally and intellectually. I've done a lot of things that I couldn't do before due to lack of emotional support. I am much happier."

At follow-up we also find another source of strength in Joan. At the point of separation she not only had a stable and well-paying job, but she also had developed a satisfying extramarital relationship. Asked about the man she was dating at baseline and had married by follow-up, Joan replies "I knew him before I separated. I didn't necessarily feel I would marry him but I knew there were people out there I could relate to. But the main thing was that I'd always been working and making a very good living. I thought about it maybe for three years occasionally but I never told him. The day I told him I left." In other words, Joan's slow and deliberate approach to separation gave her time to really prepare for the separation in many different ways—in considerable contrast to the experience of her husband, who essentially received a one day's notice!

Martha Madigan: A Year of Grace

In contrast to Joan Mikel, Martha Madigan did not contemplate an emotional separation for three years nor was she dating prior to separation. She did, however, have about one year to prepare since her husband told her that he was unhappy and wanted a trial separation. Martha's initial reaction was that she could not handle even a trial separation and she tells us at the first interview that she would have done just about anything in the last year of the marriage to keep it going.

Martha is a 38-year-old former fashion columnist for a local newspaper who now works as public relations specialist for a clothing manufacturer. When we first meet we find her to be petite, thin and elegant, with shoulder-length red hair. She is wearing beautiful designer clothes, including a cream color silk blouse and matching gabardine slacks. Her spacious flat is tastefully decorated with Oriental rugs and leather furniture and has a beautiful view of the Pacific Ocean.

Martha was married when she was 28 and her husband was 26. They have a 6-year-old son. Her spouse, an advertising executive, made most of the decisions in the family and she relied on him for most things except money. A major reason for the separation was "different values on money, lack of communications in all verbal areas, and girlfriend."

About four months before they separated, Martha began to suspect her husband was having an affair since he was calling for another woman in his sleep. She described as being the most stressful thing that happened during her divorce "not knowing the truth about why my husband was fooling around and seeing his friend's secretary. He would not tell me, but talked more than three to four times in his sleep. I confronted him after he talked during his dreams and I asked him to go to a doctor. Prior to this, I knew nothing about his affair."

Martha reports that the reality of divorce became clear at this point, when she found out about the affair. She was extremely upset but by the time of the separation she felt things would work out for the best. The combination of these four months and the additional eight months that had passed since her husband's first indication of problems gave Martha time to think about what might happen, and to get a more positive view of the future. In fact, although her husband was initially most in favor of the separation, by the time of our first interview (about four months after separation), Martha herself is most in favor of it.

At this first interview she reports being in excellent health, has only two psychological symptoms, is "pretty happy" and reports experiencing numerous positive emotions such as feeling excited, pleased, proud and on top of the world. Martha feels that she "has taken a big leap and accepted the unknown." She says that the greatest benefit resulting from the separation has been her complete "change of attitude. I feel like fifty pound of weight has been lifted off me. He was very negative." Now she feels "more positive and more competent. Others have pointed out to me my good characteristics."

By follow-up, Martha describes major changes in herself: "I am a much happier, related person. I truly enjoy my awareness of myself, . . . I find myself very fortunate and blessed and continue to find myself happier and happier. . . . I am very realistic about my own life and future. I was previously always concerned about my husband's jobs, habits and terrible, terrible overspending habits. I learned independence the hard way."

Now happily remarried to a businessman who owns his own small company, Martha contrasts her new and old marriages "360 degrees different! I married a man five years my senior who had similar values to mine. Our communications are very good, we manage to do a lot together in our marriage and enjoy sports together. We live in our budget. Our boys, one each, are very compatible and love each other. They are almost two years apart—10 and 12 years old. We are very lucky and have a lot in common, and have a lot of fun." For Martha Madigan, the one year of preparatory time was sufficient to allow for substantial reappraisal of the marriage and her own prospects for a good life. In consequence, she landed on her feet and quickly made the transition to a new and more satisfying life.

Emmy Lou Danford: Quick in Beginning, Slow in Resolving

Emmy Lou, a 39-year-old bank teller, kicked her husband out of the house within an hour of learning he had been unfaithful. She explains the circumstances underlying the decision to separate: "Another woman. That was the main thing. You have no idea what's going on at all and all of a sudden you get a bill for a hotel and you weren't there. And then he even owns up to it! He spills his guts out! That did it right there. And I never had an idea."

During their marriage Emmy Lou's husband made most of the decisions in the family and she relied on him for just about everything, including companionship, guidance, money and practical matters. Her husband also had a major say in how their three young daughters were raised. The couple spent most of their time together and they shared almost all of their household jobs as well. Curiously, Emmy Lou believes that she was the boss in the family, despite feeling she did not have a life of her own.

Emmy Lou was initially most in favor of the separation, but by the first interview, five months later, neither she nor her spouse is in favor of it. In fact, they have decided to postpone any further legal action. As Emmy Lou explains: "We're letting it ride for a few months until we decide if we'll get back together." This remark indicates that they are neither resolved about staying together nor separating. This state is most like the ambiguous, liminal phase of a rite of passage where the individuals are betwixt and between their past and future roles.

On the Revised Trauma Scale, Emmy Lou reports most problems occurred at the time of the separation, including difficulties sleeping and working, and feelings of loneliness, anger and depression. On the Bradburn Scale she reports being "not too happy" and she has 17 out of 42 psychological symptoms, far above the average. She considered her health to be fair and had seen the doctor twice in the previous year for nerves and just to "see how I was getting along."

Three years later we learn that Emmy Lou reconciled with her husband about eight months after the first interview. She explains at the second interview that she was least angry with her husband at the filing of divorce. "I felt I was really going to lose him, so some of the anger just went away. I couldn't express myself. He said I could have anything I wanted. Then I just didn't want anything. He never hassled me."

This choice to reconcile, however, does not seem to have clarified the ambiguity about whether or not to divorce. Emmy Lou still says that she was most in favor of a divorce originally and that now she is still most in favor of a divorce. In fact, she comments spontaneously that she "still thinks about it." This suggests that she is stuck in the liminal phase of being both betwixt and between her past role as a wife and not yet truly committed to either staying married or getting divorced.

Emmy Lou feels differently about her husband now. "I am more cautious now. He looks different to me. I see him in a different light. I see things I couldn't see before in him." The relationship struggles along. "We love each other but can't get along with each other. But I think we were so wrapped up in what we were doing ourselves that we didn't see each other, respect each other. But I think I'm the one doing the changing." Her damaged sense of trust and belief in the potential of the relationship has now extended into massive self-criticism. The separation has resulted in her having: "Less confidence. A lack of self-esteem. No assertiveness. All those good things. I'm trying to get those back. That's why I'm reading these great books (she points to the *Erogenous Zones* on the table). I thought I was a great person. I was going great guns there. I guess that was the problem. I never saw the other woman. You have to learn to deal with it. That's life, I guess."

In contrast to the first interview, Emmy Lou now considers her health to be poor and reports many more somatic complaints: nerves, hair falling out, obesity, pain in the side and numerous visits to the doctor. Her psychological symptoms have increased dramatically from 17 at baseline to 30 now. In addition, she still reports being "not too happy" and has felt angry, depressed, bored and restless in the last week. She reports feeling only one positive emotion, once, in the previous week. One leaves Emmy Lou with the feeling that at some point she and her husband may have to confront the reality of a broken marriage, and more specifically that Emmy Lou really needs to spend some time thinking it through instead of continuing simply to react to the stresses of life.

SUMMING UP

The central point of this chapter has been to show that the speed of passage through the transition of divorce has relevance for adaptation. Commonly seen as something that is more a result of prior conditions than important in its own right, speed of passage emerged as strongly associated with the well-being of people who are divorcing. Analyses focused on three major findings: (1) speed of passage is in fact influenced by several antecedent conditions, such as age at marriage, duration of marriage, who was most in control during the marriage, and who was most in favor of divorce, (2) the duration of the periods of Anticipation and Separation is important to subsequent adaptation, and (3) the overall time taken to pass through dissolution may strongly influence later adaptation. Both analyses and cases have underscored the fact that people undertake the transition of divorce in the context of a dynamic psychological and social environment, with the timing of certain marker points being a key factor in terms of understanding how well people fare.

The predictors of both timing and adaptation represent conditions within the marital situation that in many ways reflect social independence or perhaps even maturity. The best predictors of timing are measures of the quality and structure of the marital relationship. For example, women who moved more quickly from decision to separation were less likely to feel they had been boss in the marriage, relied less on their spouse for companionship and guidance, and had been married for shorter periods of time.

In this chapter we considered the relevance to adaptation of three time periods: from decision to separation, from separation to petition, and from separation to the first interview. The length of all three periods did appear to affect adaptation, even after controlling for a number of antecedent conditions such as control over the divorce and length of marriage. Timing of what we have called the Anticipation Stage showed the greatest influence on adaptation, followed by total elapsed time from separation to interview. Since the amount of time taken from separation to filing a petition had the least effect, the findings suggest that the legal act of petition does not represent a highly salient marker point in the transition of divorce. On the other hand, the overall amount of time spent in the passage from decision to the present (i.e., the point at which the respondent was interviewed) provided the strongest explanation of adaptation: those who had had the most time in which to adjust generally seemed to fare better. This latter finding would suggest a vindication of the old adage, often cited in the bereavement literature, that "time heals all wounds."

Overall, our findings suggest that different demands are placed upon women at different points along the divorce process. What Melichar and Chiriboga (1985) call the point of "virtual separation" initiates a period of inner, psychological adjustment. The function and significance of this period may resemble what Parkes and Weiss (1983) describe as a period of forewarning in their studies of bereavement. This period they found to be vital to the subsequent well-being of surviving spouses; the dynamic seems to be that having advance warning helps people to think out the implications of the stressor before having to take any definitive action. It is a time to think, rehearse, and perhaps above all, really make sure that the divorce is the only way to resolve the problems faced in the marriage.

The act of physical separation, on the other hand, really brings home to both those who are divorcing, and to friends and relatives, that the marriage has failed. Because it is a more public act, physical separation may initiate a cycle of adjustment that is more focused on relations with the outer social world. Friends and parents have to be informed, insurance benefits and automatic deposit procedures must be changed, the employment benefits office must take action; essentially the entirety of one's role and status set is transformed (Cline and Westman 1971). Simultaneously, new social expectations begin to surface that may be exciting or troublesome: the idea of dating other people was often frightening to our participants, especially those who had been married for longer periods and felt they had lost all their "singles skills." These various demands for readjustment are not specific to divorce; they are well defined in the general literature on how stress affects social relations (e.g., Clausen 1988; Fiske and Chiriboga 1990; Vaillant 1977).

The findings suggest the need to consider two overlapping adjustment processes, one beginning at the point of what might be called emotional separation and the other at physical separation. The overlap between the two adjustment processes is determined in part by the antecedent conditions and in part by how long after the first process the second began. A situation in which a spouse leaves without warning may necessitate two concurrent changes, even if his (or her) leaving were viewed favorably. The unexpected separation is analogous to the case of unexpected widowhood, at least until the differential social responses to widows and divorces begins to be felt (e.g., Lopata 1979; Kitson and Lopata 1978). The point from which "time heals," in short, will vary according to the specific situation people face.

In conclusion, our findings provide evidence that the timing of major events in the transition of divorce plays a central role in the process of marital dissolution. This latter process is complex, and timing is certainly only one of the many factors that can provide insights to the clinician or counselor providing support to people who are undergoing the difficult transition from married to single life.

VIEWS OF THE SELF AND OTHERS

7

THE SELF-CONCEPT OF DIVORCING PERSONS

Cathy Birtley Fenn, David A. Chiriboga and Linda S. Catron

Emmy Lou, the 39-year-old black woman first introduced in chapter 6, sits on her hidabed sofa, talking to the interviewer. "Since my separation," she comments, "I don't have as much faith in people as I had before, and I will never put that much faith and trust in one person again. . . . [I feel] less confidence, [suffer from] lack of self-esteem, no assertiveness—all those good things. I'm trying to get those back." In contrast to Emmy Lou, 40-year-old George Worthington, a white male, feels "a lot more confident. I'm living by myself, doing things on my own. I'm having to deal with growing and being successful at everything I've tried. Nothing is turning sour, everything is turning to gold."

DEFINING THE ISSUES

As health professionals, we know or at least suspect that the potential for psychological damage is far greater among the divorced and recently separated than it is among the happily married. We also know that the majority of persons who undergo a set of stressful life events, such as those that surround the marital breakup, will not develop severe and enduring psychic dysfunction. Why do the self-images of some persons wither during divorce while those of others flourish? Do men and women inherently face different challenges? How does one's self-image affect perceptions of the divorce process, and how fixed are one's perceptions about oneself anyway?

We address these questions in order to gain a better understanding of how the self-image is affected by divorce and which constellations of self-images suggest a possible need for clinical attention. Since our concern is with the individual's own self-assessments, we shall refer to "self-image" rather than "self-concept," the more familiar term. Our approach has been to explore the broad spectrum of qualities that together make up the individual's self-image. We also examine the ways in which positive self-images can serve as resources in times of stress and, alternatively, why other self-images may have potentially deleterious consequences for adaptation.

At this point the reader may be wondering why we are including self-image as a key variable in divorce. The major reason is that self-concept variables play an influential role as mediators of stress. More generally, personal resources such as a positive self-image have long been viewed as important predictors of behavior by personality theorists (e.g., Lecky 1945; Maslow 1954; Rogers 1951).

Self-Image and Stress

The self-image plays a meditating role in the basic stress paradigm that was outlined in chapter 3. In general, "Research on self-systems is relevant to psychological stress because it deals with motives and values which can be threatened and thus are crucial to stress reactions (Lazarus 1966, 61)." Self-esteem, in particular, has been advanced as both a buffer against the actual experience of distress and as a factor associated with stress resilience (Janis 1974; Goldschmidt 1974; Pearlin and Schooler 1978; Murphy 1974). White (1973, 95) states quite bluntly, "No adaptive strategy that is careless of the level of self-esteem is likely to be any good."

As a multidimensional construct, self-image includes components with the potential to be either deficits or resources. For example, low self-esteem or low sense of mastery may reinforce an individual's sense of incompetence or inadequacy to respond to a challenge. Other factors may enhance an individual's ability to cope. In this section, we will discuss in greater detail some studies that concern the relationship of self-image to the stress response, focusing particularly on results from the divorce literature.

Cognitive Appraisal and Self-esteem. Cognitive appraisal has long been advanced as a critical element in the stress paradigm (e.g., Arnold 1960; Lazarus 1966; Lazarus and Folkman 1984). Appraisal involves the process of evaluating potentially threatening events in terms of whether they actually are threatening. This evaluation depends, at least in part, on whether one perceives oneself as competent and resourceful. Lazarus (1966; Lazarus and Folkman 1984) has postulated that high self-esteem may reduce personal vulnerability to threat and therefore act to reduce levels of perceived threat. Implicit to this point of view is the idea that an individual's perception of self, rather than objective reality, is crucial to the way in which he or she will filter stressful information. In turn, the perceived degree of threat may influence whether the individual's response will be adaptive or maladaptive.

A promising avenue of research has focused on the protective function of the self-image. In their investigation of the effectiveness of coping strategies, Pearlin and Schooler (1978) found that low self-denigration, high mastery, and high self-esteem reduced the effect of role strain on stress. Lazarus and Folkman (1984) also postulate that self-esteem may reduce one's vulnerability to threat and therefore facilitate adaptation. These formulations give credence to some of the early experimental studies of the mediating effects of the self during stressful situations (e.g., Gerard 1961; Harvey, Kelley and Shapiro 1947).

The Self in Bereavement. Self-images have also proved to be central to our understanding of bereavement, a stressor with many parallels, but—as we have mentioned repeatedly—important differences, to divorce (Bohannan 1970; Freund 1974; Kitson and Lopata 1978). In Freud's ([1917] 1957) classic work on mourning and melancholia, for example, pathological grief is characterized by loss of self-esteem. Bereavement may bring latent self-images to the fore that may help or hinder the success of the grieving process, and may prompt reevaluation of the self (Horowitz et al. 1980).

For many, the disruptions caused by grieving will lead to a reestablishment of a positive sense of self. For people who are unable to reestablish a positive self-image, the result may be an increasingly negative spiral of stress, blows to self-esteem and more stress, and so on, that can lead to mental as well as physical illness (e.g., Bengtson and Kuypers 1985; see also chapter 3).

The Self in Divorce

The loss of a spouse through divorce may effect the self-image in ways similar to bereavement. Clinical investigators of marital disruption have acknowledged the potentially devastating impact of divorce on self-esteem (Hunt and Hunt 1977; Weiss 1975), and several have emphasized the importance of achieving a new sense of identity (e.g., Bohannan 1970; Wiseman 1975).

While there are relatively few empirical studies, the importance of self-concept for postdivorce adjustment has been suggested (e.g., Blair 1970; Hetherington, Cox and Cox 1976). In the following sections we will discuss the role of the self as portrayed in studies of divorce. We will then present our own research on the predictive capacity of self-images, and the implications of this research from a life span and longitudinal perspective.

SELF-IMAGE AND THE STRESS OF DIVORCE

We have mentioned that positive self-images may protect the individual against psychological disturbance under conditions of high stress (Pearlin and Schooler 1978; Rosenberg 1979). Not much is known, however, about the self as a buffer against stresses specific to divorce. It may well be that self-images exert very little in the way of protection. For example, Weiss (1976) reports clinical evidence that during the separation phase of divorce the self-concept frequently is thrown into a state of flux. Individuals may vacillate between euphoria linked with heightened self-confidence, and depression accompanied by low self-esteem.

Passage of Time and Stages of Divorce

The marked shifts in self-image are clearly time-dependent. While Weiss does not comment on whether instability of the self-image is related to the amount of time separated, Herman (1974; see also chapter 6) suggests that after marital separation, the passage of time is associated with greater self-awareness, as well as with resolution of identity issues. In her study, Herman compares stages of divorce with the classic stages of grief developed by Kubler-Ross. The last stage, "acceptance," is a period of reckoning with the self. She argues that this is the period in which persons can begin to feel good about themselves.

Similarly, whether one accepts the reality of divorce is highly relevant to self-esteem (Wiseman 1975). Once divorce is accepted as a reality, the primary task of the individual may become the reworking of identity. Persons at this stage are often open to new modes of coping and in danger of regressing to a more dependent, less adequate level of functioning (Wiseman 1975; see also Bengtson and Kuypers 1985). In addition, unresolved identity issues, which had become dormant during the marriage, may reemerge. This conflict over personal identity may occur quite early in the divorce process, due to the activation of latent self-images that have never before surfaced into consciousness (Wiseman 1975; Weiss 1975). Not only is identity being reestablished; it is also being reappraised. Behaviors such as seeking out a variety of sexual experiences are aimed at rebuilding a damaged self-concept and are a way of reworking identity conflicts.

The Significance of Change. After the self-image of divorcing persons has begun to stabilize, changes may still occur since the process of divorce can continue for some time. These changes need not be deleterious; while people in the middle of a divorce may face many practical difficulties, they may also report improved feelings about themselves. Wallerstein and Kelly (1980), for example, found a rising sense of self-esteem among younger mothers who had successful experiences in the work force. However, women in the higher socio-economic classes (as determined by their husband's education, occupation and income) often dropped to a lower social class, an assault to their self-esteem that led to long-term problems.

Many of the social and geographic changes brought about by the divorce process contribute to self-redefinition by one's self, others and society. Given that divorce is an evolving process, different self-concepts may be associated with adjustment at different stages. Hetherington, Cox and Cox (1976) studied divorced families at two months, one year and two years following the final decree. Initially, the fathers in their sample were confused about their new identity, or new lack of identity. During the first year after the divorce, they also felt less competent. In an attempt to resolve their identity problems and generally low self-esteem, men often engaged in frenetic social activity and self-improvement. These efforts seem to have paid off: their feelings about themselves showed a marked improvement two years after the divorce.

The significance of such changes in self-concept is poorly understood. The literature on the stability of self-concept in general is equivocal, and rarely if ever is concerned with changes manifest in divorce. While empirical studies provide strong support for the idea that self-concept is relatively stable (McCrae and Costa 1984; Fiske and Chiriboga 1990), others argue that it evolves and changes (Mead 1934; Morse and Gergen 1970; Lifton 1971) over the course of life. One can only speculate that self-image varies with the circumstances of divorce, and, although some perceptions may change, other, more enduring self-images will remain. For example, in the study conducted by Hetherington, Cox and Cox (1976), self-esteem was correlated with the presence of intimacy in relationships among both men and women.

While the men in their sample showed greater initial changes in self-concept, the effects of divorce on the self-concepts of the women were longer lasting.

Self-Image and Adaptation

Various components of self-image have been associated with adjustment to divorce. Using a cross-sectional design, Pais (1979) found self-image to be the most powerful correlate of adjustment among 62 women who had been divorced for approximately 15 months. A similar study of white, middle-class divorcees found that poor self-image was related to a more difficult adjustment to divorce (Blair 1970). White (1979) found men with limited social skills to have poor overall adjustment and low self-esteem. He concluded that marital separation is especially stressful for men due to the lack of the social protectiveness provided by the marital role. Poor adjustment to separation among formerly cohabiting men and women has been associated with greater discrepancies in the fit between self and ideal self (Mika 1980). In yet another study, women who experienced the least difficulty in adjusting to separation were the more self-oriented (Meyers 1976).

Overall, the literature regarding self-images, separation and divorce indicates that positive self-images are associated with successful adjustment. However, the multidimensionality of self-images is rarely explored, nor is there information on the evolving nature of the self-image of divorced persons in relation to different periods of adjustment.

WHAT WE DID: METHODOLOGICAL CONSIDERATIONS

The preceding literature review suggests that self-images are related to adjustment to divorce, and change as one proceeds through the different stages of divorce. Four research questions that relate self-image to psychological functioning evolved from this review.

Question 1. How do self-images during marital separation differ from self-images manifest several years later? Self-image resources were anticipated to increase from the earlier to later stages of divorce, while deficits in self-image were expected to decrease.

Question 2. How are self-images during marital separation related to psychological functioning during the same period?

Question 3. How are self-images at follow-up related to psychological functioning at follow-up?

Question 4. How are self-images during marital separation related to psychological functioning at follow-up?

Baseline and Follow-up Self-Concept Measures

In order to examine the multidimensionality of self-images, 13 measures were developed from one instrument, the Adjective Rating List (ARL). This rating list consisted of 70 adjectives, each of which is rated as "like self," "unlike self" or "in-between" (Lowenthal et al. 1975; Fiske and Chiriboga 1990); the list is an adaptation of one previously developed by Block (1961). After making the ratings, participants were asked to go back and circle those characteristics that they felt were undesirable. The following measures based on this rating list were developed initially in our companion study of normative transitions (for more details, see Fiske and Chiriboga 1990):

1. *Ego Diffusion:* This consisted of the number of traits respondents indicated they "cannot decide" are like themselves or not. A measure designed to assess integration of self-image, neutral responses appear to reflect ambiguity and diffusion in the self-image (Fiske and Chiriboga 1990).
2. *Interviewer-Respondent Correlations:* This measure consisted of correlations between self-ratings and interviewer ratings on the ARL. Higher correlations indicated more agreement between the interviewer and respondent. The agreement score has been indicated as a measure of fit between public and private images, and is related to adaptation (Lowenthal et al. 1975).
3. *Self-Esteem:* This refers to the number of items on the ARL that were circled as undesirable; the more circled, the lower the presumed self-esteem.
4. *Self-Concept Factors:* A factor analysis on the ARL yielded nine factors that were defined as follows: Negative Self, Dominant Self, Incompetent

Self, Desirable-Engageable Self, Vulnerable Self, Hostile Self, Masterful Self, Self-Oriented, and Socially Skilled Self. These factors reflect independent dimensions of the self-image (Pierce and Chiriboga 1979).

On the basis of previous research (e.g., Lowenthal et al. 1975; Pierce and Chiriboga 1979; Fiske and Chiriboga 1990), these 12 self-image measures were divided into two groups, those tapping into a self-image resources dimension and those tapping into a deficits dimension of the self. Resources consisted of Desirable-Engageable Self, Masterful Self, Socially Skilled Self, and Interviewer-Respondent Correlation. Images reflecting deficits included Negative Self, Dominant Self, Incompetent Self, Vulnerable Self, Hostile Self, Self-Oriented, Self Esteem (i.e., low self-esteem), and Ego Diffusion.

Baseline and Follow-up Measure of Adaptation

California Symptoms Checklist-42: This is the checklist of 42 psychosomatic and psychological symptoms (Lowenthal et al. 1975; Chiriboga and Krystal 1985) that we have mentioned in previous chapters.

Antecedent Variables: Baseline and Follow-up

There were six sociodemographic or antecedent variables examined at both baseline and follow-up. Five of these were measured in the same way at both times (Age, Sex, Finances, Children, and Confidant). Months Separated was included only at baseline and Remarriage was included only at follow-up. Most of these measures are relatively obvious in intent but one, Confidant, needs a little clarification. This variable was derived from response to the question, "Among your friends and relatives is there someone you feel you can tell just about anything to, someone you can count on for understanding and advice? Structured responses ranged from "no," to "one person" to "more than one person."

Statistical Analyses. Two basic analytic strategies were followed: analysis of variance and regression. In the examination of self-image levels and change, two-way repeated measure analyses of variance were performed on each of the 13 measures of self-image. The between-subjects factors were sex and age, with people being divided into four age categories: twenties, thirties, forties, and fifty plus. When the focus shifted to exploring the relationship between self-concept and adjustment at different stages of the divorce process, hierarchical multiple regressions were computed. Each regression had 18 predictor variables, the first 6 of which were the antecedent variables and the remaining 12, self-image variables. Note that in addition to these analyses we will, on occasion, also compare participants in the divorce study to those in the companion study of transitions.

THE PROCESS OF DIVORCE

A Preview

Before describing the specific changes we found in self-image during the course of divorce, we will provide a brief overview. The primary purpose of this chapter is to examine the multidimensionality of the self-images of men and women across the life span with respect to different stages of adjustment to divorce, the extent of change in self-measures and their relationship to psychological symptoms at two stages of the divorce process. The results suggest that:

1. For the most part, self-image "resources" increase and "deficits" decrease as one proceeds from the postseparation stage to the three-and-a-half-year follow-up. All dimensions of the self do not change; certain self-character-istics remain stable over time.
2. Self-images were associated with psychological symptoms at baseline and follow-up. After controlling for the effects of six sociodemographic vari-ables, five dimensions of self-image were associated with postseparation adjustment and three follow-up dimensions were associated with long-term adjustment.
3. Two baseline self-image dimensions were found to be effective predictors of long-term adjustment to divorce.

The specific findings and discussion of the results are presented in this and the following sections. We will first discuss the "process" of divorce as represented in baseline and follow-up differences in self-image and psycho-logical functioning. The next section will delineate those aspects of self-image associated with adjustment at baseline and follow-up. The third will deal with the capacity of the self-image at baseline to predict long-term adjustment to divorce.

Time-related Differences in Self-Concept

Changes in self-image from the first to second interview primarily reflected improvement in self-image. By follow-up, the sample exhibited significantly higher scores on Masterful Self and Socially Skilled Self than were recorded at baseline, and lower scores on Vulnerable Self. In other words, heightened feelings of vulnerability at the postseparation stage had diminished by the follow-up. The passage of a few years since the time of the initial separation was also associated with an increased sense of competence and social poise.

These findings agree with those of other investigators. Although behavior suggesting vulnerabilities associated with divorce has been observed in recently separated individuals, these usually lessen as time goes on (Weiss 1975; Hunt 1966; Wallerstein and Kelly 1980). Damaged self-esteem for example is usually repaired during the years following separation and divorce, as the individual develops a new sense of identity and "mastery" of the environment (Hetherington, Cox and Cox 1976; Wallerstein and Blakeslee 1989). In fact, the stress literature suggests that responding successfully to a crisis situation like divorce ultimately can lead to an enhanced self-image (e.g., Cumming and Cumming 1962; Chiriboga and Dean 1978).

On the other hand, while significant change from baseline to follow-up occurred for some of the self-image variables, the majority of these variables exhibited no change over time. Men and women in the sample did not differ from baseline to follow-up on Negative Self, Dominant Self, Incompetent Self, Desirable-Engageable Self, Hostile Self, Self-Oriented, Self-Esteem and Interviewer-Respondent (I-R) Correlation. This suggests some overall stability in the self-image.

Ego Diffusion: An Important Exception. The results discussed thus far indicate that either no change was found or that self-images actually became more positive. There was, however, one exception to this finding: Ego Diffusion showed an overall increase from baseline to follow-up. On closer inspection, this increase was found primarily among the women. Males actually decreased slightly in experiences of ego diffusion, but females showed a marked increase from first to second interviews.

What is the significance of this increase? The intercorrelations of Ego Diffusion with other measures of self-image provide some clues. To begin with, the correlation of baseline Ego Diffusion with other measures was very similar for both males and females. In general, correlations for both sexes indicated that higher Ego Diffusion was positively correlated with self-image deficits and negatively correlated with resources. These findings suggest that scoring high on Ego Diffusion can be interpreted similarly for both sexes.

Please recall that Ego Diffusion represents the total number of adjectives about which a participant felt ambiguous or uncertain. Ego Diffusion was developed by Lowenthal et al. (1975), who concluded on the basis of their research that the measure reflected the kind of "liminal" or transitional status described in chapter 4. Our present findings add to this conclusion by suggesting that the transition of divorce has a more profound effect on the lives of women, and, hence, is associated with greater uncertainty about who, in fact, they are. These findings also support Weiss's (1976) speculations concerning the state of identity flux created by divorce.

Given that self-diffusion scores were positively associated with self-concept deficits and negatively associated with self-resources, the marked increase in self-diffusion among the women could spell trouble. It suggests an increased lack of clarity about the role of women and perhaps a greater risk of psychological disturbance. Self-diffusion was significantly correlated with symptoms at follow-up, but not at baseline. This makes conceptual sense since, at our first contact, it would be almost an expected part of the divorce transition that there would be some lack of clarity about the self-concept.

Other Sex Differences. The results also indicated that women generally scored higher than men on two of the resources (Desirable-Engageable Self and Interviewer-Respondent Correlation); males scored higher than females on one resource (Masterful Self) and one deficit (Hostile Self). The higher Interviewer-Respondent correlation among females concurs with what Lowenthal and her colleagues (Lowenthal et al. 1975) found in their sample. While Lowenthal's group did not factor analyze the Adjective Rating List and thus did not have data on Masterful Self, Hostile Self or Desirable-Engageable Self, sex differences on specific adjectives on the ARL paralleled those found in the present study. Thus, sex differences among these divorced persons on self-image measures appear to represent fairly normative differences among males and females.

Age Differences. Age differences, found for Self-Esteem and the Interviewer-Respondent agreement score for the respondent's self-image, paralleled age differences on the same measures that have been reported by Lowenthal et al. (1975). That is, younger persons were lower on self-esteem and had lower agreement between subject and interviewer than did older persons. One implication of the latter finding is that older people in both samples were more likely to have an objective view of themselves.

Generalizability of Findings. An obvious question concerns how unique were the self-conceptions of these divorced persons. To address this question, comparisons were made with subjects from our companion study of transitions. To refresh your memory about that study, these persons were part of a longitudinal study of the impact of transitions on the functioning of average men and women. The transitions in question were normative or expectable, and included high school seniors about to leave home, newlyweds facing decisions about parenthood, middle-aged parents facing the departure of their youngest child from home and men and women facing retirement.

Our intention in comparing the Divorce and Transitions samples on self-images was to identify those areas in which the Divorce group stood out. For this reason, all subjects in the Transitions sample who had been separated or divorced were removed from the data base. Responses to the ARL by Transitions Study respondents were scaled to match the nine self-image factors developed for the Divorce Study. At both baseline and follow-up, the Divorce sample ($N = 285$) scored significantly higher on Negative Self, Dominant Self, Vulnerable Self, and Masterful Self than the Transitions sample ($N = 161$). Even though their self-image and psychological functioning had improved over time, persons in the Divorce sample had fewer self-resources and more deficits at both separation and follow-up than did this comparison sample of persons undergoing normative transitions. The fact that divorcing persons scored higher than the comparison group on Masterful Self at both baseline and follow-up suggests, however, that the divorce process may allow for growth as well as deterioration.

Summary. The results of this study indicate that as one proceeds through the divorce experience, certain "resources" of the self increase. In general, however, most of the self-image dimensions did not change significantly over the 3.5 years of study. Indeed, while the passage of time appears to have affected some perceptions of the self, the majority remain quite stable. The only increase in deficits was evident in the Ego Diffusion scores of women. While this later variable is considered to be a self-image "deficit," and was in fact related to poor psychological adjustment, the more important implication may be that increased conflict over identity is a long-term consequence of divorce for many women.

Comparisons with the companion study of transitions indicated that the Divorce respondents maintained self-images that reflected greater vulnerability and negativity. At the same time there was evidence that they believed themselves to be more dominant and capable of mastery over self and others. Since the respondents in both studies were drawn from the same socioeconomic group in the same geographic area, it can be conjectured that these differences may derive from the divorce experience, and that the self-blame and lowered self-image of divorced persons may prompt a defensive or compensatory drive towards control.

Self-image and Adjustment at First Contact

We used regression analysis to determine which self-image variables at first contact were associated with initial symptom levels. When controlling for the effects of age, sex, finances, children and months separated, five self-image variables were selected by the regression procedure. These variables were: Negative Self, Vulnerable Self, Self-Esteem, Masterful Self, and Ego Diffusion. The overall regression model accounted for a highly significant 47% of the variation in symptoms.

These self-image variables were powerful predictors of psychological functioning during the postseparation stage. Recall that the symptoms measure is a count of the number of psychological and psychosomatic symptoms reported by the respondent. Our results indicated that people with more symptoms scored higher on Negative Self, Vulnerable Self, and Ego Diffusion, but they also scored lower on Masterful Self and Self-Esteem. Negative Self was the strongest predictor of symptoms; it alone explained approximately 26% of the variance.

These results matched our expectations concerning deficit measures of the self. In other words, people who scored higher on deficit measures were more likely to manifest more symptoms. The one self-image "resource" included in the prediction model was associated with a lower symptoms score. These findings also agree with findings from other studies (Blair 1970; White 1979) where negative self-images were linked with poor adjustment and positive self-images associated with successful adjustment. The results, however, provide a richer understanding of the complexity of the self and those characteristics that are particularly salient to adaptation at the separation stage of the divorce process.

The Special Role of Children and Social Supports. The predictive capacity of the regression model was slightly enhanced by the inclusion of two interaction terms: "Children and Masterful Self" and "Confidant and Ego Diffusion." The stress literature and studies of divorce adjustment have indicated the importance of social support to adaptation, while having children has been associated with depression (Pearlin and Johnson 1977) and with generally poor adjustment to divorce (Blair 1970; Goode 1956). One reason may be that children can impede the working through process necessary for adjustment.

In the present set of analyses, we did not take into account the number of children, merely whether there were children living with the respondent. In contrast to other studies, the presence of children was generally found to be associated with lower symptoms scores. However, children seem to have a special role under certain conditions of self-image. The interaction term, for example, indicated that having children can counteract the effects of low mastery. While generally related to higher scores on the symptoms measure, low mastery was associated with less symptomatology if there were children living at home. Here then is a case where children do seem to have a positive impact on the lives of divorcing persons.

In contrast, higher Ego Diffusion, while detrimental in general, becomes worse when confidants are unavailable. This finding could be interpreted in several ways. Persons with ambiguity regarding their identity may not be well liked by others and, therefore, may have little social support. Alternatively, confidants may provide a source of self-affirmation and definition. Those without confidants may lack a vital anchor for their identity.

Self-Concept Variables Associated with Adjustment at Follow-up

We have seen that self-image at first contact was strongly related to initial levels of psychological symptoms. The same multiple regression procedure employed for the first interview material was used for the second interview to determine which self-image variables were associated with symptoms. The control variables in this analysis were age, sex, finances, children, confidant and remarriage. Negative self, Vulnerable Self and Self-Esteem were again selected as the most powerful predictors of follow-up symptoms. The regression model accounted for 43% of the variation due to symptoms, and the overall prediction equation demonstrated that self-image variables are strongly associated with measures of long-term adjustment, in the expected directions.

Another Special Role for Children. Only one interaction term proved significant in the prediction of Symptoms at time two: the combination of having children living at home and being high on self-esteem was associated with fewer symptoms. In contrast, those with low self-esteem and children living at home manifested the highest levels of psychological symptoms. One explanation for these findings was already mentioned in our discussion of why overly self-critical people have difficulty making or keeping friends and intimates. In fact, correlational analyses showed that persons with lower self-esteem generally were less likely to have a confidant and unlikely to remarry. When an individual has friends or partners with whom feelings or experiences can be shared, normal day-to-day frustrations can be released. However, without that kind of outlet, having children at home can be a strain rather than a buffer. In short, it appears that other factors associated with low self-esteem in a person (who has children living at home) may contribute to higher psychological Symptoms.

Summary. The regressions predicting symptoms at first and second interviews selected three of the same predictors in the same order of importance. These three variables were: Negative Self, Vulnerable Self and lower Self-Esteem. Negative Self accounted for 26% of the variance in symptoms at first interview and 30% for second interview data. The consistency of findings suggests that these self characteristics are important to psychological functioning and may in fact represent aspects of poor self-image that are detrimental to mental health during divorce adjustment.

At the first interview, the antecedent variables contributed 12% to the variation in symptoms, but at follow-up they only contributed 6%. This suggests that some factors, such as the availability of a confidant, are most relevant during the early stages of the divorce process. In fact, the presence of a confidant and children were significant predictors for initial symptom levels but not at follow-up. These findings will be pursued in greater detail in chapter 9.

Self-Concept during Separation as a Predictor of Long-Term Adjustment

A multiple regression was performed with baseline self-image variables as the predictors and follow-up Symptoms as the criterion variable. The purpose of the analysis was to determine whether certain perceptions about the self during the early stages of divorce could be used to identify persons who might be at risk for long-term maladjustment.

In this analysis, the effects of the following baseline variables were controlled for age, gender, finances, number of children, months separated and the presence of a confidant. In addition, since we knew that initial symptom level is a strong predictor of symptom level at follow-up, the regression included initial symptom level before any other variable. The analysis selected only Hostile Self as a predictor of long-term adjustment; Negative Self and low Self-Esteem (significant predictors in the absence of initial symptom level) did not account for additional variance when baseline symptoms was included as a predictor. And in fact, Hostile Self was not a very strong predictor: 45% of the variance in follow-up symptoms was due to baseline symptoms and only 1% was explained by Hostile Self.

The appearance of Hostile Self as a predictor, although only at a minimal level from the point of view of explained variance, suggests that it provides some unique information about prediction of long-term psychological dysfunction. The adjectives comprising the Hostile Self factor are "hostile," "guileful," "cruel" and "not fair-minded." These personal characteristics would seem to be particularly alienating to others and it is not surprising to find that Hostile Self was positively correlated with the self-image measure indicating strong self-concern and negatively correlated with the measure reflecting a Desirable-Engageable Self.

As a component of self-image, in other words, Hostility may direct one inwards and discourage social support. Hostile Self is significantly correlated with symptoms at baseline and follow-up; however, other variables exhibit stronger correlations with symptoms than it does. Perhaps, then, Hostility represents a risk factor that is not necessarily associated with concomitant symptomatology. In a clinical sense, this could be helpful.

This finding has important implications for preventive intervention. Knowing that symptoms at baseline is the best predictor of symptoms at follow-up is useful, for example, in terms of clinical intervention. It is also helpful to know that a view of oneself as hostile may identify persons at risk for long-term psychological dysfunction. Working through the feelings of hostility may be a particularly useful intervention for these individuals. For most persons, symptom levels decreased from first to second interview, but Hostility remained unchanged. While this finding is interesting, the results must be validated in other studies before they can be applied to treatment programs for the divorced.

SOME FURTHER THOUGHTS ON CHANGE

The issue of whether self-image and personality characteristics change or remain stable in adult life is controversial. There are those who vehemently adhere to the belief that personality is stable (e.g., Block 1961; McCrae and Costa 1984), while others argue just as vehemently that personality change is part of normal development (e.g., Brim and Kagan 1980; Levinson et al. 1978). A premise underlying our own approach was that if one explores the multidimensionality of the self-images of divorcing persons *both* change and stability will occur. That is exactly what the results indicated. Overall, the group exhibited no change in the majority of self-image dimensions. What change did occur, except for an increase in one deficit (Ego Diffusion), indicated increased resources and decreased deficits. A crisp picture of constancy versus stability did not emerge. Since analyses were done on divorced persons as a group, we learned that, even though a minority of persons in this group remain the same or get worse, on the average improvement in self-image occurs.

One intriguing result was the increase in Masterful Self from baseline to follow-up. Not only did mastery improve, but the Divorce sample was higher in mastery than the Transitions sample at both postseparation and the three-and-a-half-year follow-up. While divorce has obvious disadvantages, the experience appears to provide most persons with an increased sense of competence. This point is well illustrated by responses to the question: "Has divorce changed the way you feel about yourself; if so, how?" Following are some examples, taken from responses at the first contact with participants:

"I like myself as a person, a lot more self-confident; feel I can handle whatever comes along." (female)

"I thought I needed someone to stay with me and now I realize I can make it on my own." (female)

"More control of my life." (female)

"I don't have anyone telling me how terrible I am anymore. I found out that I'm much more capable than I probably gave myself credit for." (probe) "The water pipe broke; I got the water shut off and taken care of. With the kids he was an authoritarian figure. I wasn't sure I could do it all on my own. In fact, the kids are doing better than they were. I handled the money before but I had someone to answer to." (female)

"It gives me a certain feeling of self-reliance and also I feel positive about making a necessary decision." (male)

"I feel a lot more confident, but I don't know whether to attribute that to my divorce. I'm living by myself, doing things on my own. I'm having to deal with growing and being successful at everything I've tried. Nothing is turning sour. Everything is turning to gold." (male)

There are a variety of reasons that might explain this increase in mastery. The absence of negative feedback about themselves that they were accustomed to receiving from their ex-spouses may be all that is needed to help some persons feel more competent. The divorce provides others with increased social contacts from which they derive positive feedback and a sense of effectiveness. This last sequel to divorce was mentioned particularly by many of our middle-aged women in response to open-ended questions concerning the impact of divorce and deserves further discussion due to its life-course implications.

The experience of "making it" and the new skills acquired through the divorce process may provide an important resource for the divorced person, one which promotes adaptation. The literature on stress and adaptation places great emphasis on the importance of mastery and perceptions of control to successful adaptation (Mandler 1979; Pearlin and Schooler 1978; Seligman 1975). Brim and Kagan (1980) contends that personality does change throughout the life course, and states that this is especially true regarding feelings of mastery. It appears that persons undergoing divorce experience growth in the self (increased mastery and social skills, decreased vulnerability) as well as deterioration (increased Ego Diffusion). Even in the midst of great external change (divorce), however, change in self-image was selective rather than universal. Such findings echo the conclusion of William James (1950; see also McCrae and Costa 1984), who felt that by age 30 the character had solidified to the extent that further change was relatively unlikely. There is a persistency to our self-images, even for those experiencing divorce.

Self-Image and Adjustment

Another important focus of this study was on the relationship between self-conceptions and psychological functioning. The same three variables, Negative Self, Vulnerable Self, and low Self-Esteem, proved to be powerful predictors of increased symptomatology, especially at the first contact. No attempt was made in this study to select persons with different psychiatric profiles or to subdivide the sample into different levels of psychological functioning. The regression analyses, however, provide information about the self-characteristics that would be expected among divorced persons with severe psychological dysfunction. Following are two brief case studies of persons who scored high on symptoms, Negative Self, Vulnerable Self, and low on Self-Esteem.

CASE STUDIES

Emmy Lou (Follow-up)

Emmy Lou, the mother of three teenage girls, was mentioned at the beginning of this chapter, and in several other chapters as well. A high school graduate who works full time, she has reconciled with her spouse by the second interview. When asked if divorce has changed the way she feels about herself, she responds, "Less confidence. Lack of self-esteem. No assertiveness. All those good things. I'm trying to get those back. . . . I thought I was a great person. I was going great guns there. I guess that was the problem. You have to learn to deal with it. That's life, I guess."

She feels more distant from other people since our first interview. When questioned about her health, she says she has gone to the doctor frequently. Her complaints included nerves, hair falling out, obesity, pain in the side and depression. When asked how her marriage now is different from before, she states, "I'm trying to be more understanding and it's killing me. I'm trying to be more tolerant and it's killing me. It's depressing. I'm more subservient now. I try not to complain or talk about the things that are really bothering me or tell him off when I should, when he needs it."

When asked what sorts of things she tends to think or daydream about, she replies, "How much fun I used to have when I was younger, how well [spouse] and I got along. We did more things together. The kids were still babies and I had a better outlook on life in past times." Overall, Emmy Lou imparts a sense of a crushed ego, of a person who feels that even a troubled marriage is better than what she can do by herself.

Bob Philips (Baseline Interview)

Bob is a 27-year-old working man who graduated with a B.A. from college and got married at age 23. When asked what kinds of things influenced the decision to separate and perhaps divorce, he says "I had no identity. I lost myself—couldn't identify myself." This is consistent with the fact that he scores very high on Ego Diffusion. The greatest difficulty with the process of divorce so far has been "Letting go of the marriage, the person, trying to accept it." The divorce has changed the way he feels about himself: I feel ashamed of myself for some things I've done to my wife—my lack of maturity in the relationship and my inability to communicate when needed." In response to questions regarding his social support network, he states that his friends don't contact him anymore and that he has no one to count on.

When asked what sorts of things he tends to think or daydream about, he said, "Shortcomings about myself. I see myself in another position in life, higher economic level, more social."

Further Thoughts on Adjustment

These case studies illustrate poor adjustment to divorce. Responses to loss have often been discussed within the framework of pathological and normal grief. For example, in *Mourning and Melancholia*, Freud ([1917] 1957, 243) states: "Mourning is regularly the reaction to the loss of a loved person, or to the loss of some abstraction which has taken the place of one, such as one's country, liberty, an ideal and so on."

Freud ([1917] 1957, 244) goes on to note that "The distinguishing mental features of melancholia are a profoundly painful dejection, cessation of interest in the outside world, loss of the capacity to love, inhibition of all activity, and a lowering of the self-regarding feelings to a degree that finds utterance in self-reproaches and self-revilings, and culminates in a delusional expectation of punishment."

According to Abraham (1927) as well as Freud ([1917] 1957), hostility toward the self, self-criticism, self-denigration and narcissistic self-preoccupation are all components of pathological grief. They attribute this to a preexistent ambivalent relationship with the deceased. Aggression that was previously directed at the lost object becomes directed towards the self. More recently, Horowitz et al. (1980) explored the treatment of pathological grief with psychoanalytic or brief therapy. They concluded from their research that the symptoms of pathological grief are intensifications or prolongations of states found in normal grief and describe them in terms of the "re-emergence of self-images and role relationship models that had been held in check by the existence of the deceased person" (p. 1157).

This activation of latent self-images has also been observed in persons' response to divorce (Wiseman 1975). In the present study, those variables that were found to be the most highly associated with psychological dysfunction among divorced persons have remarkable similarity to the components of pathological grief. At both baseline and follow-up, self-denigration (Negative Self), self-rapprochement (low Self-Esteem) and vulnerability (Vulnerable Self) were strongly associated with pathology.

A separate analysis was done for the purpose of identifying characteristics of the self at baseline that could be used to predict long-term psychological dysfunction; Hostile Self was the only variable (beyond baseline symptoms) that could identify persons at risk for symptoms three and a half years later. The following brief case study is of a person with a high score on Hostile Self at both the first and second interviews, and with high levels of symptoms at the second interview.

Tina Tighter Revisited

We have already encountered Tina in chapter 3, where the focus was on stress and Tina fell into the Loser category. At first contact, Tina is a 40-year-old working woman who has two daughters and a son. She reports that the greatest difficulty with being divorced is loneliness. The loneliest period of her life she says is "Now," and the reason is that she has not been getting along with anyone and that she gets in arguments with everyone. When asked what she does about this situation, she replied, "Nothing."

At follow-up, approximately three and a half years later, Tina is living alone, is dating no one, and states that her greatest difficulty is finances. She reports feeling suicidal, more distant from other people since her divorce, and she has no friends or relatives she can count on.

Tina's life serves to illustrate Parkes's (1971) position that hostility provokes hostility and that persons with disordered mourning create situations in which they are repeatedly rejected by others. Since the measures of self-image in this study were perceptions of the self, rated by the respondent, they are considered internalized feelings about the self as opposed to observed behavior towards others. In this respect, the content of the Hostile Self measure could be considered as reflecting inward directed hostility. Many scholars have shown that hostility directed towards the self and others is associated with pathological grief and mourning (Abraham 1927; Bowlby 1980; Freud ([1917] 1957); Horowitz et al. 1980). The results of the present study suggest that this characteristic is particularly salient in identifying divorced persons at risk for long-term psychological dysfunction.

SOME CONCLUDING COMMENTS

Throughout history, people have been curious about the internal processes that make them human and distinguish them from other animals. Both the "mind" and the "soul" are concepts which have traditionally captured interest and eluded understanding. Among social scientists, these ideas have taken the form of the "self," the "ego," "identity" and others.

William James (1950) is noted for his work on the self and laid the foundation for others interested in understanding this concept. Contemporary scientists who theorize about the self are considering "psychological processes" that guide and determine behavior. However, there are many different terms and meanings in usage (Rosenberg 1979).

Researchers have demonstrated fairly conclusively that self-conceptions do affect behavior (Gerard 1961; Harvey, Kelly and Shapiro 1947) and that self-image plays an important role in loss-related stress (Horowitz et al. 1980). Studies of specific stressful events such as divorce have demonstrated the critical role of the self in relation to postdivorce adjustment (Blair 1970; Pais 1979). Our own results have provided a more detailed portrayal of self-characteristics, one that goes beyond global reports of "good" and "poor" self-image. It was demonstrated that changes in the self-images of divorcing persons over a four-year period generally reflect improved self-images; however, this longitudinal perspective also indicated that the majority of self-images are stable and enduring.

We have tried in this chapter to highlight those dimensions of the self that may identify persons at risk for short- or long-term psychological dysfunction, and found evidence that components of self-image are in fact intertwined with components of mental health. The results underscore the perspective that in order to understand how individuals respond to stress, we must understand their self-image in a multidimensional way. Overall, the results provide some provocative support for the position, advanced in chapters 3 and 4, that during the early stages of a transition, the individual's self-images may be particularly susceptible to change, especially change of a negative nature. Whether we view this as a manifestation of social breakdown syndrome or the experience of a nonnormative transition, the result is the same: robbed of the underpinnings of identity, the individual must confront what remains of selfhood during a time when others may be labeling the self as nonproductive, overemotional, a "bad parent" or "troubled."

Gradually, if new roles and new social skills are built up, positive self-images can emerge. Critical to this evolving reconstruction of the self may be factors that we turn to in the following two chapters. The first is identification with others, especially parents. The second is the sense of personal mastery or control, a construct that is at once part of the self-image and part of the social realities with which the self is confronted.

8

VIEWS OF THE OTHER: ISSUES OF SELF-IMAGE AND IDENTIFICATION

Ann Coho, David A. Chiriboga, and Linda S. Catron

In the last chapter we discussed the self-image of our divorcing subjects, and compared their self-images with those of persons undergoing more normative transitions. We found that in some dimensions there were signs of deterioration in the self-image of those in the throes of marital dissolution, but there were also clear indications that this was a toughening or growth experience for many, and that there was movement in the direction of a more positive sense of self by the time of the follow-up.

Our interest in self-image was sparked by the assumption that divorce may rob many people of major components of their social identity. The reason is that, at least as viewed by many personality specialists, one's identity is wrapped up in the multiple social roles occupied by the individual. Losing a major social role, such as the marital, may remove the linchpin of identity. Moreover, subsequent problems in identity disorganization and changing role definitions can be acutely disruptive to ongoing life adjustment. In this chapter we continue to examine issues surrounding identity, but broaden the scope to explore how our subjects viewed other people, and especially the extent to which they identify with others. Our basic concern is whether or not identification with others is associated with psychological wellness during the process of divorce.

SEMANTIC IMAGES OF SELF AND OTHERS

While most research on self-image employs structured instruments ranging from the vintage Gough Adjective Checklist to Rosenberg's (1979) self-questionnaire, the technique of choice for studying identification is often a more clinically oriented approach: the semantic differential. Using variants of the Semantic Differential Rating Scale developed by Osgood, Succi and Tannenbaum (1957), subjects can rate themselves and others on a series of bipolar opposites. For each set of bipolar opposites, such as hot and cold, the task is to decide how close each target person stands to each extreme or opposite. Since the same adjectives are used to evaluate each target, the results can be compared across targets.

Literally hundreds of studies have employed the semantic differential, applying it to concepts as diverse as commercial products, animals, prominent personages, navy enlistees, schizophrenics and geometric designs (Osgood 1962). The literature on marital relations and divorce is more sparse, but still informative concerning self-image and identification.

Self-Image, Identification and Divorce

According to Kelly's (1955; see also Mead 1934) cognitive-motivational theory of development, a self-image develops through interaction with others. The many years of interplay between parent and child can produce a shared space between them, constructed of shared past experience. This sharing imparts an empathetic understanding that facilitates the development of role- or perspective-taking (Kelly 1955). Similarly, the years of married life may affect how one perceives the world. It could be argued that to the extent that one perceives oneself to be like the ex-partner, one may have problems accepting the realities of divorcing. That the more one perceives eligible partners as like oneself, the better off one is; and that the greater the perceived similarity with parents, the better off one is.

There have been some provocative studies of self-image and identification in divorce. For example, Sobata and Cappas (1979) used the semantic differential technique to study changes in images of self and others among those attending a lecture series on divorce. In pre- and post-test comparisons, views of Myself became more positive and stronger after the courses. Divorce, Separation and The Present were all rated more positively, while Former Spouse was rated more negatively.

While the investigators interpreted these results as demonstrating the efficacy of the lecture series, of greater relevance to this chapter is their idea that how one views others has a bearing on how one views oneself, and may reflect one's personal well-being. Luckey (1960a, 1960b, 1960c), for example, studied marital satisfaction in 81 couples. Each partner rated him- or herself, spouse, ideal self, mother and father on an adjective checklist; the degree of congruence between self and these others was then calculated. Satisfaction in marriage was related to congruence between the husband's self-image and wife's image of him. Happiness, a more generalized indicator of well-being than marital satisfaction, was related to the degree of congruence between the husband's self-image and his image of his father, and to the congruence between wives' images of their husbands and their fathers.

Luckey's data also suggested that when both husband and wife agree that the husband is close to his own ideal (which tends to be like his image of his father), and as she desires him to be (which tends to be like her image of her father), both are happier. Moreover, less satisfied husbands perceived their fathers as being less loving, cooperative and responsible than themselves. These several findings serve to emphasize that how one views social others, including self, holds significance for morale.

The findings reviewed above have been replicated. Stryker (1964), for example, found that congruence between self-image and images of self held by spouse was associated with less marital dissatisfaction. Taylor (1967) reported that a greater similarity between self-image and spouse's perception of self was related to positive marital adjustment, while Kotlar (1965) found that congruence of perception was related to wives' adjustment scores. In another study, marital satisfaction was higher when the wife accurately perceived her husband; the husband's accurate perception of wife was not related (Stuckert 1963).

Several clinically oriented studies have examined the concept of identification as it pertains to symptoms of anxiety and depression. In one early study, for example, the semantic differential was used to measure the degree of "inferred identification" between college students and their parents. Low-anxiety males manifest greater profile similarities with Father, low-anxiety females manifest greater profile similarity with Mother (Lazowick 1955). On the other hand, high-anxiety subjects of both sexes manifest greater similarities between their ratings for the adjective Unpleasant and the following other targets: Father, Mother and Family.

Overall, the literature suggests that for persons in various stages of marriage and divorce, the similarities between images of self and selected others are associated with well-being. In part the importance of similarities and dissimilarities may evolve from the process of identification, especially with parents. In part the importance may reflect the process of disidentification, as well as the way in which we develop attraction or rejection of others.

SEMANTIC STRUCTURE: AN INITIAL LOOK

As a means of balancing out the information provided by the more structured Adjective Rating List, we included in our follow-up interviews a semantic differential instrument, the Social Image Scale (SIS). In administering the SIS, subjects are asked to rate five target persons (Self, Mother, Father, Ex-Spouse and Present Partner) on ten bipolar adjectives. The adjectives included good-bad, clean-dirty, slow-fast, hard-soft, heavy-light, fair-unfair, excitable-calm, hot-cold, active-passive and strong-weak.

One of our first concerns in looking at the information was whether it conformed to the three general factors often reported by researchers using the semantic differential technique. These consist of an evaluative factor, a potency factor and an activity factor; together these three factors are often referred to as the EPA dimensions of meaning.

Although the three factors emerge with some consistency in the literature, a host of other factors may emerge, depending on the scales and concepts under consideration (Osgood 1962). For example, the factor structure may be more "diverse" when ratings are made for concepts related to human personality, such as Mother or Good Friend. Borgatta (1964) and Norman (1963) suggest that when adjective ratings are used to assess people, at least five major factors can be identified. The overall conclusion that can be reached is that there may be greater diversity in the dimensionality perceived in personal than perceived in nonpersonal concepts.

In other words, it may not be appropriate to rely on the standard EPA structure when looking at how divorcing persons assess themselves and others. We checked on this issue, using a sophisticated technique called confirmatory factor analysis (Joreskog and Sorbom 1981). Basically what we did was pose a theoretical model based on EPA and determine how well the data, for men and women separately and together, fit EPA. What we found was that in fact there was no resemblance at all between how our data were organized and the evaluative, potency and activity factors (Coho 1984).

We also found that men and women differed substantially in factor structure. Men tended to employ rather generalized rules of classification that cut across targets. For example, in one set of analyses combining data from all five targets we found among men what might be called a "decency" factor that included items from Myself, Father and Present Partner. Women, in contrast, tended to view each target as a distinct phenomenon that required specific classification. Each of their factors tended to include items from one target. While these gender differences are interesting, and indeed relevant to what we found later, they also suggested the impossibility not only of using the EPA Scales but of using scales derived from our own factor analyses.

VIEWS OF THE SELF AND OTHERS: ANALYTIC STRATEGIES

Because the EPA scales and our own factor results were not very useful, we needed to find another way of using the data to compare ratings of self with the others. What we finally selected were similarity coefficients. For each subject, we computed the correlation between selected targets. For example, we determined the correlation for each individual between the 10 ratings on Self and the same 10 ratings on Ex-Spouse. This approach approximates the "inferred identification" analyses of Lazowick (1955) and others.

All in all, 10 similarity coefficients were computed for each subject. These provided data on the similarity/dissimilarity between: Myself-Father, Myself-Mother, Myself-Ex-Spouse, Myself-Present Partner, Father-Ex-Spouse, Father-Present Partner, and Present Partner-Ex-Spouse.

The similarity coefficients became a new set of variables, which in turn allowed us to begin to examine the implications of inferred identification. For example, what are the implications of perceiving one's Present Partner (if available) as similar to one's Ex-Spouse or Father or Mother? Much of the clinical literature suggests that a man may be seeking his mother in selecting a wife or partner. Conversely, there is the suggestion that a woman may be seeking her father in selecting a partner.

We also did a number of checks on the appropriateness and possible biases that might result from the analyses. For example, one question was whether people without a "steady" differed systematically from those who had developed a steady relationship by the second interview. This was important because those without a steady would be eliminated from analyses where comparisons with Present Partner were being made. Comparing the relationship of baseline and follow-up total symptoms count with similarity coefficients involving the other nine targets, we found that the correlation matrices for subjects with and without present partners were of similar pattern and magnitude (Coho 1984).

Identification and Symptoms

In this section we will look at the correlations between symptoms and inferred identification patterns just for men and then just for women. The report for the men we studied can be quite brief. Baseline symptoms did not correlate at all with the 10 indices of identification, and follow-up symptoms manifest only one significant correlation. However, this single correlation was an important one: men with more symptoms at follow-up were less likely to see themselves as similar to their Father. This finding suggests that men who have a weaker identification with their father will in the long run experience greater problems with the divorce.

Identification and Symptoms for Women. More associations were found for women than was the case for men. For example, during both impact and long-term phases of divorce, those with more symptoms perceived less similarity between Myself and Mother. This latter finding of course parallels the relationship found for Father among males. For both impact phase and long-term follow-up, the more symptomatic were also less likely to perceive similarities between Father and Present Partner. Just at the impact phase, there was a trend for the more symptomatic to see less similarity between Myself and Ex-Spouse. Just at follow-up there was a trend for the more symptomatic to see less similarity between Myself and Present Partner.

Age, Gender and Identification

In reviewing the results presented thus far, one general conclusion is that persons who are manifesting greater symptomatology perceive less similarity both between themselves and others and between significant others. Before speculating any further about these findings we examined the role of two factors that might affect degree of inferred identification: age and gender.

Gender played a significant role in three of the ten similarity indices and results parallel what we found when computing factor analyses: men seem to generalize more when thinking about people, women seem to differentiate more. Here, though, the differentiation of women, compared to men, was specific to one target: the Ex-Spouse. Women were significantly less likely than men to view Myself as similar to Ex-Spouse, and also were less likely to perceive similarities between Ex-Spouse and Present Partner. Perhaps naturally, women were also less likely than men to see similarities between Mother and Ex-Spouse: for men this is a comparison between two women, and for women it involved a cross-gender comparison. Overall, the pattern of differences suggests that women were more likely than men to view themselves, their present partner and their mothers as distinct from their ex-spouse. This may imply a more complete separation among women than men. That is, the results may imply that women make a cleaner break with their former way of life (and spouse), a break that, as described in chapter 4, should theoretically be associated with greater adjustment.

Age played a role in just one instance. The oldest subjects, in this case consisting of those aged 50 and over, viewed themselves as most like their fathers, regardless of gender. Those subjects in their twenties were next-highest in identification with their father, while those in their thirties and forties were least likely. These results suggest that adult children may have to distance themselves from their fathers during the stage of life when one is generally consolidating family and work. Although we have no evidence, being in the process of divorcing may affect paternal identification most critically during the middle years of adulthood.

ANTECEDENTS AND CONSEQUENCES OF PARENTAL IDENTIFICATION

The issue of parental identification has received considerable clinical literature, and was found in our data to play a critical role in adjustment. For these reasons we examined the antecedents of parental identification, and also explored the construct validity of the way we ended up looking at parental identification.

Our approach to assessing parental identification was simple: we took the similarity indices for Myself-Father and Myself-Mother, and dichotomized the scores for each index by means of median splits. We then created a typology, based on the median splits, that consisted of four cells: 1. low identification with both mother and father; 2. low mother, high father; 3. high mother, low father; 4. high identification with both parents.

Some Basic Differentiations in Parental Identification

We entered 21 variables in three sequential or "forced entry" sets, following a discriminant analysis technique that was designed to show which variables help in classifying people correctly into the four cells. Gender was entered first, since it was assumed that gender is a "given" at birth and therefore precedes any experiences to follow. Surprisingly, there was no difference by gender in type of parental identification. We had expected, at the least, that women would show higher levels of identification with mother versus father, and vice versa for the male subjects. However, Osgood's (1962) conceptualization of the semantic differential as a measure of unconscious processes might well be reflected in this finding. From his position, both parents can play important and formative roles, and therefore for both male and female subjects there should be a range in levels of identification.

The next set of variables to be entered were those tapping childhood stressors. As a group, childhood stressors (the same as those discussed in chapter 2) played a significant role in differentiating among the four types of parental identification. Parental divorce and separation from one's parents on bad terms were particularly important in helping to distinguish between those high in parental identification from those who were low. Those low in parental identification were more likely to report both types of childhood stressor, and also seemed more likely to have lost a sibling during childhood. Including childhood stressors produced a 75% accuracy rate in placing high parental identifiers and a 49% accuracy rate in predicting low parental identifiers. In contrast, 27% of the high father/low mother identifiers and 15% of the high mother/low father identifiers were categorized correctly.

These results support the conclusions reached in chapter 2 that childhood experiences exert a long-term influence. Specifically, childhood stressors related to parents may affect the extent to which the adult identifies with his or her parents—which in turn seems to have consequences for adaptation.

The third set of predictors included indices of sociodemographic status: age, ethnicity, income, religiosity, presence or absence of children, number of siblings, proximity of relatives and number of visits with relatives. When we added these variables the accuracy of group classification was not improved dramatically. Overall, the percentage of cases correctly classified went from the 45% found just with gender and childhood stressors, to 50% when sociodemographic variables were added. This increase was primarily a result of income, which reduced the accuracy of classifying the two extreme types slightly, but increased the accuracy of classifying high mother/low father identifiers from 15% to 32%, and of high father/low mother identifiers from 27% to 40%.

Seeking the Meaning of Parental Identification

Up to now we have been looking at the antecedents and correlates of parental identification and have made the assumption that the way in which we measured identification made sense. However, having found that our typology generally leads to findings that make sense is not enough, and for this reason we turn next to the issue of construct validity.

Our first step was to take the four-cell typology of identification and consider whether the self-image factors discussed in chapter 7 distribute in any meaningful and systematic way across the four cells. The statistic used was the one-way analysis of variance, where the typology provided levels for the main effect. The findings are presented below, grouped according to the self-image factors:

Negative Self. The results were highly significant. High parental identifiers scored lowest on negative self-image, followed by men *and women* who were high in identification with father but not mother. The remaining two types were equally low.

Dominant Self. Only a trend was found, a trend indicating that high parental identifiers were lowest in dominance, while the low parental identifiers maintained the most dominant self-image.

Incompetent Self. Again only a trend was found. The low parental identifiers maintained self-images reflecting the greatest sense of personal incompetence.

Desirable Self. The results were not significant but paralleled those previously reported: the high parental identifiers were most likely to see themselves as having a desirable self-image. Low parental identifiers were low in the sense of having a desirable self-image.

Vulnerable Self. While not significant, the results again found high parental identifiers appearing to be psychologically more robust: they scored lowest on sense of self as vulnerable.

Hostile Self. While not significant, low parental identifiers scored highest on sense of self as hostile. High parental identifiers were intermediate.

Masterful Self. Again no significant variation was found, but low parental identifiers saw themselves as low on mastery while high parental identifiers scored highest in this area of self-image.

Self-Oriented. Not significant, the low parental identifiers scored highest on self-orientation (which reflects selfishness or self-absorption).

Socially Skilled Self. Here significant results were found. The low parental identifiers were lowest in the sense of self as socially skilled, and the high parental identifiers were highest in this sense of self.

From these results the impression emerges that parental identification does have a bearing on the basic sense of self, at least as maintained during divorce. High parental identifiers are less negative regarding themselves, and also see themselves as more socially skilled. In other words, they see themselves in a more positive light and as interpersonally skilled. Interpreting these results in the context of the findings for childhood stress, it can be inferred that the way in which we evaluate how good or bad we are may be related to our early relationships with parents, and to patterns of identification.

The Self in Relation to Past and Present Partners

We next looked at how two specific indices of identification, Myself-Present Partner and Myself-Ex-Spouse, varied across the four-cell typology of parental identification. We were interested in whether greater parental identification was more likely to result in viewing both Present and Past Partner as similar to self. Our interest arose from the assumption that high parental identification might make the self-image strong enough to admit similarity with many people, the ex-spouse as well as present partner. To consider the issue, we chose once again the one way analysis of variance.

Results fit in with our expectations for the similarity index for Myself-Present Partner, but the Myself-Ex-Spouse index failed to produce significant variation. Highly significant, the results for the first comparison indicated that those with low parental identification were least likely to view themselves as like their present partner, while high identifiers were most likely to view themselves this way. One explanation is that high parental identifiers identify strongly with others in general and that they may empathize with others more readily than those with low parental identification. However, it also may be that high identification with the present partner is simply a by-product of viewing parents, self and others in generally more positive terms.

Regardless of which interpretation is correct, there does appear to be some specificity: perceptions of the Ex-Spouse were not associated with level of parental identification.

Parental Identification, Stress and Symptomatology

At the initial contact, those who identified strongly with both parents averaged nearly 9 symptoms, while low parental identifiers and the two other groups averaged approximately 11. These differences were not statistically significant, but they became highly significant at the long-term follow-up, when high identifiers averaged 7 symptoms, low identifiers averaged 10 symptoms and the remainder fell in-between.

Here then we have confirmation of the results from the self-image data. Not only do high identifiers see themselves more positively and low identifiers more negatively, but low identifiers are considerably more symptomatic. Since the differences are indicated at baseline but emerge more strongly several years after the separation, these findings suggest that low identifiers may experience long-term problems. What we do not know is whether these problems are related specifically to the divorce experience or simply reflect their usual condition.

To carry the analysis one step further, we also looked at reports of positive and negative stress, both during the impact phase and in the long run. Again the results matched our expectations. The high identifiers consistently scored lowest on the total negative life event score: they averaged 49 during impact and 44 at follow-up, whereas the low identifiers averaged 64 and 65, respectively. High identifiers scored 82 on total positive events at impact and 80 at follow-up, compared to 69 and 67 for the low identifiers. These differences did not reach the level of significance for the impact phase analyses, but at follow-up the differences for negative life events were significant.

CASE STUDIES

Joan Mikel Revisited

We first met Joan Mikel in chapter 6, when discussing the issue of timing. As the reader may recall, Joan spent approximately three years deliberating before informing a very surprised husband that she wanted a divorce. She then sailed through the divorce process, saying that she is "very happy" on the Bradburn Scale at both interviews and reporting only one psychological symptom at baseline and one at follow-up.

Joan is one of the most highly identified with both her mother and father. She typifies the high identifiers not only in her general resilience to the stress of divorce, but also in reporting no childhood stress. Joan was only a little troubled originally by becoming separated, and not at all at the time of the first interview, four months later. She did seek help from a friend and a counselor. About who was most helpful, she says "Well, I guess the counselor, but all she said was do what you want to do. I didn't seek too much help." Asked who could have been more helpful, she said: "no one could have been since I didn't seek out help. Maybe if my ex hadn't been so emotional it would have been even easier."

Joan's greatest difficulty has been "overcoming my guilt feelings about ending the marriage." Additional difficulties included the fact "my husband was very persistent in trying to get back together." She also misses the "contact with the mutual friends that I am not keeping up with and the relaxation of one close relationship."

Her divorcée friends tell her that "the breakup is not the end of the world. Temporary problems are far outweighed by future good situations." For the last year, she has been "going out with a man I met at work. We work together and we were in very close physical contact in the back of the sales office." She says that initially she liked the "Companionship. The interest in each other. The working together. The sex." She used these words to describe the sex: "innovative, fantasy, whips, leathers and fulfillment." According to Joan, sex: "can contribute greatly to a relationship. You must be able to communicate your sexual needs to your partner." She tells the interviewer that her separation has "increased the frequency and enjoyment" of her sex life.

Joan's favorite activity is to "spend time with my lover" because she likes the "feelings of sharing, caring, and closeness." Her second favorite thing to do is "reading because it stimulates my thinking." In fact, Joan says that "the relationship with my lover, traveling and my job" are the activities that helped her the most during the separation. Now she thinks and day dreams more about the future, specifically "How I can get more involved in my job so that I benefit the most. I also think about avoiding the same mistakes of the last relationship. I must spend a lot of time with my male companion and be aware of his needs."

By follow-up, Joan has been working for two years in a public relations job in addition to her full-time sales position. Her new spouse is also in sales and is the same man she was dating before separation and living with at the time of the baseline interview. He has two children, ages 9 and 10, from a previous marriage.

Reflecting back on changes since the decision to separate, Joan now says "Well, I have experienced a lot of personal growth emotionally and intellectually. I've done a lot of things that I couldn't do before due to lack of support (emotional). I'm much happier." The greatest benefit of divorcing is "not having to live with my husband anymore. It's been wonderful. Just, uh, a new freedom for me to reassess my life and decide where I'm going." The divorce did change the way that she feels about herself. "I just feel like I'm a better person. More assertive. I just feel a whole lot better about myself— more positive." She also feels less dependent, more in control of her life, more responsible, and neither more nor less disappointed in life.

On the Bradburn Scale she still is "very happy" now and reports the following positive emotions as being experienced several times during the past week: on top of the world, particularly excited or interested in something, pleased about having accomplished something, proud because someone complimented you on something you had done, and that you had more things to do than you could get done. She only felt one of the less positive emotions once in the last week—that you couldn't do something because you just couldn't get going. Only once in a while does she wonder if she may not be an interesting person.

Looking on the general reactions of others Joan notes that her father had died prior to the initial separation. At first her mother mildly approved of the idea of divorce, and then strongly approved later. She lists the following relatives who live within an hour's trip: parent, father-in-law, brother and sister-in-law, grandparents and her new husband's children. She gets together with her friends and relatives about six to eight times a month. She has about five friends and gets together with them about five times a month. Most of these people felt neutral about the divorce.

About her favorite things to do: "read—it's the general broadening of knowledge." Her second most favorite thing to do is "spend time with my husband. That really should be #1. Because everything is more enjoyable when I experience it with him." Asked what activity since the separation had helped her the most to cope with things: "the time that I have spent with my husband." Asked how that had been helpful: "that includes doing lots of traveling, etc. Because I'm involved with him and love him." All in all,

Joan's ability to develop a close relationship with others, evidenced in her strong identification with both parents, has reemerged in her relationship with her new husband.

Herman Schutz: A Low Identifier

Herman Schutz is a 50-year-old building inspector who reports low identification with his mother and father. Characteristic of those with low identification, he lists 15 psychological symptoms at first contact and even more, 18, at the second contact. One clue to Herman's life may lie in his childhood. Herman reports 7 childhood stresses, including: a long separation from your parents when under 13, intense arguments between your parents, intense arguments between you and your parents, divorce of your parents, remarriage of your father or mother, separation from your father or mother due to divorce or desertion and the frequent absence of your mother or father.

With the exception of the remarriage of his mother or father, he felt very unhappy about these events and still thinks about them a lot. In fact, these early experiences were brought up repeatedly and spontaneously throughout the first interview. Herman described how his mother and father separated when he was 4 years old and how his mother remarried when he was 11. When asked what was the loneliest period of his life, Herman said: "Growing up with mother from when I was 4 till 12 years old." When asked why was it so lonely, he said: "I had no brothers and sisters and my mother worked. I got scared and I didn't cope with it." When asked how he experienced the loneliness, he said: "My heart beat fast—pain."

Troubled relationships are a way of life for Herman. He only sees his mother every two years or so, despite the fact that she lives less than 50 miles away. He never sees the two children from his first marriage.

At the point of our first interview with him, Herman's favorite activity is a very solitary one: just "being content—doing nothing." The reason, he says, is "inner peace." Inner peace, however, does not seem to come easily to him. Over its ten year duration, his second marriage had been marked by daily verbal battles and occasional physical fights as well. The couple sought therapy after separating and Herman thinks it did have an impact. Before, it had been "hit first and ask later." Now changed, he is examining the relationship.

Neither person was originally more in favor of a separation according to

Herman. However, there simply was too much violence. "We fought all the time; I broke her nose." Later when asked about what had been the greatest benefit of getting divorced, "I didn't kill anyone." Further questions suggest that his wife really initiated the separation. "I didn't want it. It was her idea. I wanted to try to work it out. We both were rugged individuals who got together in bed. We never communicated. We had secrets. We had totally separate lives. There was a power struggle. Testing each other."

Now six months into the separation, Herman sees his spouse several times a week. He saw her three days prior to the interview and stayed overnight. This is typical for the two of them to get together. When asked how he feels when with his spouse, he replies that he wants to stay with her—it feels good. He said they communicate better and said yes to the question—do you think that there is any chance of the two of you reconciling? In response to the question, what makes you think it still might be possible to reconcile, he said: "wishful thinking—hope is eternal."

His goals are to "Grow up enough to be happily married"—then he corrects himself and says "a good relationship." He says that during both of his marriages he was always afraid his wife would leave him. He adds that he is always afraid that people will leave and that he has felt this way since he was 12 years old. Right now his major difficulty is "living alone." What he misses most is "a home."

Herman is currently living with a woman he met in a bar shortly after the separation. She was also getting a divorce and he moved in with her a month ago. When asked how long he thinks the relationship will last, he says "till he gets tired of her or finds something better." For Herman sex is "extremely essential like air."

At the second interview, Herman is still living with a woman. It is not the same woman he lived with at the first interview, but the conditions of meeting were very similar: "we met in a bar—she was drunk, I picked her up and that's that. She couldn't get along with her husband and it's that simple." Asked would he consider marrying this person, he says "I shouldn't" but goes on to say yes, there is a fair chance of this taking place. He goes on to say that his girlfriend was a drug dealer from Reno before moving to the Bay Area.

Divorced, he never sees or talks to his former wife. He reflects that "the whole thing wasn't a marriage in the first place—it was a power trip. Of course I wasn't aware of it at the time—neither one of us was but we were aware of the constant battles and a divorce was the ultimate threat type idea.

No way out, something had to be done. So I got myself a girlfriend and she found out about it so we used the ultimate weapon." The passage of time does not seem to have changed Herman's outlook, or his approach to relationships.

Cheryl Chang: Personal and Cultural Distance

Cheryl Chang is a twenty-nine-year-old social worker of Chinese/Hawaiian ancestry who is divorcing her husband, a Chinese dietitian. The interviewer describes Cheryl as being small-boned, thin and petite. Her black hair is worn in a short Afro, she wears mod-style glasses and a mix of hip and oriental clothing. The interviewer finds her interesting-looking—"so oriental and yet so not. She has adopted the style and conventions of the 70s and yet somewhere in there one does experience her ethnicity." The day of the interview, she wore oriental bejeweled slippers, faded blue jeans, and a Nehru jacket.

Cheryl reports the same number of childhood stress events as Herman: 7. These include parental divorce and separation from parents on bad terms—the two presumed childhood stresses most associated with negative identification with parents. She also reports high levels of perceived childhood stress as well, rating most of her childhood at either "very low" or "dissatisfactions outweigh satisfactions." It is not very surprising that she reports high levels of psychological symptoms: 20 at the first interview and 15 at the second.

Also like Herman, Cheryl still thinks a lot about her unhappy childhood and provides evidence of disturbed social relationships. For example, she has all kinds of relatives who live within an hour's travel time from her home, including parents, in-laws, cousins, aunts and uncles, and siblings. When asked how often a month she visits them, she said clearly and definitely "zero."

Married for three years, the couple have no children. They seemed to share very little. She had numerous hobbies that she did not share with her husband, such as: going to plays, reading poetry, dancing, going to ballet, needlework, reading, painting, reading magazines. They typically spent about only 10 to 12 hours a week together, "just the time eating dinner—not deliberately, only because we were living in the same place." They "went to church but not deliberately to do it together. We did not make it a point to spend time together and took vacations apart."

Cheryl did not receive support and understanding from her parents when she told them of her marital separation. She explained: "I had warned my mother (that I was going to get a divorce), but she never takes me seriously. My mother was quite moved, i.e. saddened. It was hard for her to adjust and I had to support her in my decision. I am more strong-willed than mother. She said I would be lonely. She had a hard time understanding my feminist leanings."

About her father's reactions, Cheryl said: "My father is essentially a selfish man who hasn't given me a thought in his life. I don't think it affected him. I think he was disappointed, but I don't think it lasted very long." In contrast, Cheryl says her brother is very supportive. "He worries about me and he is probably closer to understanding my situation than my mother."

In describing her parents, Cheryl criticizes both and emphasizes the differences between herself and her parents. She speaks about her husband in a similar tone. When asked how she feels when with her husband, she replies "terrified, agitated, nervous." She explains "He has been kind of irrational. I find him defensive and revengeful now." About their relationship, Cheryl said that they "did not deliberately plan to spend time together" and that she had "a policy of choosing my fights for things that mattered."

The similarities in Cheryl's description of her father and her husband are striking, and both descriptions are very negative. It is tempting to infer that she may be in the process of rejecting or distancing herself from the "bad" father. In addition to her personal feelings towards her ex-husband and father there are cultural feelings as well. She adds this: "Comment on Asian men" to the interview. "The Chinese culture values men. Suddenly Asian women get the message that they are not highly valued. For Asian men there are modes of success and behavior, they are more rigidly dictated for men than for women. Thus, women are freed from the climb for success. Sensitivity and ability to listen are hard to come by in Asian men. What is it about being silent among Asian men? Something is ingrained in Chinese men that you don't talk about your feelings. I don't think the Chinese culture supports the exploration of your feelings." Cheryl's lack of identification may be not only with her father and her husband, but with Asian men in general.

In Cheryl's case there may be a process of rejection or distancing oneself from the "bad" father going on. At the same time, Cheryl is undergoing a toughening or growth experience moving her towards a more positive sense of self. "I feel as though I have been reborn again at 29. I feel as though it is a frightening but exhilarating sense to know that I am responsible for living my life. I've become more sensitive to music. I've begun to paint. I'm rediscovering old and true friends. I'm feeling more mobile. I delight in my solitude."

By the second interview Cheryl seems to have rejected many elements of her cultural heritage. She is living with a white self-employed artist that she has known for about two years. She relies on him very much for companionship. About this new relationship she said: "There would be a more conscious effort at maintaining our individuality. There would be more communication and better social adjustments. There would be growth I think within the relationship—less conventional is what I'm trying to say. My ex-husband believed in togetherness forever. Moe and I have doubts about the institution of marriage itself. I don't want to go through another divorce."

This new relationship seems more stable and solid than the last, perhaps because her new friend is so different from her father. As Cheryl's views of others improve, so, hopefully, will the way she views herself. This could in turn lead to better adaptation for Cheryl in the future. Perhaps someday she will be able to enjoy the happiness of having a more congruent image between her father and her partner or future husband.

SUMMING UP

Our cases have illustrated the point that something as seemingly esoteric as parental identification can be important if we want to understand how individuals fare during the process of divorce. What we found is that the way one views oneself in relation to others has a historical component: these comparisons are embedded in the conditions experienced as a child. At the same time, these views have an important relationship to well-being in the present, for both men and women.

In this pilot investigation, we encountered several surprises. One surprise was that men and women did not differ in the extent to which they viewed themselves as like either the father or the mother. This finding suggests an essential similarity between the sexes in the outcome of the identification process with parental figures, despite the probability of the process being quite different for males and females (for example, resolution of the "Oedipal" relationship).

A second surprise was the salience of early childhood stressors for parental identification outcome. Two specific stressors, parental divorce and parental separation in which conflict was evident, were particularly important in distinguishing at least between those high and low in identification with both parents. Note that loss of a parent through death, or any of the other childhood conditions, did not predict the extent of parental identification. Instead, some degree of specificity was evident: the effect was limited to a disturbed relationship.

Finally, these analyses reaffirm the notion that the way one views self in relation to others, especially parents, has clinical relevance. Those who saw themselves as similar to both parents viewed themselves at the impact phase in more positive terms and envisioned themselves as more interpersonally and socially effective. Such characteristics, one could assume, are likely to be shaped by one's early relationship with parents, in the context of a continuous and relatively harmonious experience. They may also explain why high identifiers consistently report fewer negative life events and more positive ones.

IV

CONTRIBUTING FACTORS

9

SOCIAL SUPPORTS IN THE CONTEXT OF DIVORCE

Leah Friedman, David A. Chiriboga and Linda S. Catron

In this chapter we shall navigate that extensive but foggy terrain known as social support, investigating the role that support plays in short- and long-term adaptation to divorce. Social support is one of those concepts that seems intuitively obvious until one asks oneself what it actually refers to. In point of fact, the term is often applied to quite different phenomena, which is one reason why the research findings often seem in conflict. But although there is no consensus about its definition, there is some agreement (see Thoits 1982; Turner, Frankel and Levin 1983) as to the utility of Cobb's (1976) functional assessment of social support as information leading individuals to believe they are cared for and loved, or that they are esteemed and valued, or that they belong to a strong network of communication and mutual obligation. The only point that might be added is that social support includes information helpful in alleviating the source of distress; this more instrumental component, however, might be better seen as social help rather than social support.

Cobb's portrayal of support establishes the relevance of social supports to the model, discussed in chapter 3, of divorce as a stress process. The underlying assumption of that model is that during the divorce, as in all stress situations, a number of social and psychological mediators exist and must be considered before any meaningful picture can emerge of the relationship between stress and the mental health outcome of divorce. Social support can be seen as a critical mediating factor, one that may work to make people feel better in times of crisis because they feel they are not alone and that someone cares.

In the following sections we will address four major questions. First, what constitutes the basic dimensionality of social supports, at least insofar as students of divorce are concerned? Second, how consistent do social support resources remain over the course of marital disruption? Third, what factors explain the presence or absence of support for particular types of individuals? Fourth, at what points in the stress process does social support play a role, and how does the availability and use of social support resources mediate short- and long-term adaptation to divorce? These questions will be addressed separately for men and women, since the literature suggests the importance of gender differences in the utilization and structuring of social support (e.g., Brown and Felton 1978; Chiriboga et al. 1979; Veroff, Douvan and Kulka 1981).

THE DIMENSIONALITY OF SOCIAL SUPPORT

Conceptual Issues and Problems

Often used in reference to a single measure or one-dimensional concept, the term "social support" covers a range of phenomena (Henderson 1977; Di-Matteo and Hays 1981; Cohen and Syme 1985). Our inclination in studying support was therefore to employ several distinct measures of support. As might be expected since there is no agreement on definition, there is no agreement concerning what constitutes the major dimensions of support. Several similar if not completely overlapping categorizations of social support dimensions have been proposed over the past few years (e.g., Barrera 1981; Lieberman 1982). The similarity of these categorizations seems to indicate that some fundamental constructs underlying the social support phenomenon are being tapped. These categorizations can be summarized as follows:

1. "Social resources," a dimension that describes the individual's social connections or network. The social resources dimension describes the pool of the individual's social relationships which can be drawn upon for support.
2. "Support behavior," a dimension that takes into account actual support activities or behavior. This dimension looks at relationships from a behavioral rather than structural perspective.
3. "Perceived support," a dimension that taps into the individual's perception, appraisal and satisfaction with the support available to the individ-

ual. Perceptions of social support involve "an evaluation or appraisal of whether and to what extent an interaction, pattern of interactions, or relationship is helpful" (Schaefer, Coyne and Lazarus 1981, 384). The experience of support, that is, the individual's perception of being supported, is perhaps the critical element in social support (Turner, Frankel and Levin 1983). Curiously, and as pointed out by Lieberman (1982), few studies actually make use of the "respondent's reflections" to get a truly phenomenological perspective on their support experience.

Our Measures of Social Support

Given the lack of agreement concerning what social support refers to, or how it should be measured, we tried to develop a set of measures that was defensible on both theoretical and empirical grounds. Measures were developed to assess each of the three dimensions of social support: (1) social support resources, (2) supportive behavior, and (3) the perception of support. We used two measures to assess social resources: Active Network and Confidant. Each of these measures assessed somewhat different aspects of the individual's potential support network. The behavioral dimension of support was represented by a single measure: Support Seeking. Perception of support was also represented by a single measure: Perceived Support.

Social Resources I: Active Network. In thinking about how best to measure a network, our approach was guided by the assumption that networks supply a range of options (see Weiss 1974) rather than providing varying amounts of the same thing. Different people may need different kinds of support and/or have access to different combinations of support, some of which is provided by relatives, some by friends and some by intimate partners.

What we did was simply count the number of primary relationships available to respondents by proximity and rates of interaction. The measure evaluates what Pearlin (1985) has called the "active" category of support— those supports to which a person would be likely to turn in times of need. Respondents were asked about three types of relationship: with relatives, friends and "dates." A summary score for each respondent was derived from their answers to the following five questions:

1. How many of different categories of relative lived within an hour's distance of them?

2. How many times per month they saw these relatives?
3. How many friends they had within an hour's distance?
4. How many times per month they saw their friends?
5. Were they dating or not? (Coded: no = 0, yes = 1).

For the sample as a whole, the average number of types of relatives living within an hour's distance was 1.97 (SD = 2.16); the average number of times respondents saw these relatives every month was 4.16 (SD = 7.67); the average number of friends living nearby was 6.23 (SD = 12.07); and the average number of times per month respondents saw these friends was 9.90 (SD = 10:07). At the first interview, close to half of the respondents (48.9%) were dating. To translate all these figures into a more meaningful picture, these results indicate that the average divorcing man and woman at baseline tended to live near two different types of relative and saw these relatives about four times a month; they had about six friends living nearby whom they saw close to ten times a month and they were about as likely to be dating as not.

When men and women were compared at the separation stage, we found no gender difference in overall network scores. Gender did make a difference on one of the five items that comprised the measure: women reported they saw their relatives significantly more often than did men. But although women saw more of their relatives, both women and men on the average had two types of relatives living nearby. There were no significant differences between men and women on either the number of friends they had living nearby or the frequency with which they saw them. However, by follow-up men were nearly twice as likely to have friends living nearby.

Social Resources II: Confidant. The importance of confiding relationships has been widely accepted as an indicator of the presence of support (e.g., Lowenthal and Haven 1968). The concept of a confidant is unique in including both a qualitative element (it addresses the issue of intimacy in relationships) and a quantitative element (it addresses the number of such relationships a person has). And as pointed out by Pearlin (1985), relationships characterized by intimacy may be at a different level from other relationships and hence deserve particular attention.

In the divorce study respondents were asked to indicate whether they felt they had among their friends and relatives someone they felt they could tell anything to and could count on for understanding and advice. Their responses to this question were coded "no = 1," "yes, one person = 2," or "yes, more than one person = 3." The average score of 2.62 indicated that a separated man or woman generally had somewhat more than one confidant. Only 8% reported they had no confidant, 21% reported one confidant and the majority, 71%, had more than one. With 92% having at least one confidant, it can be seen participants were by and large not lacking in having available someone they could count on for understanding and advice. However, although few were without a confidant, the literature (e.g., Lowenthal and Haven 1968) suggests that those few may constitute a high-risk group. It is important to add that men were less likely to have a confidant than women.

Support Behavior: Support Seeking. This measure was used to assess the behavioral dimension of social support. Derived from an instrument created by Pearlin and Lieberman (1976), it is based on responses to the question "Did you try to get any advice or assistance or talk to anyone about the separation or divorce?" If respondents had sought assistance they were asked to check off which of the following 13 categories of help givers they consulted: spouse, parent, child, relative, friend, neighbor, co-worker, doctor, clergy, counselor, lawyer, self-help groups, other.

Responses to these questions provide an indication of how much help with the separation and divorce the individual has sought. In comparison to the Active Network and Confidant measures which are indicators of *potential* social support, the Support Seeking measure is an indicator of *actual* social support-seeking activity.

We developed a simple summary score of the number of help-seeking categories approached by respondents. For the total sample, the average number of help-giving categories people turned to was 2.84 (SD = 2.27). The mean Support Seeking score for men, at 2.56 (SD = 2.33) tended to be lower than the mean for women (3.04, SD = 2.21). In other words, on the average women tended to seek assistance from more categories of help-givers than did men.

Perceived Support. This measure assessed the participants' evaluation of the quality of support available to them. Perceived Support was similar to the Support Seeking measure in that it assessed social support in terms of the individual's actual experience of support, rather than in terms of potential support. Information came from responses to two questions:

1. "How often are you without anyone to talk to about yourself?" (coded— never = 4, once in a while = 3, fairly often = 2, very often = 1).

2. "How often are you without anyone to share experiences and feelings with?" (coded—never = 4, once in a while = 3, fairly often = 2, very often = 1).

We added the responses to these two questions in order to obtain a summary score, with higher responses reflecting a greater perception of support on the respondent's part.

In the entire sample the mean score on perception of support was 6.45, with a standard deviation of 1.81. Consistent with findings for the measures of Confidant and Support Seeking, men perceived themselves to have significantly less support than did women. For men the average score was 6.05 (SD = .85), while for women it was 6.72 (SD = 1.73).

Intercorrelations of the Four Measures of Social Support

As you may recall, our goal was to develop relatively distinct measures of support. Our findings indicate that in this we were successful: there were generally low intercorrelations among the support variables. Support Seeking in fact was virtually independent of all other support variables. The closest association was between Perceived Support and Confidant ($r = .28$, $p = .000$). While it makes sense that persons with more confidants would perceive greater support, the relationship still is a rather weak one. There was also a tendency for people with larger networks to have more confidants and to perceive that they were supported.

While these associations make sense, more important perhaps is that the four measures of social support are essentially independent of each other, a finding that lends credence to the notion that they represent different dimensions of support. This in turn emphasizes the importance of a multidimensional approach to the measurement of support. The goal should not be to find the single *best* measure of social support but, rather, to capture social support in all its complexity by identifying the central facets of the various forms of support.

While the intercorrelations remain low, some interesting differences emerge between men and women when they are looked at separately. For men but not for women, the larger the Active Network, the higher the level of Support Seeking. For women but not for men, the larger the Active Network, the higher the score on the Confidant measure. For both men and women, the Confidant measure was significantly related to Perceived Support. The correlation was higher for women. These differences in the intercorrelations among measures of social support suggest that there may be differences in the salience of each dimension of social support for men and women.

THE CONSISTENCY OF SOCIAL SUPPORTS OVER TIME

As we turn to the issue of consistency in social supports over time, keep in mind respondents were interviewed during two very distinct phases of an evolving stress process. At the first interview they all had recently separated from their spouses and were in what could be considered the "impact" phase of divorce. By the time of the second interview, most had in some way accommodated to the necessity of change; their lives were not marked by the chaos and indecision of the earlier period.

Given the situations our participants faced at the two points, we would anticipate considerable variation in the availability, use and perceived adequacy of supports over the course of the crisis. In order to answer this question three statistical techniques were used. The first, the t-test, looks at stability of group means but is relatively insensitive to individual variation. The second, correlations, looks at the individual's consistency from one time period to the next but disregards variation in the actual level of scores. The third, Chi-square analysis, looks at general patterns of stability and change.

Average Group Differences over Time

One question that arises when studying support in a stress context is whether groups of people remain stable over time. For both men and women, there were no differences in group averages between first and second interviews for any of the four measures of support. In other words, when looked at from the perspective of group means, there was apparent consistency in each of the dimensions of social support for both men and women from one time of measurement to the next.

Correlation over Time

Consistency over time in social supports can be evaluated in ways that place greater emphasis on how individuals fare at each point. Correlations assessed whether knowing social support scores at the first interview gave us any idea of where the individual would be in the long run. For men, the correlations of Active Network ($r = .76$, $p = .00$) and Support Seeking ($r = .59$, $p = .00$) suggest reasonably high stability in these two measures between the first and second interviews. The measures for Perceived Support ($r = .29$, $p = .00$) and Confidant ($r. = .27$, $p = .00$), however, were much less stable.

A very different pattern is revealed in the correlations of social supports for women. Neither Active Network ($r = .36$, $p = .00$), nor Support Seeking ($r = .36$, $p = .00$), nor the Confidant measure ($r = .33$, $p = .00$) was particularly stable over time. Perceived Support ($r = .51$, $p = .00$) demonstrated the highest stability for women and this stands in marked contrast to the results for men.

Overall, then, while the group averages held relatively constant over the years of the study, the results of the correlations showed that for certain social support variables there was less stability than for others. We also found that there was generally less stability in the social supports of women compared with those of men, and men and women also differed in terms of which measures were most stable. For men the most stable measures of support tapped the structural and behavioral dimensions of support, while for the women the variable that displayed the highest consistency tapped the perceptual dimension of support.

The Chi-Square Analyses

We used the Chi-square statistic to provide information on how many people had roughly the same or different levels of support when we reinterviewed them. When men's Active Networks were compared from first to second interview, considerable consistency was apparent: 61% of the men manifested the same level of network activity at both measurement points. What change was found tended to be in the direction of an expanded network: 28% of the men reported having a larger Active Network while 11% reported a smaller Active Network. In short, the Active Network of men was relatively stable over time; when change occurred, it was more than twice as likely to occur in the direction of adding to the Active Network. This suggests that the experience of divorce may have prompted these men to enlarge their social networks.

More than half of the men remained constant in their access to a confidant, with approximately 22% increasing and another 22% decreasing such access. Essentially the same distributions were found in Support Seeking and Perceived Support. The only difference is that slightly more men (27%)

decreased in the number of people talked to about the divorce and slightly more (25%) increased in their perception of support. Both these latter results are expectable since by the second interview the level of negative events had decreased. In other words, there was less need of Support Seeking and, as we have reported later in this chapter, people with lower levels of stress are more satisfied with their levels of support.

Among women, about 45% fell into the same categories of Active Network at both time periods; nearly 23% reported fewer resources and 32% reported an expanded network. As was the case for men, in other words, when change did occur, it tended to be towards a larger rather than a smaller Active Network. This growth in network, evident for both sexes, suggests that men and women were accomplishing the third transitional task; reintegration back into society. They had become less isolated by the second contact.

The number of confidants available to participants was quite stable. We found that over 18% of women declined in number of confidants reported, 13% reported an increase, and an impressive 69% remained in the same category at both times. In other words, what well may be the linchpin of support, the presence of people with whom one can truly be free and open, is likely to remain anchored through time.

Stability was less evident in Support Seeking, where we found that only 46% of the women reported talking to the same numbers of people, 31% talked to fewer people and a surprising 23% talked to more people. Thus, somewhat less than half the women talked to the same number of people at both times; of those women who changed, more reported talking to fewer people than talking to more people at follow-up. Comparing men and women, men again appear to be somewhat more stable than women on this measure, as they were on the Active Network measure. However, the direction of change was similar for those men and women who changed on this measure, both reporting talking to somewhat fewer people about the divorce at follow-up. Despite the reductions, it is noteworthy that substantial numbers of men and women were in fact still seeking advice and support nearly four years after their separation.

Nearly 52% of the women reported the same level of Perceived Support at both interviews, but at the second interview 20.5% reported less Perceived Support and 27.6% reported higher Perceived Support. Women and men were very similar in the amount of change they displayed in this measure of support from baseline to follow-up.

Summing Up: Consistency over Time in Support

Substantial levels of consistency in the social supports of men and women are evident as they pass through the transition of divorce. This consistency is particularly striking given that participants were interviewed at a point of major upset as well as some years later. To expand on this last point, it should be emphasized that as a major, nonnormative life event, divorce by its very nature can be very disruptive of social networks and systems of support (Thoits 1982; Weiss 1975). Hence we had expected that the period of time between the first and second interviews would be accompanied by substantial change, not consistency, in social support.

There are undoubtedly many factors which cooperated to produce the levels of stability observed in this study. Timing of measurement, for example, can influence findings (Thoits 1982; House 1981; see also chapter 6). Since it may take a while for stress to exert its full effect, measurements taken earlier in the transition could miss its impact on social support; measurements taken late in the process, similarly, could miss change entirely since support could have ebbed and flowed in the intervening time period. Since we first interviewed people an average of six months into the period of separation, we can assume that the transition would generally have progressed sufficiently to have exerted some impact on participants. And despite the fact that three and a half years is a relatively long time, our data suggest that divorce for most people was not entirely a "done deal" at follow-up.

More possible is a durability to supports, even during times of strain. Perhaps the much-publicized changes associated with divorce—new friends, disruption of old networks, new lifestyles—have been overemphasized. A majority of people appear on the whole to keep their basic or "core" social connections intact throughout crises like divorce. Aneshensel and Frerichs (1982) and Ferraro, Mutran and Barresi (1984) provide longitudinal results supporting such a consistency hypothesis. There is no question that some divorces result in major changes in living patterns and social relationships, but this may be true for fewer people than the media and popular opinion would lead us to believe. Furthermore, some elements of support systems would seem to be naturally resistant to change: for example, relatives and those close enough to be considered confidants.

Is Consistency Adaptive? A related point is that consistency in social support may itself contribute to the reductions in symptomatology we found during the course of the study. If supports are relatively consistent in availability over the months and years of divorce, could this very consistency have a major stabilizing effect and facilitate coping with the many problems attendant on the breakup of a marriage? To follow up on this question, we computed change scores for confidant availability. What we found emphasized what we already know: men and women differ markedly in the significance of supports.

Our scoring system divided people into those who had fewer confidants at the second interview, the same number, or more. We first looked at psychological symptoms reported at the second interview and found a tendency for men with greater consistency in availability of confidants to report more symptoms than other men, while women who were consistent over time reported fewer symptoms than other women. These findings indicate that consistency is in fact linked to better functioning, but only for women. Associated with greater symptomatology, consistency among men may indicate a continuing need of support rather than an ongoing part of normal life.

A significant interaction between gender and consistency was also found for our measure of overall happiness as measured at follow-up. Unlike the case for symptoms, where women averaged higher scores than men, the sexes were equal in happiness at follow-up. As would be expected on the basis of the results for symptoms, the least happy men were those who were consistent in confidants since the first interview; the happiest were those who had experienced a decrease. In contrast, the happiest women were consistent in confidant availability.

All in all, these results strongly suggest that an ordinary part of life for well-adjusted women is to maintain consistency in an inner circle of friends that, incidentally, usually includes more than one person. Men, on the other hand, may expand their inner circle as a means of resolving problems, but in normal circumstances operate with a more restricted group of close friends.

DIFFERENTIAL ACCESS TO SOCIAL SUPPORT

One of our goals was to see if the stress process model proposed in chapter 3 could help explain why people vary in their access to social support. To explore this issue we tried to predict each of the social support measures on the basis of three sets of variables: social background factors, divorce context factors, and exposure to negative events. These three sets were chosen on the basis of literature and theory. Both social background factors and negative events, for example, have been reported to be associated with level of social support (e.g., Veroff, Douvan and Kulka 1981; Liem and Liem 1978; Dean and Ensel 1983; McFarlane et al. 1983). As for the divorce context variables, some researchers (e.g., Goode 1956; Chiriboga and Cutler 1977) report such measures to predict adaptation to divorce, while others find no association (e.g., Brown et al. 1980). Whether or not context variables (in this case, length of marriage, time separated, control over divorce) affected adaptation through their impact on the supports was of interest.

It turned out that the three sets of predictors were generally unrelated to the four dimensions of social support. One individual measure, however, did exert a modest but significant effect on the availability of support: Negative Events. For both men and women, higher levels of stress were associated with people feeling they had less adequate levels of support. McFarlane et al. (1983) and Dean and Ensel (1983) noted a similar relationship between perception of support and stress exposure.

To a small but significant extent, high stress was also linked to increased Support Seeking, but only for men. What seems to happen is that while men generally are less likely to seek support, increased stress leads them to increase Support Seeking to a level where their support system approximates that of women. As suggested by our findings for consistency, then, we see that while males may characteristically rely less on supports than do women, they do respond under conditions of stress.

For divorcing men, the relationships between Negative Events and Perceived Support, and between Negative Events and Support Seeking provide additional information on their use of social support dimensions. Under conditions of high stress, we found that men talk to greater numbers of people about the breakup of their marriage, yet perceive themselves to be less supported. There are a number of possible explanations for this phenomenon. First, there may be a time lag involved. Even though men sought more support at times of greater stress it does not mean that they instantly received its benefits and this delay creates dissatisfaction. Second, men staggering under the burden of many stressors may devalue their support because it is not a magical cure. Finally, since men generally maintain a more frugal support system, they may have to work harder to obtain any support, and what they obtain may not suffice. This last possibility might be labeled a "deficit" hypothesis, since the point is that the support systems of men may be less adequate in the face of crisis.

THE ROLE OF SOCIAL SUPPORT DURING THE IMPACT
PHASE OF DIVORCE

As a means of assessing the contribution of social supports in understanding adaptation, we examined four conceptual domains encompassed by the stress process model of divorce: (1) predisposing factors, (2) social stressors, (3) psychological mediators, and (4) social mediators. Level of psychological symptoms was the outcome measure of interest.

1. *Predisposing factors* are seen here as durable personal and social characteristics as well as structural characteristics directly linked to the divorce that can lead to greater or lesser vulnerability to its impact, for example, age, income, number of years married, number of months separated (e.g., Rabkin and Streuning 1976). Two separate sets of variables were used to measure predisposing factors: a set which measures social background characteristics and a set which measures divorce context characteristics.
2. *Social stressors* are those life events which occurred within the same general time frame of the separation and divorce and which had the potential to further disturb life patterns. The summary measure of all negative events reported for our Life Events Questionnaire over the year prior to the interview became our measure of social stress.
3. *Psychological mediators* here include the person's appraisal of the stressfulness of the divorce, and his or her self-esteem.
4. *Social mediators*, like psychological mediators, concern the resources available to an individual which can reduce or modify the impact of stress. We considered social supports as the mediators of interest, and included the four measures of support that have been described in prior sections: Active Network, Support Seeking, Confidant, and Perceived Support.

In our model of the stress process, both predisposing factors and exposure to stress are hypothesized to precede and affect stress appraisal. Stress appraisal is placed before self-esteem in the ordering since appraisal is hypothesized to have a direct effect on self-esteem, but the literature is unclear about the exact role of supports in the stress process. Since support can potentially enter into the stress model at several points, our first procedure was designed to clarify at which point support may be most helpful.

Supports and Some Precursors to Maladaptation

As we have just mentioned, social support can affect the stress process at several different points. In a series of hierarchical multiple regression analyses, we actually explored the effect of placing social supports at different steps in the model. By adding in social support at various stages of the hypothesized stress process, it was hoped that more could be learned about the role of social support as a mediator in the processes antecedent to the development of psychological symptoms. Specifically, we looked at the utility of supports when trying to predict several personal characteristics evident during the impact phase of divorce: divorce-related distress, self-esteem and psychological symptoms.

When the level of divorce-related distress during marital separation was the dependent variable, the set of support variables was entered between social background, divorce context and negative events and distress, to see whether support made a difference to stress appraisal; it did not. In a second analysis, in which self-esteem became the dependent variable, measures of social support were entered immediately after distress; support did not make a difference in the level of self-esteem.

Supports as a Predictor of Symptoms During the Impact Phase. Our next step was to consider what happened when we entered support measures immediately after self-esteem, with psychological symptoms as the outcome measure. It was at this stage of the process that social support had its effect. Social support was associated with the development of symptoms in divorcing persons, with higher levels of support being associated with fewer psychological symptoms. This relationship existed independently of the person's exposure to negative events, appraisal of stress or self-evaluation. Some variations in the role of support, however, were noted for men and women.

Men. For recently separated men, neither social background nor divorce context factors were associated with psychological symptoms. In contrast, the experience of Negative Events during the past year was related very significantly to symptoms; Negative Events explained a substantial 15% of the variance in symptoms. To a lesser extent, appraisal of the divorce as stressful was also associated with symptoms: the appraisal of stress explained 4% of symptoms ($p < .05$). Those lower in self-esteem were the most likely to be symptomatic; self-esteem explained 18% of the variance in symptoms ($p = .00$).

We next entered our set of social support variables, which contributed 7% ($p<.05$) of explained variance in symptomatology. Both the Support Seeking (Beta = $-.16$, $p=.06$) and the Confidant variable (Beta = $-.14$, $p=.09$) contributed at trend levels. For men, having people to confide in and seeking out people to talk to about their separation tended to be associated with a reduction in psychological symptoms.

We next added a set that looked at whether social supports might make a contribution more indirectly, through an interaction with negative events. The idea here was that social supports might be most helpful in the context of negative stressors but possibly have no effect on symptoms under conditions of low stress. Overall, the set of interactive terms did not contribute significantly to the prediction of symptoms; however, the interaction of Negative Events and Support Seeking was associated at a trend level (Beta = $-.25$, $p=.09$). As we had anticipated, men who were lower in Help Seeking when confronted with high stress tended to report more psychological symptoms.

Thus for data collected at the first interview, the men who reported more symptoms were those who reported more Negative Events during the year preceding the interview, higher levels of distress over the impending divorce, lower self-esteem and fewer supports. There was also a suggestion that men who did not respond to high stress loads with more help-seeking efforts did more poorly. This last finding builds on the notion, advanced when we were discussing consistency of supports, that the key to adaptation among men is whether they temporarily reconfigure their support system in response to stressful conditions.

Women. Unlike the case for men, the social background variables did contribute at a trend level ($R^2=.06$, $p=.09$) to the prediction of psychological symptoms in women. Of the five social background characteristics, number of children (Beta = $-.15$, $p=.08$) and level of education (Beta = $-.20$, $p<.05$) made the strongest contributions. Women with more children and women who had attained higher levels of education reported fewer psychological symptoms during the impact phase. Both conditions may act as a buffer; one question of significance is whether the presence of children is effective only in the short run.

For women as well as men, the divorce context factors were not helpful in predicting symptoms. However, Negative Events explained 14% ($p<.00$) of the variance; this relationship was almost identical to that found for men.

Stress appraisal was not associated with symptoms for women, but women lower in self-esteem were more symptomatic; 7% of the variance was explained ($p = < .00$).

When we added the support variables an additional 8% of variance ($p < .00$) was accounted for. Of the four social support variables in the set, only Perceived Support (Beta $= -.24$, $p < .00$) actually contributed significantly. Women who perceived themselves to be highly supported were less likely to experience psychological symptoms during at least the early stages of divorce.

Finally, we added the set that tapped into the interaction of stress and social support. Neither the overall set, nor any of the individual variables, contributed to prediction. Overall, those women who had fewer psychological symptoms were less self-critical, experienced fewer negative events over the past year and had more children, education and perceived support.

Supports and Stress: Some Comments

The failure to find effects of social support on divorce-related distress and self-criticism, two elements critical to the evolution of a stress response, was surprising. In contrast to the findings of Pearlin et al. (1981), social support in the present study did not add much to an understanding of the stress process itself. Further, none of the sets of interaction terms was significant at any point in the stress process.

Perhaps the reason social supports demonstrated only a moderate effect on other components in the stress process lies in the nature of separation and divorce itself. Earlier in the chapter we noted that divorce may not disrupt the support system as much as previously thought; it appears that many people are able to preserve their core support systems during divorce. This does not mean, however, that the divorce process is not accompanied by internal turmoil and does not create major demands for reassessment and readjustment. Marital separation and divorce can upset or destroy many of a person's well-entrenched positions in the social and economic order. They can also challenge people's most valued concepts of themselves.

In fact what our results suggest is that social supports do play a role, but they are not helpful with everything. Appraisal of divorce as distressing for people caught in the impact phase was so inevitable that the support of others could probably do little to alter it. Turning to another key element in the model of divorce stress, that of self-esteem, it appears that multiple factors contribute to the likelihood of low self-esteem, for people going through marital separation. Failure at one of life's primary tasks, that of developing and maintaining a successful intimate relationship, may lead to negative self-evaluation, guilt and possibly even a tendency to believe the criticism hurled by ex-mates (Hetherington, Cox and Cox 1976; Wallerstein and Kelly 1980; Weiss 1975; White and Bloom 1981).

That a person should be troubled over the divorce, and also low on esteem could in short be viewed as expectable components during the acute stage of this life crisis. The really critical issue is to prevent these processes from turning into chronic responses. What seems most meaningful in the findings just presented is not necessarily the failure of social supports to affect the intervening process but the strength of supports in helping to prevent the distress and self-derogation associated with separation and divorce from becoming incorporated into more permanent and nonyielding aspects of psychological functioning, as indicated by the development of psychological symptoms.

It may even be argued that some awareness or appraisal of stress over the breakup of the marriage, and some feelings of low self-esteem, can be productive and perhaps essential elements of a process of working through feelings and doubts aroused by marital disruption. There is evidence that divorce provides opportunities for growth as well as destruction (Chiriboga et al. 1979). Distress over the divorce and self-criticism may be necessary pathways to that growth. Not to be troubled or upset over so major an event may indicate denial or avoidance of a natural grieving process—an emotional lacuna that could lead to serious problems down the road. Low self-esteem, if not carried to extremes, may help to make people aware of their contribution to the breakup of their marriage and this, in turn, may refocus their attention not on blaming others but on the need to adapt to new conditions.

We also found that for women the interaction of social support with stress exposure failed to predict symptoms. This finding is noteworthy mostly because it fails to confirm what is sometimes called the "buffering" hypothesis. In order for buffering to take place, an interaction between stress and social support is assumed, with higher levels of stress being mediated by high levels of support (Thoits 1982). What we are left with, as a result of all these analyses of social supports in the context of separation, is that for women, as indeed for men, there is a salutary effect of social support on psychological symptoms, the more worrisome, chronic and intractable level of disturbance.

THE ROLE OF SOCIAL SUPPORT IN LONG-TERM ADAPTATION

The powerful impact of divorce upon emotional well-being has been well documented in a number of studies (e.g., Goode 1956; Bloom, Asher and White 1978; Chiriboga 1979b). Although longitudinal studies are rare, Wallerstein and Blakeslee (1989) suggest that divorce can exert an impact five and even ten years after separation and divorce. We were interested in the question of how this psychological turmoil plays itself out over time and how social factors such as social support affect this evolution. The long-term follow-up provided the opportunity to answer a central question of this chapter: what is the role of social supports in long-term adaptation to divorce?

We approached the prediction of long-term psychological adjustment in a manner similar to the hierarchical regression approach used for the prediction of adaptation during the period surrounding marital separation. The social background and divorce context sets were entered first, since without dispute they represent conditions external to the conditions assessed at the time of the second interview. Since prior symptoms have often been found to be predictive of subsequent symptomatology (see Monroe 1983, for a discussion of this issue), the baseline score for symptoms was then entered in step three as an independent predictor of follow-up symptoms.

The remainder of the measures in the hierarchical set multiple regression derive from time-two administrations of the same instruments used at baseline and the sets were composed of variables identical to those used earlier. The social background and divorce context sets were not repeated because of their obvious temporal precedence. Each set was entered into the regression in the same order as it was at time one. The decision was made to enter the follow-up social support information after self-esteem, on the basis of the results from the analysis of symptoms at the impact stage of divorce.

Long-Term Symptoms among Men

Overall, the regression analysis predicted 52% of the variance in psychological symptoms at follow-up (MR = .72, $p < .01$); this is more than the 49% explained at baseline. However, only baseline symptoms and stress appraisal at the second interview contributed significantly to prediction. Level of symptoms at the first interview contributed an impressive 25% ($p < .001$) to the explained variance in symptoms at follow-up. Stress appraisal at the second interview predicted 7% ($p < .01$) of time-two psychological symptoms. Together, then, these two variables explained almost one third of the change in symptoms from first to second interview.

While the set of follow-up social support variables as a whole did not contribute to the explanation of variability in psychological symptoms, perceptions of support made an independent contribution to the prediction of long-term adaptation (Beta = −.32, $p < .05$). Men who had higher levels of Perceived Support at follow-up reported fewer symptoms.

Overall, men who had reported high levels of symptoms at baseline were very likely to report them at follow-up. Further, men who were more distressed about the divorce at follow-up were also significantly more likely to be experiencing psychological symptoms at that time. Neither Negative Events experienced in the year prior to the follow-up interview nor self-esteem, both of which were very important to the prediction of symptoms at separation, played a role in men's adaptation at follow-up. And, as noted above, time-two social supports had a much diminished role in determining time-two adaptation. However, perceptions of support, which did not play a role for men at baseline, contributed significantly to well-being at follow-up: those who felt they received more support fared better in symptoms.

Long-Term Symptoms among Women

For women, the regression analysis predicted 66% of the variance in psychological symptoms at follow-up (MR = .81, $p < .00$). The level of symptoms reported at the first interview explained 46% ($p < .00$) of the variance in follow-up symptoms. To a very significant extent women who had more symptoms at baseline were more likely to report symptoms at follow-up. Clearly then, for both men and women, one of the best predictors of long-term adaptation is how they do in the short run.

Of remaining sets of variables, only Negative Events, with a contribution of 8% (Beta = .35, $p < .00$), significantly added to the variance explained in time-two symptomatology. Women who experienced many negative life events in the year prior to the second interview were much more highly likely to increase in symptoms by the second interview.

Neither the way people appraised divorce-related stress at the second interview, nor their level of self-esteem predicted long-term adaptation in women. Appraisal had not been a significant predictor for symptoms recorded at the first interview, but low self-esteem had been a significant predictor. When we turned to social support at the second interview we found that this set also did not make a significant contribution. As was the case for men, however, the follow-up measure of Perceived Support independently predicted follow-up symptoms at a trend level (Beta = −.16, p = .07). This was similar to but weaker than the role played by Perceived Support for women at baseline. Women who at follow-up perceived that they were well supported tended to have decreased more in symptoms than had those who did not feel supported (recall that generally all participants experienced some decline in symptom level by follow-up).

Summing Up. The fact that only initial symptom levels provided a unique contribution to the variance of follow-up symptoms, together with the results of earlier analyses of the impact of initial levels of negative events, stress appraisal, self esteem and social supports on symptoms at first contact, suggests that variables assessed at the first interview exert their influence on long-term adaptation by affecting psychological well-being during the crisis phase of divorce. Those who adapt in the short term may have more psychological resources for coping with the long-term difficulties that arise. Those in greater distress in the crisis phase may have entered onto a downward spiral of continued difficulty and distress.

Supports and Distress in the Long Run: Concluding Comments

One of the most obvious differences between the factors influencing adaptation at follow-up and during the crisis stage of separation/divorce was the reduced role of social supports. At baseline, social support variables made significant contributions to the explanation of the variance in the level of psychological symptoms among these divorcing men and women. At follow-up, the set of follow-up social support variables failed to reach significance for both men and women. Only follow-up Perceived Support made an independent contribution to explained variance in follow-up psychological symptoms, and for women this was only at a trend level.

We have already reported in previous chapters that the best predictor of time-two symptoms was time-one symptoms. This relationship between earlier and later symptoms has been reported frequently in the literature (for examples, see Monroe 1983; McFarlane et al. 1983). It will be recalled from the previous section of this chapter that baseline social supports contributed significantly to the prediction of time-one psychological symptoms. This finding argues for the importance of social support at the time of impact or crisis in the divorce process. The separation period has been frequently viewed (Bloom, Asher and White 1978; Chiriboga and Cutler 1977; Goode 1956) as the time of greatest stress in marital disruption. Higher levels of depression have been found among the separated as opposed to the married, widowed and never married (Dean and Ensel 1983; Pearlin and Johnson 1977). Indeed, elevated symptom scores were found at baseline (as compared to follow-up) for both men and women in the present study.

CASE STUDIES

All of the cases we present in this book demonstrate in one way or another the all-pervading importance of social supports in the lives of divorcing men and women. One consistent theme identified in the present chapter is the tendency of men to have more deficits in all dimensions of support (see also Chiriboga et al. 1979). This tendency is not unique to the present study; it in fact was labeled a "lethal" trait by Jourard (1964) in discussing the greater vulnerability of men to interpersonal conflict. Some have alluded to a "John Wayne Syndrome," described as one where a male is more likely to demonstrate affection and love to a horse than to another person. Among our cases, Ben Bennett has elements of this syndrome, with his sole source of social support appearing to be his dogs until he finally finds another woman to marry.

Emmy Lou Danford: Isolated but Trying Hard

Emmy Lou Danford is the slightly plump 39-year-old black bank teller and mother of three teenage girls who has already been described in chapters 6 and 7. Exemplifying people who spend very little time from decision point to separation, as well as those with a poor self-image, Emmy Lou filed for divorce from her husband of 17 years immediately after discovering he was having an affair. Although she reconciled with her husband about eight months later, she was still considering divorce at the time of the second interview. Emmy Lou is one of the few Divorce Study subjects to demonstrate a marked increase in psychological symptoms when interviewed for the second time.

A crucial factor contributing to Emmy Lou's downward spiral is the disruptions and weakening of her social support system over the course of her marriage. She had depended upon her husband almost exclusively for support and in his absence had few other sources of social support to fall back on. In fact, Emmy Lou did not feel that she had a life of her own when she was living with her husband. They spent most of their time together on the weekends and evenings, and she relied on her spouse very much for companionship, guidance and more material things. Throughout both interviews, she refers to her husband in warm and endearing terms. For example, she says at baseline that "He's going along with everything I want—which is kind of hard. He's so nice." At the second interview she refers to him as "sneaky, but a good person."

At the first interview she says she is without anyone to talk to about herself, to share feelings with, and she feels distant from people. She wonders if she may not be an interesting person and she often avoids going to places because she would be alone. The greatest difficulty she has experienced in the process of divorcing has been: "meeting new people—new men." She misses "male companionship" most. However, she explained that "having sex for having sex leaves me depressed. I have to have feelings and like the person." Asked if she has experienced any problems in meeting or dating people she replies that "sometimes I get to the point of going out, then back down."

Emmy Lou has, however, been dating since the separation, and it has helped. "He's good [to ask] for advice," she says of a man she is seeing. "He's an older man and likes to give advice. We've been going out about a month or two though I've been talking to him for four months. We met because we work together. He was new on the floor and we just started talking. He likes to listen and talk. He'll listen to me, contribute to the conversation."

When asked how long the relationship will last, she responds "I can't say —it's not a heavy thing." By follow-up, of course, we find that the relationship had not lasted and Emmy Lou later reconciles with her husband. She says "Sex means love. . . . I'd say, it's satisfying and gratifying. Really it just means love to me. I can't have sex with just anyone. I'm not a run-around. I'm square. I thought I couldn't. I tried and I can't."

Emmy Lou reports several forms of social support at the first interview. For example, she does have a few friends that are hers and not her husband's, but she only goes out with them to dinner parties or movies once every three or four months. Other supports include a women's group and a public health nurse, with the most helpful being the women's group. This group has given her "information on jobs, improvement through education, sharing what we're all going through. But we invited our male friends to come—they started saying we were queer. And the group fell apart. It was sad." At follow-up, she provides additional detail about the group: "I belonged to a support group the union organized at the bank. We all were single women. We had rap sessions on dealing with divorce and separation. We had brunches, we would go out and have meetings at each other's houses. I enjoyed kicking it around with other people. When we [my husband and I] got back together he didn't want me to be in it any longer." At both baseline and follow-up, Emmy Lou mentioned that her husband had discouraged her from partici-pating in this enjoyable and informative source of social support.

Another loss in social supports concerns relations with her relatives. Emmy Lou saw her relatives about four times a month when she first separated, but by the time of the follow-up interview she is seeing them just once a month, if that. She explains this reduction as due to the fact "They've been trying to tell me what to do about my life and they're taking sides—my family not his. I still visit his mother, father, sister, but he won't visit mine and they won't come here."

Her children are pivotal to her well-being. At the first interview one of her favorite things to do is: "See happiness in my girls. I like to see the joy on their faces. They are genuinely happy. They don't put on." But even at the first interview, changes have occurred in her relationships with her children, "We've gotten closer but they're bossier—they seem to be trying to take over where their father left off—like little women." Asked how the divorce will affect her children, she said: "I don't know—though the younger one said, 'It's OK Mom, all our friends' parents are divorced.' So, really, it's no big thing as far as they are concerned. They ask about him, want to do things with him, and go by his house."

By the second interview her relationship with the children has deterio-rated. "They seem to take my husband's side of things always. There's a negative thing between us now. The 16-year-old calls me 'Fat Fannie.' I don't like that." She has also suffered another blow to her already fragile social support system: her mother died several months prior to the interview.

On a more positive note, Emmy Lou now has one friend that she can tell almost anything to and she sees her twice a month. She has made some new friends since the first interview and when asked if she had learned anything from them, she said: "Divorce is *ugly*." She adds that "I'd like to work on myself—become more balanced, able to cope with situations as they come up better." She likes to sit and relax so that "I can regroup and can get started again." About her plans and goals for the future she has this to say: "try to adjust to deal with myself, that's my biggest problem." She also wants "to lose weight. I want to just concentrate on me for the next five years. I want to be selfish."

Ruth Rud: Isolated but Improving

In contrast to Emmy Lou, Ruth Rud shows marked improvement between interviews in both psychological and physical health. For example, she went from 31 psychological symptoms and 24 doctor's visits at first interview to 20 symptoms and 10 visits at the second interview. Ruth is a 60-year-old office worker with a seventh-grade education who had very little social support at the time of her separation from an abusive husband. Her only child, a son, died in a childhood accident. She describes her married life as a living hell, but now worries about getting sick and having no one to care for her. She misses having a social life and she has no one to talk to.

Ruth lives in an immaculately clean, small apartment, with lots of pictures decorating the walls. She offers tea while describing the circumstances leading to her separation: "I was afraid of my husband, because he drank and got abusive and threatened to kill me." Despite his frightening behavior, Ruth is still attached to her spouse. In fact, Ruth saw him the Sunday prior to the interview because he was ill and she was doing his wash, cleaning his house, and cooking his meals. About this she has "mixed emotions—I like to think that he has changed but I know he hasn't. I feel obligated to take care of him when he's sick." She does not, however, think there is any chance they will reconcile, "but I haven't given up hope."

Ruth thinks most often about the past: "About what has gone by. Where I went wrong. If I should have done things differently. How much of my life I've wasted and now I end up being alone. I think how things would have been, if I had done things differently. I would have been better off if I'd have ended the marriage when I was 30 years old instead of now at 60."

At our first meeting Ruth wonders if dating would be helpful to her, but has not met any men who are interested. She thinks that she now has more peace of mind since she has separated, but also feels that "being alone is hard." Ruth indeed feels very alone. As mentioned previously, her only child died many years ago and she recently had to put her pet dog to sleep. She feels that her husband "never allowed me to have friends, so now it's hard for me. He'd always break off relationships 'cause he'd cuss or embarrass me and I'd then not encourage people to visit. I always loved to entertain."

Ruth's life exemplifies the finding that less support is associated with greater symptomatology and that the more stressed subjects feel that their support is less adequate. At our first interview she has no network, few social supports, no social behaviors and scores low on perceptions of support. She seems uncertain about what to do with herself. Her relatives live more than one hour away, and she never visits with them. The same for friends. She feels very isolated and states that she is very often without someone to talk to and share experiences and feelings with. Ruth did, however, report having a brother she believes she can tell anything to. She contacts her brother two to three times a month. She saw him a few days before the first interview. He is ill and Ruth cared for him in addition to her husband.

When it comes to help seeking, Ruth reports seeking help from relatives, neighbors, a lawyer and doctors. She ranks doctors as being most helpful and made 24 visits to doctors during the past year. Doctors in fact seem to represent an important source of support to this basically support-deprived woman. She does not belong to any organizations, and does not have any friends who were especially hers and not her husband's. Her main source of support during the marriage was her husband and she never did things like go out to dinner, parties or movies without her husband. Not surprisingly, she reports that she did not have a life of her own while married.

Her personal chaos is reflected in the fact that Ruth has no goals and feels "compelled to live a day-to-day existence." Her Life History Profile is a steady progression downward from 9 at age 5 to 1 at her present age of 60 and she does not make any projections beyond age 60. Her favorite activities are walking and reading—both solitary activities. She reports feeling "lonely, remote and depressed" on the Bradburn Scale. At both baseline and follow-up, Ruth reports herself to be a religious person, and she attends services at least once a week.

At the second interview, Ruth has seen the doctor 10–15 times in the past year, an improvement over baseline. She now has 20 out of 42 symptoms, also an improvement. She now sees a sister three or four times a year and has five friends living within one hour's trip. She sees them twice a month. She has made new friends since the divorce, but still has problems meeting people because when she gets off work, she goes home. But she says "I'm hoping when I quit work, I can do better."

She now has a larger network and her perception of support is higher. She has goals and plans to expand her social activities. Her symptoms are fewer at follow-up, although still fairly high in number. She views her life as much more satisfying at follow-up and appears more optimistic about her future. While she never goes on dates, she would like to do so.

By the second interview Ruth feels she "wouldn't remarry. Old men are dirty. Old men are worse than old women and I don't want to take care of and wait on someone else. It would be my luck that he'd get sick and I would have to take care of him." Clearly, Ruth does not want to be obligated to provide non-reciprocal care giving for a sick, elderly man much as she always has for her husband.

Her Life History Profile now is markedly different: 9 at age 5, down to 3 at age 20, up to 6 at 30, down to 1 at 55 and up to 8 at current age where it remains. Now, Ruth sees her life extending to beyond the age of 90; at the first interview she was unable to project a year beyond her current age. One possible explanation for her improved health and vitality at follow-up is relief from her abusive husband. A further indication of her improved health is that she now reports some goals: travel, bridge parties and school. She explained: "I like to travel a lot and want to take a trip around the world on a freighter."

Overall, Ruth illustrates our point that the negative consequences of an impoverished support system are most apparent during the period of marital separation. By the second interview, her health and psychological symptoms have improved substantially, and she also is rebuilding her social supports. The improvements can be attributed to relief from a psychologically and physically abusive husband, opportunities to find new sources of social support, new hobbies and interests. This renewed vitality is seen in her reduced, albeit still high, psychological symptoms.

THE MULTIDIMENSIONALITY OF SOCIAL SUPPORT: CONCLUDING THOUGHTS

One of the themes we saw in conducting a number of case reviews, including the two we just presented, is that the various dimensions of social support seem in some ways to be related to how individuals cope with divorce. To pursue this theme in more quantitative terms, we correlated several impact stage variables related to supports with one of the coping variables described in the second chapter: Help Seeking. People who told us at follow-up that they used Help Seeking as a coping strategy were in fact more likely at the impact phase to talk to others about the separation. Interestingly, they were more likely to talk to the person they had separated from, to their parents, to counselors and to people in general. They were not more likely to talk to friends, presumably because most of our participants sought out friends; the help-seeking strategy seems to involve going beyond the friendship category.

Returning to what we have reported in this chapter, there seemed to be six basic points made by the data:

1. By and large, social support measures were relatively consistent across the time span of the study.
2. Only a modest amount of the variability in any of the dimensions of social support was predicted from background variables.
3. Social support measures played a limited but still important role in the explanation of psychological symptomatology during the impact phase of divorce. Social support had a direct additive effect on symptoms and very little evidence was found for interactive effects.
4. Social support measures were less associated with symptoms at follow-up than at baseline, suggesting that their major contributions to personal well-being may come at the time of crisis rather than for long-term well-being.
5. A number of findings corroborated the multidimensional conceptualization of social support.
6. There were a number of differences in the way social support and the stress process model operated for men and for women. Of particular importance is that maintenance of a stable support system may be more important for women, while for men the important thing may be to respond to stress conditions by temporarily expanding and activating the system.

Social Support as a Multidimensional Concept

Rather than discussing each of these points, we will here focus primarily on one: that the domain of social supports is multidimensional. Social support was conceptualized in this chapter as multidimensional and it was operationalized in a way that attempted to capture at least some of its underlying dimensions. Several findings of the study attest to the multidimensional nature of social support. Consider for example the fact that there were low but still significant intercorrelations among the four variables chosen to operationalize the dimensions. This suggests that the variables represented different underlying constructs.

Further, in the context of the stress process model, different background factors were related to the various support variables. Perhaps, most importantly, the support variables differed in their impact on psychological dysfunction. Others who have conceptualized and measured social support as multidimensional have produced similar findings (e.g., Caldwell, Bloom and Hodges 1983; Schaefer, Coyne and Lazarus 1981). Further, there were differences in which of the support dimensions appeared to be salient for men and women. Overall these findings can be taken to indicate that the different measures of support represent different aspects of support.

Gender and Multidimensionality. The differences in which of the social support dimensions were important for men and for women were intriguing. At this point, of course, it is only possible to speculate about the meaning of these differences. Apparently for men the behavioral and structural aspects of social support were most salient to adaptation. When men were stressed, taking support-seeking action appeared to be psychologically helpful. A commonly held belief is that men are in general reluctant to seek support from others; on the other hand, they are supposed to be oriented toward action, toward "doing something" about their problems, and in the case of some of these divorcing men, the action orientation may have overcome the general disinclination to seek support.

The other aspect of social support that tended to be significant for men was the presence of confidants. Perhaps men rely psychologically on the structural givens of their lives; the presence of confidants and colleagues may have a supportive effect in itself, whether or not the men actually turn to these potential sources of support. Women, on the other hand, appeared to respond at a different level. For women, it was only when they perceived themselves as having relationships of intimate emotional exchange that the relationships were associated with good outcome—that these relationships appeared to protect against the development of symptoms. For women, the important aspect of support appears to be not what they potentially have access to but what they actually experience in their relationships.

Dating as a Form of Support. One type of social support we have not covered to this point has to do with dating or sexual partners. In several early analyses concerning the impact phase of the study, we considered the role of dating in some detail. Although having dating relationships generally was a positive experience, there were some intriguing sex differences that highlight the different ways men and women relate to others. In short, the happiest men were those who were dating only one person, while the happiest women were those who were dating more than one person (Lachman 1977).

While this finding would seem to fly in the face of our stereotypes about male behavior, it does make sense. If men tend to rely on their wives as confidants, they may be in some sense seeking a replacement. Here we should also point out the fact that when men and women were asked, at the impact phase, who ideally could help them the most with the divorce, a number of men responded that their wives could. None of the women made such a response about their former husbands! Women, on the other hand, tend to have a number of confidants. For them, the experience of multiple partnerships or dating relationships may provide important strokes to self-esteem.

Clinical Implications and Directions for Future Research

Two of the more important and clinically relevant findings from the analyses have been (1) that short-term adaptation sets the stage for long-term psychological well-being and that social supports have a direct impact on short-term adaptation and (2) that different dimensions of social supports matter for women and men. This strongly indicates the need for intervention at the point of impact and it also points out the necessity for tailoring support to the different requirements of men and women. Men may need interventions that allow them to play an active part while women may need the opportunity for longer, more intimate contacts.

Our results stress the importance of multidimensional approach to the study of social support. The notion of multidimensionality in turn points to the need for greater specificity in thinking about and measuring social supports. Social support comes in different forms, from different sources, in different ways, and to different types of people. It is not a unitary concept, and simply to know that someone has a smaller or larger social network, or a specified frequency of social contact, tells little about their vulnerability to stress.

10

WHO LEAVES WHOM: THE IMPORTANCE OF CONTROL

H. B. Wilder and David A. Chiriboga

Each of the preceding chapters has examined factors that contribute to the tremendous variability in how people respond to separation and divorce. One psychological factor suggested to have major importance but which has been examined only superficially in past studies is control over the initiation of divorce. Those who have considered it seem to agree (e.g., Weiss 1976; Krantzler 1973) that control is a pivotal concept in understanding people's reactions to divorce. Unfortunately, control is also a concept that is difficult to measure because people's reports of control are subject to the vagaries of social desirability, self-justification and other problems associated with retrospective bias.

Control and Stress

One reason why control may be a pivotal concept lies in its key role in the stress process. Mandler and Watson (1966) and Sells (1970) were among the first to emphasize the deleterious consequences of a perceived lack of control in a stressful situation. Some 14 years later, Lazarus and Folkman (1984) drew much the same conclusion in studying both life events and day-to-day hassles. Ample evidence exists that control can play a powerful role in mitigating the effects of stress and that lack of control can be an important factor in creating and heightening stress reactions (e.g., Bandura 1989; Seligman 1989).

THEORETICAL SIGNIFICANCE OF CONTROL

Control has received attention from social scientists for over 50 years. It has been written about under many names and under the auspices of many theories. One of the earliest advocates for the importance of the general sense of personal control was Alfred Adler. In establishing what he called a "will to power," Adler (1969) cast the construct as predicated on an evolutionary need to master the environment in the best possible way.

During the decades that have passed since Adler first introduced the basic concept, writers have continued to stress the primacy of control. According to one expert, "man's primary motivation propensity is to be effective in producing changes in his environment. Man strives to be a causal agent, to be the primary locus of, causation for, or the origin of, his behavior; he strives for personal causation" (deCharms 1968, 269). White (1959, 1960), in a series of papers written from an ego psychology point of view, proposed much the same thing with what he called a competence model.

The concept of competence subsumes the whole realm of learned behavior whereby the child comes to deal effectively with his environment. It includes manipulation, locomotion, language, the building of cognitive maps and skilled actions, and the growth of effective behavior in relation to other people. . . . The directed persistence of such behavior warrants the assumption of a motivation independent of drives, here called effectance motivation, which has its immediate satisfaction in a feeling of efficacy and its adaptive significance in the growth of competence. Effectance motivation can be likened to independent ego energies in the psychoanalytic scheme. (White 1960, 138)

Lack of perceived control has been isolated by writers of various theoretical persuasions as a central factor in psychopathology. Sociopathy (e.g., Melges and Bowlby 1969), depression (e.g., Brown and Harris 1989; Melges and Bowlby 1969; Seligman 1975) and indeed multiple areas of both physical and mental illness have been related to lack of perceived control (Rodin 1986). Seligman (1975) has marshaled impressive evidence that organisms are capable of learning not simply that their actions bring about desirable or undesirable consequences, but that their actions have no effect on the environment. He argues that this perception, termed learned helplessness, is an important element in many dysfunctional patterns of human adjustment.

RESEARCH ON CONTROL

Research on control has been organized along one of two major lines. The first, which subsumes the bulk of existing research, involves studying the effect of control across situations; here we will call this "general control." The second looks at control in the context of specified situations, and can be thought of as "situational control."

General Control

Research on general control often considers control as a dimension of personality, and has dealt almost exclusively with perceptions of control, rather than with actual control. Based almost always on self-report, it has usually drawn upon subject reactions to broad philosophical statements about the control the respondent tends to feel over life in general.

One of the most accepted approaches to studying general control is Rotter's (1966, 1990) theory of perceived locus of control. For Rotter, individuals differ with regard to the extent they perceive life circumstances as resulting from their own behavior and permanent characteristics, as opposed to chance. A large body of evidence supports the notion that locus of control is a generalized, cross-situational expectancy (Rotter 1966; Strickland 1989). Many differences have been found between individuals on the Internal-External (I-E) Scale Rotter used to measure the construct. For example, those with an internal, as opposed to an external locus of control, tend to show more initiative in attempting to control their environments (Phares 1965; Seeman 1963) and solving personal (Phares, Ritchies and Davis 1968) and behavioral problems (James, Woodruff and Werner 1965).

Externality has been associated with feelings of inadequacy (Fish and Karabenick 1971; Ryckman and Sherman 1973) and with low mood levels (Gorman 1971). Other studies have reported a relationship between external locus of control and self-descriptions of depression (Warhime and Foulds 1971), low self-esteem (Fitch 1970) and neuroticism and maladjustment (Hersch and Scheibe 1967).

Situational Control

Research on situational control is concerned with measuring the effect of various modes of control over specific problems. Investigations of situational control have been conducted within a variety of settings. At one end of the spectrum has been laboratory research on aversive stimuli designed to minimize the influence of subjects' perceptions of the experimental contingencies (i.e., Haggard 1943). At the other end have been the studies in which respondent perceptions were of primary interest. These include works of particular relevance to this chapter, such as the field work of Goode (1956), in which divorcees were asked who initiated and carried through on plans to divorce. A relatively complex theoretical approach to studying control within a specific context is the cognitive appraisal viewpoint (e.g., Lazarus and Folkman 1984). In this approach, coping is seen as developing from transactions between characteristics of the person (including physical and mental state) and the conditions of the environment.

As with general control, research into situational control has revealed the complexity of the concept. In an early review of the literature on control over application of aversive stimuli, Averill (1973) found that control could be divided into three types. The first was direct behavioral control over the environment. Components of this type of control included ability to regulate administration of the stimulus (i.e., how, when and by whom the stimulus will be administered) and stimulus modification (the capacity to avoid or terminate the stimulus, etc.). Cognitive control, the second, involved providing the subjects with opportunities to reinterpret or obtain additional information concerning the aversive events. The third type of control, termed decisional control, provided the subject with ability to choose among two or more conditions under which to receive the stimulus.

The importance of control in the situational context is well established. Several large-scale studies have underscored the impact of negative life events outside the control of the individual. In one study, negative events beyond personal control were particularly important in discriminating persons with high versus low scores on psychiatric impairment (Myers, Lindenthal and Pepper 1971). In another, correlations between life events and impairment scores were the greatest for events classified outside the respondent's control (Dohrenwend 1973).

Uncontrollable and/or unpredictable life events have been linked with depression (Paykel et al. 1969; Brown and Harris 1989), self-reported tension and distress (Vinokur and Selzer 1975), accidental injuries (Bramwell, Masuda, Wagner and Holmes 1975), back pain and headache (Luborsky, Docherty and Penick 1973), sinus problems (Wolf 1954), coronary heart disease (Glass 1977; Rahe 1968) and various common physical symptoms (Wolff

1968). Field studies with the aged indicate that loss of control leads to withdrawal and depression (Schulz and Aderman 1974) and even to early death (Ferrari 1962; Schulz and Aderman 1973).

Control and Adaptation: A Complex Association

There is a temptation, when reviewing the wealth of information linking control with adaptation, to conclude that lack of control is synonymous with pathology. The relationship between control and psychological functioning, however, is more complex than it first appears. First, many theoreticians have stressed that abdication of control or power to others is often an active adaptation strategy. Fromm (1941), for instance, in *Escape from Freedom*, his famous analysis of the rise of fascism, identified acquiescence to authoritarianism as a mechanism a society adopts to avoid the collective uncertainty and anxiety which are part of the price of maintaining personal liberties. Rank (1945, 64), at the level of the individual, commented earlier on "the longing for release from self responsibility through the other."

In more recent times, control has come to be viewed as a complex phenomenon, forged of elements from both personality and the situation. In the review of the literature on control and aversive stimuli cited earlier, Averill (1973) found that behavioral, cognitive or decisional control could lessen, heighten or have no effect on stress, depending on the meaning of the stimulus and the mode of control to the subject. One interesting finding was that subjects generally preferred to be able to regulate administration of the stimulus, even though this rarely led to lower short-term physiological arousal. This may be related to the reports (e.g., Davidson and Bobey 1970) that a cognitive appraisal style which focuses on threatening events and searches for cues regarding potential harm may lead to greater distress in the short run but improved adaptation in the long term.

In view of the many facets of control and its various effects over time, it is surprising that so little work has been done to develop its richness. In particular, almost no work has been done to compare the effects of situational and general control. However, there has been considerable attention paid to the development of locus of control scales that focus on particular areas of concern. One example is the Health Locus of Control (HLC) Scale, which may be superior to Rotter's I-E Scale in predicting health behaviors (Wallston, Kaplan and Maides 1976). For the HLC, respondents react to items purported to measure their health-related expectancies, such as "Whenever I get sick it is because of something I've done or not done." This analytic approach can be seen as an attempt to focus the general control perspective onto a situational topic.

CONTROL AND DIVORCE

Research into the relationship between control and stress, then, demands a certain complexity. Research into the relationship between control over the divorcing process and postdivorce adjustment has, for the most part, failed to come to grips with this complexity. Results have also been somewhat equivocal, due in part to the relatively perfunctory treatment the variable of control has received.

A large number of studies (e.g., Blair 1970; Hill, Rubin and Peplau 1979; Lenihan 1979; Meyers 1976; Nevaldine 1978; Waller 1930; Wallerstein and Kelly 1980) have found significant correlations between an active role in the decision to separate and successful postseparation adjustment. These studies for the most part have followed the lead taken in Goode's (1956) landmark study on divorced women. Goode asked divorced mothers in their twenties and thirties questions concerning who was originally in favor of divorce, who favored it most at the time of actual separation and who was to blame. He found that women who believed they shared control with their spouses over the separation and divorce demonstrated less stress than those who either initiated the divorce or resisted it. He also found that those who were older experienced more stress than those who were younger, regardless of their level of control.

In general, Goode's (1956) findings with regard to stress must be viewed in light of the cross-sectional nature of the project. It has been suggested (Krantzler 1973) that, in comparison with men, women tend to experience greater initial turmoil, but work through their difficulties more quickly. Women in Goode's sample who were initially high in stress, therefore, might have been found to fare relatively well if they had been followed up. Bondurant (1977) found, with an evenly mixed (though relatively small) group of men and women, few significant differences in adjustment between those who initiated and those who resisted separation.

Several studies have failed to find a relationship between locus of control and adjustment to marital separation (e.g., Pais 1979; White 1979). This is likely due to the kinds of problems which prompted development of measures such as the previously mentioned Health Locus of Control Scale, namely, the relatively poor predictive value of items which tap abstract philosophical attitudes rather distant from the situational context being studied.

To date, no serious attempt has been made to develop a control measure relevant to the situation of marital separation and divorce. Such an attempt might include attitudinal components, such as the degree to which the respondent felt he or she was the "boss" in the now-dissolved family, as well as behavioral indicators, such as independence from spouse in social activities, or taking an active hand in budgetary matters. Further, no study has rigorously attempted to explore the relationship between general sense of control and situational control over the divorce, and no study has related these psychological indicators of control (either general or situational) to behavioral indicators, such as independence from spouse in social activities, feelings of being "boss" in the family or an active hand in budgetary matters. Most research has been cross-sectional and therefore has been unable to track the effect of either type of control over time.

In summary, the literature relating control to divorce and separation indicates that control in the situation of separation is associated with successful adjustment. Contrary to the considerable amount of research into control and adjustment in contexts outside divorce, little or no effect is noted for general control. Extremely little research into the longitudinal effects of control has been conducted, with no attempt made to compare the effects of situational and general control.

Implications of the Literature

With the general literature, as well as that devoted to marital separation and divorce, providing little guidance in the construction of hypotheses for a study of this type, we were left only with the conceptual contours of the variables. The general control measure envisioned for this study was conceived to tap a relatively stable trait, the characteristic level of mastery over life events an individual perceives him- or herself to have. In terms of stability, it was seen as comparable to the locus of control of reinforcement construct (i.e., Rotter 1966), although its emphasis was primarily on aspects of lifestyle within the marriage prior to separation.

The situational control measure, by virtue of its focus on an event relatively limited in time, was seen as comparatively transient. General control in this study comprised that portion of the self-concept related to sense of general competence and behavioral items which pertain to a sense of control over one's life prior to the separation. Situational control was measured by items related to perceived control over the divorcing process. The predictions for this study flow primarily out of these concepts of the variables.

HYPOTHESES AND METHODS

The literature has demonstrated effects both for control over the specific situation and for control as a cross-situational expectancy. Analyses conducted for this chapter sought to explore the effect of perceived situational and general control on the adjustment to divorce. Measures of situational and general control were the independent variables, and the dependent variables were psychological symptoms and morale. The following hypotheses were formulated concerning perceived control before and during the marital separation process and longitudinal adjustment:

Hypotheses

1. Short-term adjustment will be more influenced by situational than by general control. That is, respondents high in situational control at baseline will show better adjustment at baseline than those low in situational control, regardless of their level of general control.
2. Long-term adjustment will be more influenced by general than by situational control. That is, respondents high in general control at baseline will show better adjustment at follow-up than those low in general control, regardless of their level of situational control.
3. Situational and general control will have an additive effect on adjustment, in the predicted directions of Hypotheses 1 and 2. That is, respondents who are high in situational and general control at baseline will show the best adjustment at follow-up, followed in order by those high in general and low in situational control, those high in situational and low in general control, and finally by those low in both types of control.

These hypotheses can be summarized in the four-cell typology presented in figures 2a and 2b. Actual analyses used to examine these hypotheses were relatively straightforward. For the most part, they involved discriminant analysis procedures whereby we could compare how each of the four types stacked up against the others.

Figure 2a

Anticipated Adjustment Levels within Four-Cell Typologies at Baseline

		Situational Control	
		High	Low
General Control	*High*	Best Adjustment	Poorest Adjustment
	Low	Good Adjustment	Poor Adjustment

Figure 2b

Anticipated Adjustment Levels within Four-Cell Typologies at Follow-up

		Situational Control	
		High	Low
General Control	*High*	Best Adjustment	Good Adjustment
	Low	Poor Adjustment	Poorest Adjustment

How We Developed Our Measures of Control

The Divorce Study included a variety of questions tapping both general and specific feelings of control, and one of the first steps in our investigation was to examine the most appropriate treatment of the concepts. Preliminary analyses suggested that the concepts of situational and general control, in the context of divorce and marital separation, can be treated as multidimensional. For the situational control measure, we looked at five questions that tapped the degree to which respondents perceived themselves to have had control over the process of marital separation. Factor analysis indicated two distinct domains were covered by answers to these questions: who favored divorce and who was to blame for divorce. These domains also appear distinct from a conceptual point of view, since an individual might favor (and even initiate) divorce, and at the same time view the spouse's attitudes and behavior as creating the necessity for a separation.

Measures of general control were drawn from two sources. The first was the Adjective Rating List described in chapter 7; the Masterful Self factor was taken as one index of general control. The second consisted of the same set of 26 questions on lifestyle prior to separation that was cited in chapter 3;

analyses identified four relevant factors: reliance on the spouse, decisional control, social independence and the perception of having had a life of one's own while married. Together, the one self-image factor and the four lifestyle factors appear to tap relatively distinct behavioral and attitudinal components of a general sense of control over life prior to separation. The coherence of these control measures and the significant findings obtained with them support the argument for developing control measures specifically relevant to the phenomena being studied, especially when examining an experience with the unique mix of features present in marital separation and divorce.

The next step was to sum indices into two composite scores, one for situational control and one for general. These composite measures turned out to be uncorrelated with each other, a finding consistent with Darsa's (1976) conclusion that no significant differences exist between initiators and noninitiators of divorce on perceived locus of control. This result suggests that in divorce, situational and general control may be conceptualized as independent, neither acting as an important predictor of the other.

A key question in regard to the two types of control was what characteristics would predispose respondents to be high in one or another type of control. An interesting finding with regard to both of the control measures was the fact that few of the demographic variables served to predict control. Gender was the only significant predictor of situational control, with women feeling more in control of the divorce than men. For general control, education was the sole significant predictor, with those high in education more likely to be high in control.

Another point about pathways to control should be made. We have already seen that women score higher on situational control. In the area of general control, education was the key. Given the generally lower levels of education for women than for men in this sample and across the nation, this finding underscores the importance of education for women as a route to greater perceived control over their lives, both before and after divorce.

WHAT DID WE FIND?

This section will focus on the influence the two types of control exert upon short- and long-term adjustment. Because of the marked gender differences, discussion will center on the patterns among men and women in the relationship between control and adjustment. As an overview, for men both types of control were found to relate to adjustment at baseline, but with only situational control having an effect on follow-up adjustment. For women, only general control influenced adjustment, both at baseline and follow-up.

Gender Differences in Levels of Control

Concerning the issue of who experiences which type of control, the results of this study corroborate those of other projects. We found that women were twice as likely as men to be high in situational control, which is consistent with other published reports that women are more likely than men to make the final decision to separate, among both married (Goode 1956; Ross and Sawhill 1975; Wallerstein and Kelly 1980; Zybron 1965) and unmarried couples (Hill, Rubin and Peplau 1979). This phenomenon has been explained on the basis that women are more sensitive to difficulties in the marriage, more likely to initiate action aimed at improving the relationship, and, once convinced that these problems cannot be solved, more likely to sever the union (Bernard 1972; Chiriboga, Roberts and Stein 1978; Hill, Rubin and Peplau 1979). Goode's (1956) research, however, suggests that men maneuver women into the position of making the decision.

The finding that men were more likely than women to be high in general control is also consistent with the literature. That is, men are generally more likely than women to endorse an internal locus of control (e.g., Feather 1968). One explanation for higher levels of internal control in males rests with the traditionally greater male access to socioeconomic advantages, an advantage that is corroborated by the generally higher education and income levels for men than for women in this study.

Women. When we employed discriminant analysis procedures to examine the findings for women, we first created groups by contrasting those high and low in situational and general control scores. We found that women who were high in both types of control showed good adjustment at both baseline and follow-up. These were women who had considerable resources both within and outside the marriage and who took an active hand in the decision to end it. It is not at all surprising that they should have adjusted better than all other groups, both in the short and the long term. Women who were low in both types of control showed poor adjustment at baseline and also at follow-up. This finding, too, contains few surprises. These were women who were low in perceived resources before separation and experienced the process of divorce in a relatively passive manner. It is possible that, in some ways at least, this group embodies the stereotype of women who are socialized into a passive stance with regard to men (see Gould 1976; Maccoby 1990). The groups of particular interest, however, were those who were low in one form of control and high in another. Women who were low in situational and high in general control showed consistently good adjustment, in the long as well as the short term. Conversely, those who were low in general control and high in situational control showed poor adjustment, both in the months following separation and approximately three and a half years later.

This underscores the essential importance for women of a sense of control over life prior to separation. This is consistent with findings of others who have employed some of the data employed in this study, although in different contexts. Chiriboga and Thurnher (1980), for instance, found that having an independent lifestyle during marriage was associated with higher morale and fewer symptoms for women in the months following separation. In chapter 3 many of the same measures covering life prior to separation were used that here were incorporated into the measure of general control. As you may recall, the basic finding was that for younger women, greater happiness was associated with less reliance on the spouse for practical matters, greater control in choosing their own and the spouse's employment, doing the shopping but not the cleaning, and having independent hobbies and interests. For women over forty, the importance of work diminished. However, the happier respondents were characterized by recreational independence and not relying on their husbands for companionship.

The poor adjustment over time of those women who were high in situational but low in general control is highly reminiscent of the findings of Wallerstein (Wallerstein and Kelly 1980; Wallerstein and Blakeslee 1989). In a longitudinal study of divorce, they identified a substantial proportion of women who took the initiative in terminating what they perceived to be an unacceptable marital situation, but who had relatively few skills and resources with which to construct a new life. Most of the women in this category reported considerable unhappiness as much as ten years after divorcing and some regretted having acted to obtain a divorce. The bittersweet quality of situational control for women in this study is amplified by those few significant correlations between situational control and the Bradburn mood items that did not associate better adjustment with higher levels of control. For women at the first contact, being high in situational control was associated with feeling unable to get going and a lack of accomplishment. Such unexpected relationships between control measures and the other variables were found only for women, not for men. It appears that women who are low in general control, but who "rise to the occasion" face a more difficult task in coping with the effects of divorce than those who are higher in control before separation, even if the latter have the divorce "foisted" upon them.

Men. The picture with regard to the influence of the two types of control on adjustment for men is somewhat obscure during the months immediately following separation, but clearer for the period several years later. Although both types of control had an effect on short-term adjustment, it cannot be stated that the effect of one type was significantly stronger than the other. Men who scored lower on situational control reported significantly more symptoms and tended to report lower morale. At the same time, men higher in general control were significantly happier. At follow-up, however, only situational control influenced adjustment, with men who had been high in situational control ending up being happier and tending to report fewer symptoms.

As with women, more detailed information on the relative influence of the two types of control was obtained by examining the means of the combined situational/general control groups. Those high in both types of control exhibited consistently good adjustment at both contacts, while those low in both showed poor adjustment at both contacts. Focusing on the groups who were high in one type of control and low in another, it is possible to discern a shift over time. Men who were low in situational and high in general control showed good adjustment in the months immediately following the separation, but were doing relatively poorly several years later. On the other hand, those who were high in situational control and low in general control showed poor adjustment at baseline, but relatively good adjustment at follow-up. In essence, the positions of these two groups in the adjustment hierarchy shifted over time.

In assessing these results the question arises, why did this shift occur? Much research suggests that, after an initial period of disruption, functioning gradually returns to or exceeds the predivorce level (Hetherington, Cox and Cox 1976; Wallerstein and Kelly 1980). Did one of these groups reverse this trend and deteriorate over time? Did both improve over time, one more than the other? Or did one improve and the other remain the same?

Examination of the means for the combined situational/general control groups provides some answers. It appears that one group improved while the other remained more stable. The high situational/low general control group reported a mean of 9.6 symptoms at baseline and a reduction to 7.3 at follow-up. The low situational/high general group, on the other hand, remained roughly stable, with 8.8 symptoms at baseline and 8.0 at follow-up. A similar trend can be seen in morale. The high situational/low general group improved in happiness while the low situation/high general actually showed a slight decline in happiness. The significance of their decline in happiness is highlighted by the fact that the sample as a whole decreased significantly in symptoms and increased in morale between baseline and follow-up (Fiske and Chiriboga 1985). In other words, those in the low situational/high general group went sharply against the overall trend toward improvement in function. These individuals showed signs of remaining in what for many respondents had been a stressed state generally associated with the period of life immediately following separation.

These findings are consistent with the clinically based picture of the reaction of many men to the divorce situation drawn by Krantzler (1973). Although not specifically addressing the issue of situational versus general control, he depicted a large number of men as tending to postpone facing the emotional demands of separation by throwing themselves into work or other pursuits. He contrasted them with women, whom he described as facing the emotional demands of separation more straightforwardly, suffering more in the short term, and recovering more quickly than men. Krantzler concluded that men who put off the work of adjustment to their new postseparation lives ultimately have to pay the price for their denial. The results of this study support this conclusion and indicate that the price may be to remain frozen at a suboptimal level of psychological and physical functioning.

At a theoretical level, the men in this low situational/high general control group may illustrate the so-called "facilitation" effect which has been noted in laboratory studies of the learned helplessness phenomenon. A common paradigm in this research is to give subjects an unsolvable task, followed by a solvable one. Learned helplessness theory, as originally formulated, predicts that there should be a decrement in performance as compared with a level determined before exposure to the situation of helplessness. Several studies, however, have obtained the seemingly paradoxical result that performance can actually be facilitated by exposure to the unsolvable task (Hanusa and Schulz 1977; Roth and Kubal 1975; Tennen and Eller 1977; Wortman et al. 1976).

In their critique and reformulation of the learned helplessness thesis in light of attribution theory, Abramson, Seligman and Teasdale (1978) offer a "rebound" explanation for this facilitation effect: "it seems reasonable that compensatory attempts to reassert control might follow helplessness experiences, once the person leaves the situation in which he believes himself helpless" (p. 61). It may be that, for the men in the low situational/high general control group, the impact phase of separation—that time leading from the first serious mention of divorce to the act of filing—can be viewed as a helpless situation, over which they have little or no control. If this is true, it may be that several months after filing (in the period when the baseline interview took place), these men have initiated compensatory attempts to feel in control and a kind of "facilitation" effect on adjustment may be noted. What of their failure to show the expected improvement with time after divorce? Abramson, Seligman and Teasdale (1978) continue: "Such compensatory rebound might be expected to dissipate in time and be less strong in situations very far removed from the original helplessness training" (p. 61). The poor longitudinal adjustment of this group is consistent with this prediction.

The explanation proposed by Abramson, Seligman and Teasdale (1978) implies that the perceived general control of the men in this low situational/ high general group might decrease over time. Unfortunately, the absence in this study of measures for control obtained at follow-up make the testing of this supposition virtually impossible. In addition, although the predictive value of each type of control for adjustment over time was ascertained for subgroups of the sample, these findings cannot establish a definitive causal link between perceived control and adjustment. The question of the extent to which attributions of control affect adjustment ("I'm in control, so I must be doing well"), as opposed to adjustment influencing attributions of control ("I'm doing well, so I must be in control") remains. That respondents might associate control with adjustment is not unreasonable to suspect, since the social desirability of personal control is well-established (Cone 1971; Hjelle 1971; Joe 1972; Leary 1957). One approach to this difficult problem would be to measure perceptions of control prior to divorce, to determine the relationship between fluctuations in perceived control and psychological and physical functioning. This highlights again the previously discussed need for longitudinal research on control.

CASE STUDIES: TWO GROUPS AT RISK

One way to flesh out the data concerning control and adjustment to divorce is to examine cases which seem to reflect patterns common to a particular group. This can be particularly helpful in situations where the realities underlying statistical trends are not immediately apparent. Two groups in this study which emerged at risk for long-term adjustment and for which the results are somewhat confusing are the high situational/low general control group of women and the low situational/high general control group of men. The cases which follow have been selected as representative of their respective groups. Although each case has unique elements, they reflect the broad outlines common to the group, and discussion of them provides a chance for greater understanding of the human dimensions of perceived control in the context of adjustment to marital separation.

Emmy Lou Again: "You have to learn to deal with it."

Emmy Lou Danford, a high situational/low general control female, was first introduced in chapter 6. She differs in one major respect from the general group of high situational/low general general group of women, and from the sample as a whole: by the time of the second interview she has been reconciled with her husband for over two years. However, in many other ways she seems to typify the turmoil faced and the coping patterns adopted by this group.

Emmy Lou graduated from high school and has worked as a bank teller for the last five years. She left her parents' home at 18 to enter her first and only marriage, and gave birth to her first daughter one year later. She had worked steadily from the time her girls were toddlers. This had long displeased her husband, but she felt forced to have a job in order to supplement the family income.

Emmy Lou describes her husband as making the decisions concerning what job he should take, what car the family should buy, where to go on vacations and where to live. She stated that prior to separation she relied very much on him for companionship, guidance, money and practical matters, and that during that time she had not had a life of her own. As the reader may recall, she initiated the separation upon finding out that her husband was involved with another woman.

Although Emmy Lou is unique in many ways, the context of her separation seems to typify the setting for marital separation among the high situa-
tional/low general control women. Preseparation reliance on the spouse is
great, especially with regard to money and practical matters, and there is a
feeling of being forced to take action to break up the union, in reaction to
the husband's unacceptable behavior (having a lover, profligate spending,
physical or mental abuse of her or the children, ignoring what she deems
important obligations of the marriage, etc.). It is for this reason, it seems,
that women in this group tend to blame the husband, while describing
themselves as more in favor of the divorce than he is. The common perception seems to be, "he drove me to it."

The picture of her life during the period of separation emerges as one of
struggle. When asked how separation changed the way she felt about herself,
she replies: "I really work at things instead of taking them for granted." She
hopes that divorce might hold the promise of positive change: "I'll probably
just go on . . . get a higher income, get more education." However, the
hope is tenuous: "I hadn't thought about *next* year." When asked to cite a
benefit of separation, she cannot. When asked to identify the most stressful
part of separating, she answers, "Making all the decisions in my life . . .
everything: house, work, kids, whatever had to be done."

Emmy Lou's feelings of emotional turmoil during the early stages of
divorce are representative of this group. Marriage, however difficult, has
been an essential source of stability. To find herself outside this union is a
stunning blow, regardless of the fact that she herself instigated the change.
Like many others who generally are low in perceived control but take charge
of at least the early stages of divorce, Emmy Lou was largely unprepared for
the difficulties of a new life. For example, she became sexually involved with
another man during the separation. Asked by him what he might do to
increase her pleasure in lovemaking, she draws a complete blank. Her
attempts at getting help appear to have been intermittent and plagued by
doubt. She visited a psychiatrist once, but "just couldn't go back to him" a
second time.

The unexpected difficulties played a strong role in Emmy Lou's decision
to reconcile with her husband, but reconciliation did not solve her problems.
At the second interview we find that life has not been very pleasant for Emmy
Lou. Asked how her life has changed since the separation, she replies: "I
don't have as much faith in people as I had before . . . [I have] less confidence."

The separation, and the events which led up to it, have inflicted a wound which has not yet healed, over three years later. It appears that whatever sense of control she had over life before separating has since withered. She reports that she still thinks often of divorce, that the loneliest time for her was the period after she got back together with her husband and that she is still plagued by loneliness. She has been to see a doctor five or six times within the previous year for "nerves, hair falling out, obesity, pain in the side . . . depression." As we have noted before, she demonstrates a marked increase in psychological symptoms between interviews, checking 29 items from the Symptoms Checklist at follow-up, an increase of 12 from baseline.

Emmy Lou looks back on the decision to reconcile and wishes "I didn't go through with it. At that time I was so docile it was sickening. I did whatever he told me to do." She reports that now, "I'm trying to be more tolerant and it's killing me. It's depressing. I'm more subservient now. I try not to complain or talk about the things that are really bothering me." This is in marked contrast to her memory of the separation, when "I got more accomplished with the house and everything else than we had the whole time we were together." She describes herself now as more dependent, less in control of and more disappointed in life since the separation.

Although her decline is dramatic, Emmy Lou reflects themes common to the stories of women in this group: Separation has presented an immense challenge and they haven't been completely able to meet it. Attempts to assert control over their lives have not worked out. Economic struggles are often cited: child support has been insufficient or simply not paid by the husband, respondents have been unable to earn the salaries for which they had hoped, division of property has created unanticipated hardship. For example, Emmy Lou, in recounting what led up to the reconciliation, recalls being told by a lawyer that "everything would be split down the middle— including my retirement."

Typically for this group, she describes herself at follow-up as more distant from people. Her three daughters, with whom she became particularly close in the early stages of separation, now ally with their father against her, ridiculing her for the weight she has gained in the past three years. Her mother, who was sympathetic during the separation, is now dead. Sources of support in her earlier attempts to establish a new sense of control over her life have vanished.

Daniel Waterman: "I told her who I was, but she didn't believe me."

Daniel was a member of the low situational/high general control group. In many ways he is an extreme of the trends in the low situational/high general control group of men. He clearly illustrates the sharp contrasts between the two types of control seen in this group.

A white male and father of a two-year-old girl, Daniel is 32 years old at the first interview. He had been married four years prior to separation. Although he holds a master's degree in English Literature, at the time of the initial interview he is working as a part-time laborer at a lumber yard. He plans to quit in the near future and become a professional motorcycle racer. For several months he has been living in a rented condominium and devoting much of his time to poetry and motorcycling, interests that had also occupied him during his marriage.

He estimates he spent 60 hours per week apart from his wife pursuing these activities: "There was a question whether she could physically handle those things or psychologically. She never worked that out. . . . She would help but she wouldn't really get involved in it with me. With motorcycling, she'd go to a few of the races . . . two or three times in all those years." Art and the motorcycles (he has two) apparently displaced large portions of their family life. Asked who decided where to go on vacations, he replies: "We never took one together. That was one of the things she got uptight about."

Independence and the freedom to pursue interests outside the marriage, typically important to the low situational/high general control group of men, emerge as vital to Daniel. Asked if he had a life of his own while married, he replies: "I made sure of it. That's why we're not together. . . . I told her who I was, but she didn't believe me." He describes the separation as having been his wife's doing. "Well, it was really all her trip, but the 'straw that broke the camel's back,' as she put it was: She phoned me at work, something I had repeatedly and specifically asked her *not* to do and said she had an 'urgent' message. . . . Her 'urgent' message was she wanted to go to the show with a girlfriend. . . . But the real issue was the fact that I refused to cut back on the time I spent in training for races. She thinks I'm a fanatic and can't deal with it." In allocating blame for the breakup, he identifies "me for getting married and her for not accepting who I am." If he was culpable, it was for having entered into the union in the first place.

This typifies the initial low situational/high general control male reaction to separation: "The divorce was her idea; I had things to do and she just couldn't handle it." Little pain is expressed. At baseline, Daniel marks six symptoms (well below the group average) and registers an Affective Balance Subscale total of 14 (positive moods just outweighing negative moods).

In cases such as Daniel's, autonomy takes on such importance as to raise the question of a basic lack of commitment to the marriage. Describing how his life has changed since the separation, he states, "It's more relaxed. I've always considered myself relaxed, but now I don't have someone asking [me] to give less of myself to my activities and asking me to do menial things. I hate to do menial things like take out the garbage." In outlining other reasons for the divorce, he remembers, "I was uptight about being a father. That's another reason for the divorce. . . . I even stopped sleeping with my old lady for fear of being a father. . . . I was a shit to her when she was pregnant. She had to call me at another lady's house to take her to the hospital the night she was going to have the baby."

In articulating the benefits of the separation, Daniel speaks at length: "I'm improved as a racer in terms of not being hassled about my training. And I've gotten into the kind of living space I've wanted for years, which she didn't. I like living in the condo. I have a lot of space in which to write my poems and build my body's endurance for motocross." Asked to specify what has been difficult about the separation, he mentions being apart from his child and "not being part of a family unit." It is for this reason that he occasionally thinks about reconciling with his wife, "because she's the mother of my daughter, not because I have very deep feelings about her."

It is relatively common for the men in this group to think about reconciliation, as if they believed of their wives, "she's blowing off steam; she'll come around." These men tend to be conditional in their approach to the idea of reconciliation and to focus on the need for the wife to change. Talking about getting back together, Daniel states during the baseline interview that "there is a chance, maybe in the future. She's finding I wasn't so bad, after all. . . . But she's smoking now and I could never live with someone who smokes. She'd definitely have to stop that." If reconciliation is to occur, it must be on his terms. He entertains some hope that this may happen. Describing how his wife has changed since the separation, he notes: "She has become more of a realistic person. She accepts me more as a human being now."

In short, at baseline, everything seems to be going well for Daniel. He is free from demands that previously hindered him in the pursuit of his interests and is living the kind of life he has long desired. He has some concern about being away from his daughter and no longer being part of a family. However, he has some hope that his wife may change and fully accept him, making a reconciliation possible.

At follow-up nearly three years later, Daniel still appears to be doing relatively well. He has continued to live in the condo, still devoting most of his time to poetry and racing. His Affective Balance score was 17 (positive moods clearly outweighing negative moods, an increase of three over baseline). He expresses overall enthusiasm for his life.

However, there are subtle signs that the flush optimism of several years earlier has begun to fade. Although he has plans to quit work soon, Daniel has still not carried out his plan to become a professional motorcyclist. He now checks 12 items from the Symptoms Checklist (well above the group mean), twice the number he marked at the first interview. In addition to what he reported at baseline, his feelings are now often hurt, he must do things slowly in order to avoid mistakes, others often annoy him, he is sometimes so depressed that it interferes with his ability to function, and he has trouble sleeping. He has made very few changes from baseline in the Adjective Rating List. However, he now rates "withdrawn" and "easily embarrassed," words he previously said did not apply to him at all, as highly descriptive of him.

Reasons for this change are hard to find. Daniel, in most of his responses, presents himself as an energetic and happy person. An occasional clue, however, does surface. He has recently increased the amount of time he spends with his daughter and wishes he could spend even more. However, when they are together, "she says 'I wish you and Mommy would have stayed together.' When a lady comes over to visit me, she says, 'Are you going to stay the night?' It seems important to her that her mother remarried this past December." Speaking of his ex-wife, he states, "she really needed somebody who wanted to take care of her. She's not really an independent person and I am, but she found someone very like her. She likes to come off that way [being independent] and actually that was one of the things that really attracted me to her. She seemed really strong but what it was was stubborn and self-directed." In spite of her remarriage, he does not completely rule out their getting back together, saying only that there is "very, very little" chance. He dates occasionally, has no "partner" and no prospects for or interests in marriage.

Daniel at follow-up is hard to read, like most men in the low situational/ high general control group. Some signs of decline, or at least failure to achieve expected improvement, are present, but hard to interpret. A common theme among this group seems to be a diffuse and only partially articulated sense of disappointment. The drive, the single-mindedness, the satisfying sense of having life on the run which has served them too well in their extramarital lives and which seemed to be serving them well in the marriage have failed either to preserve or to reestablish their home lives. Although affection for the ex-wife is reported to have long since died, there is a pronounced tendency to maintain some form of unfriendly attachment: prolonged haggling over the financial settlement, arguments over the children, a lingering anger that the ex-wife "bailed out" while the husband was going through a particularly difficult time professionally.

It is as if there were still an element of disbelief, an inability to fully accept that they were "fired" as husbands. Moderate confusion persists about how this has come to pass, how things could have gone so well and then gotten so messy. With few friends available for talking these kinds of concerns over with and an emphatic refusal to seek professional help, their own explanations must suffice. Daniel's reaction to a question concerning talking with others during the separation is typical: "She wanted me to but I felt we were both intelligent enough and if we couldn't work it out, a disinterested third party couldn't help." With no outside input, the confusion continues. With on-going emotional demands, such as those placed on Daniel by his daughter, this confusion may even intensify over time.

IMPLICATIONS FOR RESEARCH AND SERVICE

The results presented in this chapter underscore the importance of sex differences in coping with divorce and point out the need for further research into variations between men and women in the area of perceived control and adjustment to marital separation. Based on the formal data analysis and on impressions derived from reading cases, there is support for Krantzler's (1973) contention that women face separation straightforwardly, while men avoid or postpone facing the emotional demands of divorce. There is also evidence supporting Wallerstein and Kelly's (1980) claim that lack of a preexisting sense of control over finances and practical matters may disproportionately affect the long-term adjustment of women.

One intriguing finding was that women who cope like men and men who cope like women may do better. If, for simplicity, the tendency to face head-on the emotional demands of separation is designated the "female pattern" and the predilection towards focusing on practical concerns before and during separation is labeled the "male pattern," there is some suggestion in these findings that men who incorporate some of the "female pattern" and women who utilize some of the "male pattern" in coping with marital separation may have the best prospects for long-term adjustment.

In reviewing the elements in the composite measures for situational and general control, another topic with implications for service and research is the ways in which control has differing implications for adjustment to divorce and adjustment to marriage. Take, for example, social independence, treated here as a component of general control. It may be that independence from the spouse in this area bodes well for coping with divorce. It does not at all follow that social independence, at least as measured here, had positive implications for the adjustment of the respondent while married. Taking a vacation separately from the spouse might be indicative of a highly autonomous, well-functioning individual, free from the compulsion to share all possible recreation time with the partner. It might as likely indicate an insecure individual with poor negotiation skills, ill-prepared for the give-and-take of married life, who *has* to vacation alone or have no vacation at all. In this regard, past criticism of the individualistic bias of the locus of control research (Furby 1979) is germane. Although control in this study tended to be associated with adjustment, it is probably a mistake to assume a one-to-one correlation with psychological health and skills for successful living.

Regrettably lacking in this study was a measure of the respondent's satisfaction with the level of control reported. In reviewing cases, it became apparent that such information might help illuminate variations in adjustment. Many individuals who were high in general control, for instance, seemed pleased with that fact. Others, however, who found themselves experiencing higher levels of general control than they were accustomed to were quite unhappy. Future research should attend to this important variable.

Finally, although not examined at all in this study, the question of the stability of perceived control over time appears to have important implications in the study of the relationship between control and adjustment. Very little research on perceived control has been conducted using a longitudinal perspective, although locus of control, for instance, is conceived to be an enduring personality trait (Rotter 1990). It might be assumed that a variable such as the general control measure used in this study, which is predominantly focused on the area of marriage would be less stable over time than Rotter's (1966) Internal-External Locus of Control measure. No studies to date, however, appear to bear on this question. Also needed is process research to illuminate the fluctuations in situational control. The predictive value of situational control for the adjustment of men at the three-and-a-half year follow-up implies that this type of control was not highly unstable during the period measured, and suggests that research on control from a time perspective might entail hitherto unexpected complexity.

Summary

At least three groups of men and women have been identified who may be considered at risk with regard to long-term adjustment because of their patterns of situational and general control. For both men and women, those low in both types of control emerge as being at greatest risk. For women, those who were initially high in situational but low in general control—those who "rise to the occasion" appear also to be at risk. For men, those who were initially low in situational but high in general control, and who may appear to do relatively well in the months following separation, emerge at risk in the period three and a half years later. These findings substantiate the view that appreciable differences exist between the sexes in the relationship between perceptions of control and adjustment to divorce.

11

MINORITY ISSUES IN THE STUDY OF DIVORCE

Barbara Yee, David A. Chiriboga and Linda S. Catron

As we reviewed the analyses for this book, we found to our chagrin and dismay that we had fallen into a common analytic trap. Because we lacked large numbers of minority respondents, we generally "control" for the effect of minority status in our discussions. While controlling for minority status allows us to make broader generalizations about the findings, it also means that we have not, up to this point, paid particular attention to subgroup differences. To correct the omission, this chapter provides information about the fate of those in the sample who represented minority populations.

The specific groups we will be discussing include three that may not seem very surprising and one that is. First we will explore the ways African Americans, Hispanic Americans, and Asian Americans go through the divorce transition and highlight factors that predict their adaptation to divorce. Then we will turn to a group of people who revealed themselves to be homosexuals, but who were leaving heterosexual marriages.

Before examining the findings, we will highlight several major issues to consider when studying divorce among minorities, and also consider what is known about divorce in these groups.

THE STUDY OF MINORITY FAMILIES IN THE CONTEXT OF DIVORCE

An obvious starting place when considering any topic related to minority families is the question of cultural differences. Individuals often adopt distinctive beliefs and values from their cultural heritage about marriage, children and spousal relationships, and how to deal with or resolve family problems. For instance, cultural norms provide guidelines for marriage rules and prohibitions regarding marital fidelity or modes of communication (Maretzki 1977). Cultural norms also may dictate whether divorce is selected as a viable alternative for resolution of serious marital problems, and may also affect subsequent adaptation to the divorce process.

For certain cultural groups and especially among more traditional individuals, divorce may not be considered a possible escape from an unhappy marriage since cohesion of the family is maintained at all costs. For example, during the pilot phases of our study, informants told us that in traditional Bay Area Chinese families of the past, a divorce was impossible under normal circumstances. However, if the wife became visibly dysfunctional to the point of requiring institutionalization, this justified the necessity of divorce. In addition, if an individual from a traditional family chooses divorce and the family does not endorse this decision, they may not provide support during the divorce transition. In fact, steps may be taken to intervene.

Another issue to consider is the multiple stressors, such as racism and discrimination, experienced by many individuals from minority backgrounds. These stressors often translate into poorer resources, a further barrier for some of these individuals in their ability to cope with life's troubles. Their often disadvantaged status may make minorities more vulnerable to the problems associated with separation and divorce. For instance, the lower socioeconomic status of many minority women may place them at increased risk for poor adaptation because they lack the educational or financial resources that would assist in their adaptation (McCubbin and McCubbin 1988).

A third factor to consider is the increasing heterogeneity manifest in minority marriages over the last three decades. Overall, minority marriages have increasingly become more heterogeneous and focused on complementary characteristics rather than mere similarities (Maretzki 1977). American-born Asians have intermarriage rates as high as 50% or more (Kitano and Chai 1982; Kitano and Yeung 1982; Tinker 1982). Likewise, Mexican American outmarriage rates are over 50% in California, but are lower for Texas or New Mexico (Marguia and Cazares 1982). The potential for marital problems based upon cultural differences between the marital partners and subsequent adaptation is becoming increasingly evident.

DIVORCE AMONG MINORITY GROUPS

Despite the growing body of research on minority families and divorce little is known concerning divorce and adaptation among different minorities. Most of the empirical work simply examines the rates of divorce among minority groups in comparison to their white peers and calculated demographic risk factors associated with divorce. These studies find that blacks are at higher risk for marital separation and divorce. Hispanic, Asian and Pacific Islanders are at lower risk for marital instability. One can draw no conclusion about the rates of divorce for the American Indian community, but studies suggest that the rates of divorce for urban Indians are higher than for those living on the reservation (Staples and Mirande 1980). In a comparative study of marital instability trends among Mexican Americans, African Americans and Caucasian Americans from 1960 to 1980, based on census data for the Southwest, a trend of increasing marital dissolution during these years was found for all groups (Frisbie, Opitz and Kelly 1985). Mexican Americans had the lowest prevalence of marital instability and there was no convergence between their pattern and the trend found for Caucasian or African Americans. These patterns held despite controlling for age, age at marriage and socioeconomic status.

African Americans

To the extent that minority issues are addressed, the large majority of studies examine black and white differences in divorce rates. Staples (1985) attributes the instability of the African American family to a conflict between family ideology and structural conditions which prevent the African American male from fulfilling normative familial roles. He suggests that the roles for African American males in the family are restricted to economic provider and family leader; a majority of African American males have been unable to fulfill these roles due to limited access in employment opportunities. Other social characteristics place African Americans at higher risk for divorce. In comparison to Caucasian Americans, African Americans are more likely to live in urban areas, have greater independence of women, and marry or have children at an earlier age. In addition, African American wives tend to have a higher education and income level than their husbands (Cherlin 1981; Staples 1985).

In a study of husbands' marriage order and the stability of first and second marriages of Caucasian and African American women, Aguirre and Parr (1982) found that the most important predictor of unstable first marriages among women is whether the husband has prior divorces. This predictor is even stronger among African Americans. Albrecht, Bahr and Goodman (1983) report that Caucasians are less likely to experience marital dissolution than are African Americans in either first or second marriages. Second marriages of whites are more likely to end in divorce or separation than are first marriages, while the reverse is true for African Americans. African Americans may be more predisposed to divorce due to the higher prevalence of social characteristics that have been associated with marital instability, such as first marriages at younger ages and poverty (Teachman 1986).

Rankin and Maneker (1988) found that marriages that involve African American husbands and Caucasian wives were much shorter in duration and had fewer or no children. In addition, both partners were likely to have attained relatively high levels of education and husbands were more likely to have been married previously. Homogenous African American couples (i.e., black American husband and wife) were likely to spend more time from separation to divorce in comparison to the other combinations (i.e., African American husband—Caucasian wife, Caucasian husband—Caucasian wife, Caucasian husband—African American wife). As indicated in chapter 6, this longer duration between separation and divorce may have implications for better divorce adaptation.

In a study of child visitation patterns following separation in African American and Caucasian families, Isaacs and Leon (1988) report that: (1) African American respondents were less likely to have a regular visitation schedule; (2) African American fathers generally lived further away from their children following separation, a factor which helped explain why many essentially abandoned their families; (3) African-American women were more likely than white women to move in with their parents following separation; (4) African American women discussed the children less frequently with their former spouses; and (5) African American women were more likely than white women to be the ones who decided to separate. Frequency of visitation was best explained by factors other than race per se, such as mother's self-reliance, extended family support, the father's residential proximity and the decision to separate (Isaacs and Leon 1988).

Davis (1985) has examined competence and stress among African American and Caucasian middle-class respondents who were married or divorced. As was the case in our own research, she found that greater distance in time from separation to divorce was associated with decreased distress, but she also reports no association between control over the divorce and distress. Davis found no evidence of race differences in locus of control, coping style or social adjustment. Overall, her study suggests that middle-class African Americans resemble their Caucasian middle-class counterparts in divorce adjustment.

Hispanic Americans

Frisbie (1986) reports that a strong family orientation generally diminishes the likelihood that divorce is picked as a solution to marital problems. On the other hand, higher education and greater acculturation to the norms of American society were associated with greater likelihood to dissolve marriage for Hispanic Americans. In Frisbie's study of divorce in the southwestern United States, Mexican Americans were the least likely to divorce when compared to other Hispanic American groups, but highly educated Mexican Americans were more prone to divorce than less educated Mexican Americans. Cuban Americans mirror the divorce trends in the Caucasian population; Puerto Rican Americans had the highest probability of divorce. This variability of divorce among Hispanic Americans has been attributed to educational and acculturational differences in the acceptability of divorce as a solution to marital problems.

In a study which examines the mental health of single mothers, Wagner (1988a) found that Mexican Americans were less supportive of divorced or separated mothers. Mexican American women who were Catholic and whose fathers were in blue-collar occupations, felt they were criticized, were not supported and were more emotionally upset than a comparable group of Caucasian women. Wagner's findings suggest that there may be little support or even negative sanctions for divorcing Mexican American women who are from more traditional families. These conditions would make the divorce process and subsequent adaptation to the divorce even more difficult for Mexican American women.

Wagner (1988b) has also found that Mexican American and Caucasian American women have different networking styles. Caucasians had fewer relatives available for support and relied more heavily on their friends for support. The situation for Hispanic Americans was more complex. There were pronounced generational differences in the Mexican American sample. For the American-born generations, the friend network grew increasingly more important over time while the family network decreased in support. In contrast, Mexican-born women are more kin-oriented and may become more socially isolated because there are fewer relatives to rely upon and friendships do not provide adequate substitutions.

Asian and Pacific Islander Americans

Some time ago Romnzo Adams (1937) categorized a variety of ethnic groups on the basis of organizational features. Asians were categorized as members of cultures that traditionally had strict rules, regulations and expectations that resulted in an organized approach to life (Adams 1937). In contrast, the traditional attitudes of Hawaiians had fewer organizational restraints on their behavior than the Japanese or Chinese Americans. The implication is that the percentages of outmarriages and divorces would be smaller in the tightly controlled social groups such as Japanese or Chinese Americans than in less tightly controlled groups such as Hawaiian Americans.

Lind (1964), a student of Adams, did a study of interracial marriage and divorce rates in Hawaii for the years between 1958 to 1962. He found that the outmarriage divorce rates for Hawaiian, Korean, Puerto Rican, Filipino and Caucasian Americans were lower than for those couples where the partners were married to someone from their own ethnic group. In a further analysis of Lind's data, Sanborn (1977) demonstrates that divorce risk was higher for Caucasian women married to Chinese or Japanese American men. These latter two ethnic groups have traditionally had the lowest divorce rates in Hawaii. Blood (1969) suggests that the solidarity of family structure in these groups creates incompatibility between the traditional Chinese or Japanese American husband and his more emancipated Caucasian wife, and is one of the chief culprits for marital strife. The least divorce-prone marriages in Hawaii were of Caucasian men with Puerto Rican or Filipino American women. Sanborn attributes this to greater compatibility between sex roles in the family. Caucasian males married to more traditional wives have a higher likelihood of marital harmony.

In a panel study (1968) of first marriages and divorce in Hawaii, Schwertfeger found that outgroup marriages were generally more likely to end in divorce. There were no differences in the likelihood of divorce proneness for Hawaiian or part-Hawaiian American women, and Caucasian and Portuguese American men in outgroup marriages. Groups showing the lowest divorce rates are Japanese and Chinese Americans. There is also remarkable stability of ingroup Chinese American marriages—not a single marriage between two persons of Chinese ancestry ended in divorce in Hawaii over a nine-year period. Caucasian and Portuguese American males show the lowest divorce rates when they marry Chinese and Japanese American females. This pattern does not hold for Caucasian and Portuguese American women marrying Chinese American males.

Waldron, Ching and Fair (1986) studied children and their parents coming to a divorce clinic in Hawaii. They found that outmarriages failed earlier (i.e., in the first seven years) than inmarriages. Ingroup marriages stayed together longer but had an increasing tendency to fail after eight years. Depression was a common response among the parents who did not make the decision to divorce, whereas the divorce decision created relief among the parents who made the decision to divorce. Mothers with professional or managerial positions were less depressed and anxious, and more angry and relieved than mothers in other types of occupations. Generalizations to other samples of divorced individuals may be limited.

Iu (1982) found that the degree of ethnic identification and sense of economic independence for Chinese American women helped predict their level of marital satisfaction and their attitude toward divorce. Iu also reports that Chinese American women who held a strong ethnic identity were more likely to hold a conservative view on divorce, were more likely not to consider divorce in marital conflict situations and were more likely not to choose divorce as a solution to marital problems. Family violence and infidelity were conditions most likely to provoke considerations of divorce among Chinese American women. Iu's research highlights three points. First, more traditional Chinese women and their extended family would not consider divorce as an option for marital difficulties. Second, if divorce is undertaken, the more traditional Chinese American woman may have more difficulty adapting because she is torn between her traditional beliefs and the divorce decision. Third, more acculturated Chinese American women have a greater likelihood of accepting divorce as an alternative to serious marital difficulties.

While at first glance, this literature on divorce among Asian and Pacific Islanders seems contradictory, the patterns make intuitive sense but must be empirically tested. First, the four studies cited have been done at four disparate periods of time: Adams in 1937, Lind in 1964, Schwertfeger in 1968 and Waldron et al. in 1986. Cohort and generational factors, such as acceptability of outmarriages and stigma of divorce among Asian and Pacific Islander groups could account for wide variation in rate of outmarriage across these four studies. Second, the findings may not be contradictory at all but examine the rate of divorce in outmarriages at different levels of analysis (i.e., rates of outmarriage regardless of ethnicity and sex of marital partners). Thus, comparison between studies may not produce similar results. An intriguing hypothesis is that rates of outmarriage are dependent upon which cultural beliefs regarding sex roles in marriage are held by each marital partner. Therefore, overall rates of outmarriage divorce are dependent upon who is married to whom and each marital partner's sex role beliefs.

Existing Limitations in Research

Existing research on divorce among minority groups focuses upon the incidence of divorce proneness in these populations and ignores or overlooks how minority groups deal with this stress condition. Currently, we know that the cultural values or acculturation level, and the socioeconomic and educational status of individuals have a significant impact upon divorce adaptation. First, as mentioned before, cultural values which place more importance on family solidarity than the happiness of individual family members provide strong barriers to both the decision to divorce and to positive divorce adaptation. Cultural values also influence the types of social supports available for the divorcing individual and his or her children (Fine and Schwebel 1988). Second, low economic and educational resources inhibit many minority individuals' capacity to cope with divorce and its aftermath. The present chapter is an exploratory attempt to examine factors that relate to the divorce process and divorce adaptation for minority individuals.

DIVORCE: THE LAST STRAW OR RELIEF?

In our sample we had 243 Caucasian Americans, 25 African Americans, 11 Hispanic Americans, 8 Chinese Americans, 4 Japanese Americans, 6 Filipino Americans and 13 who were classified as "Other" (they included people from India, Pakistan, Iran, etc.). Eighteen Chinese, Japanese and Filipinos were combined to form a single Asian American category since their separate numbers were too small to be analyzed. Henceforth, in order to save space, we may periodically eliminate mention of "American" when discussing the ethnic groups but the reader should keep in mind that these are ethnic groups living in the United States.

The sex distribution of respondents among the ethnic groups varied.

There is a more equal distribution of males (42.4%) and females (57.8%) among the Caucasian and among the Hispanic Americans (54.5% male versus 45.5% female). In contrast, there were more female respondents in the African (20% male, 80% female) and Asian American subsamples (33.3% male, 66.7% female). The disproportionate numbers of females in the African and Asian subsamples may have significant implications for those groups and in our discussion of the divorce process and adaptation. This should be kept in mind while ethnic differences are discussed because the literature suggests that males and females vary in divorce adaptation.

There were significant educational differences between the ethnic groups. Caucasian Americans had higher educational status when compared to all minorities combined. Asian and Hispanic Americans had slightly lower educational status than Caucasians, while African Americans had significantly lower educational status than all other groups. The significant educational difference between Caucasian and minority respondents were attributed to the low educational status of African Americans. Minorities also had lower income than Caucasians in this sample. The widest disparity was between Africans and Caucasians. Hispanics were almost at parity with Caucasians, while Asians had lower income than Caucasians.

The reader should keep in mind that the Hispanic Americans in this sample are more highly educated and have higher incomes than the majority of their counterparts in the U.S. Hispanic American population. These characteristics of the Hispanic respondents, due in large part to the fact that the Hispanic community in northern California is made up of families who have lived in this part of the country for generations and exhibit relatively high levels of acculturation, have implications for the divorce process and adaptation. Higher education and income provide much-needed resources for the divorce process and subsequent adaptation.

The minority respondents were slightly older than their Caucasian American counterparts in this study. While the average age of the Caucasians was about 29, the African Americans averaged 32.0, the Hispanic Americans averaged 34.5, and the Asian Americans averaged 29.4. Minority respondents also had slightly more children than Caucasians in the sample. The Caucasians averaged 1.2, the Africans averaged 1.6, Hispanics averaged 2.8, and Asians 1.9. Hispanics had significantly more children than the Caucasian group.

As indicated earlier, the acceptance of divorce may vary across different ethnic groups. These differences could systematically have implications for the timing of the divorce process, as well as subsequent coping after the divorce decision is made. Although not significant statistically, minorities were more troubled by the divorce than Caucasians in the sample. There are two strikes against minorities holding traditional beliefs about marriage. First, there might be ambivalence concerning the correctness of the divorce decision during the divorce process. Second, family and friends holding traditional beliefs may not support the divorce decision or the individual who made that decision. Although there is no direct test of this hypothesis in our data set, other empirical studies (see review in Wagner 1988a and 1988b) and our case-study material (for example, see the case of Karen Lai presented in chapter 4) provide support for this notion.

Earlier chapters have suggested that ethnicity and its covarying influences may affect the divorce process and adaptation of minorities. The following section will detail some qualitative patterns which have been found between the Caucasian and minority subsamples, as well as differences between African, Hispanic and Asian American groups in this study.

Indicators of Mental Health Status

We first looked at levels of psychological symptoms among the ethnic groups. As indicated in the chapter on divorce stress and adaptation, women exhibited more symptoms than men and symptoms levels dropped significantly between the impact and follow-up phases of divorce. A median split of symptomatology was created for the entire sample. At impact a little more than half the Caucasian sample (54.7%) exhibited higher symptomatology. In contrast, 64% of African, 36.4% of Hispanics and 50% of Asian Americans exhibited higher symptomatology. It appears that Caucasians, Hispanics and Asians were at lower risk at baseline than the African Americans. The Hispanics in this sample were at lowest risk at baseline. Higher levels of symptomatology for African Americans may be partially attributable to the fact that 80% of this group was female and females report higher symptomatology in the whole sample, as well as in other studies (see chapter 3 for a review of this literature).

By follow-up, a little less than half the Caucasian American sample (46%) were in the high-symptomatology group. In contrast, 56% of African, 50% of Asian, and 63.6% of Hispanic Americans fell into the high-symptomatology group. This is a stark contrast to the picture at impact.

The complexity of these changes is more easily demonstrated by the pattern of ethnic group differences for mean number of symptoms across time for males versus females. Caucasian American males reported 8.9 symptoms at impact dropping to 7.5 symptoms at follow-up. Caucasian American females reported 10.3 symptoms at impact in comparison to 8.5 symptoms at follow-up. For males and females in the Caucasian sample, there was a decrease in the number of symptoms over time. The pattern was different for the ethnic groups. African American males reported 11 symptoms at impact and the number of symptoms increased to 13 at follow-up. African American females reported 16.2 symptoms at impact and then dropped to 15 symptoms at follow-up. Hispanic American males reported 9.5 symptoms at impact and then reported only 6.2 symptoms at follow-up. In contrast, Hispanic American females had 11 symptoms at impact but reported 13 symptoms at follow-up. Asian American males reported 9 symptoms at impact and at follow-up reported only 5.4. Their counterparts, Asian American females reported 12.7 symptoms at impact with no change at follow-up (12.8).

These results suggest that both Caucasian American males and females, and Hispanic and Asian American males experienced a decrease in symptomatology over a three-and-a-half-year period. Things improved for these groups. The case study of Bill Loudon, presented at the end of this chapter, illustrates how a Hispanic male adapted to his divorce.

In contrast, symptomatology increased for African American males and Hispanic American females, and did not improve for African and Asian American females. For these latter groups, the improvement we generally found among participants did not occur. The case of Nancy Nelson, presented at the end of this chapter, illustrates the plight of an African American mother's struggle to cope with the aftermath of her divorce.

Another indicator of divorce adaptation that has been used in this study is the Bradburn Happiness Scale. Median splits were created for the Bradburn overall happiness scale. At impact, only one-fourth the Caucasian sample fell in the happier category (24%). The minority respondents (i.e., Africans = 16%, Hispanics = 0%, Asians = 16.7%) in this sample were less happy at impact than Caucasians. By follow-up, the still-significant ethnic differences in happiness grew smaller. Nearly half of the Caucasian sample said that they were happy (47.7%). Happiness grew for minority respondents as well (i.e., blacks = 36%, Hispanics = 36.4%, Asians = 33.3%). These trends may hint at ethnic differences in the acceptability of divorce. Initially, the minority respondents and their social supports may have felt ambivalent about the divorce decision and this had a dramatic negative impact on the happiness of the minority respondents. With the passage of time and healing that time provides, the minority respondents became happier and as a result the ethnic differences grew smaller.

Childhood Stressors and Divorce

One way in which ethnic groups can differ is in earlier life experiences that may predispose them to becoming at higher risk for maladaptation in the adult years. As argued in chapter 2, childhood stress may influence the individual's subjective appraisal of the stressfulness experienced in later events and the nature of adult attachments. Childhood stressors have also been discussed as having both positive and adaptive, as well as maladaptive or negative influences on adult development.

In the prediction of adaptation we found, women who identified themselves as members of an ethnic group, as well as women with lower incomes, reported more symptoms at follow-up. One other factor that seems to make a difference, at least insofar as ethnic status is concerned, is childhood stress. African Americans in comparison with Caucasians in the sample had significantly more childhood stressors. In this sample, African respondents were separated on bad terms with their parents (31.8%) in higher proportions than Caucasians (10.5%), were more likely to be adopted (18.2%) than Caucasians (1.3%), had to go to work earlier in life to support the family (22.5%) than Caucasians in the sample (5.4%) and experienced parental separation (22.7%), absence (31.8%) or death of a parent (31.8%) to a greater extent than Caucasians (13%, 16.3%, and 14.2%, respectively).

African Americans also experienced other childhood stressors to a greater extent than Caucasians, but these differences did not quite reach significance. African Americans witnessed more arguments between their parents (40.9%) than the Caucasian respondents (29.3%). African Americans in the sample were severely punished as children (18.2%) to a greater extent than the Caucasians (7.9%). A greater proportion of African Americans had parents who were divorced (31.8%) and remarried (31.8%) in comparison to the Caucasians (16.3% and 15.2%, respectively). African Americans also experienced the death of a sibling to a greater extent (9.1%) than Caucasians in the sample (5.9%).

Their greater experiences with childhood stressors may have led African Americans in this sample to be at significantly higher risk for both the incidence of divorce and maladaptation to family crises. African Americans were more likely to have had fewer parental social supports while growing up and their relationships with parents were less stable than those of their Caucasian counterparts. During childhood, more African Americans were required to contribute financially to their families, indicating that their family of origin was less economically stable than that of Caucasian respondents.

Unlike the African Americans, Hispanic Americans had about the same levels or less stress in childhood. The only significant difference between Hispanics and Caucasians is that Hispanics were more likely to have worked during their childhood (30%) than the Caucasian respondents (5.4%). Although not quite significant, we also found that Hispanic Americans experienced separation on bad terms with parents to a greater extent (20%) than Caucasians (10.5%) and were more likely to experience the absence of a parent than Caucasians in the sample (20% versus 16.3%).

While only three childhood stressors put Hispanic Americans at slightly greater risk for later maladaptation in adulthood, Hispanics experienced fewer childhood stressors than Caucasian respondents in the following areas: arguments between respondent and parents (20% versus 31.8%), severe punishment (0% versus 7.9%), parents divorced (0% versus 16.3%), parent remarriage (10% versus 15.1%), separation from parents (10% versus 13%), death of a sibling (0% versus 5.9%). In total, Hispanics in the current sample experienced less childhood stressors that would put them at greater risk for maladaptation in adulthood.

The prevalence of childhood stressors for Asian Americans was similar to that of the Hispanic Americans. In three areas they reported more stress. Asians had to go to work during their younger years much more frequently (35.3%) than their Caucasian counterparts (5.4%), had more parents who divorced (23.5%) than Caucasians (16.3%), and experienced absence from parents (29.4%) to a greater extent than Caucasians (16.3%).

Asian Americans experienced fewer childhood stressors than Caucasians in two areas: arguments between parents (17.6% versus 29.3%), and arguments between respondent and parents (23.5% versus 31.8%). These data suggest that there might be some Asian cultural constraints which put a damper on conflict resolution. Yee and Hennessey (1982) suggest that there is an avoidance of direct conflict and confrontation in more traditional individuals.

If one accepts the finding that the presence of certain childhood stressors predicts maladaptation in adulthood, then African Americans are the highest risk group in comparison to Caucasians in the sample. A portion of the African American sample experienced childhood stressors that have been linked to a steeling effect on subsequent adult adaptation (i.e., parental death or death of a sibling, see chapter 2 for detailed discussion) and a significant number of these individuals have lower symptomatology. Hispanic and Asian Americans are at lower risk for maladaptation as predicted by childhood stressors. Other risk factors in the divorce process and adaptation will be discussed in the following sections.

Divorce Stress and Adaptation

Adaptation is linked not only to childhood stressors, but to current levels of positive and negative stressors. In the current sample, a median split was obtained for those who experienced higher or lower amounts of positive life events. At impact, Caucasians experienced significantly more positive life events (53.1%) than minority respondents (37.8%). African Americans were least likely to experience positive life events (24%), Hispanic Americans had a little more (36.4%), and Asian Americans experienced significantly more positive life events in comparison to other minority respondents (44.4%).

At follow-up, approximately the same proportion of Caucasian respondents experienced high positive life events. More African Americans experienced positive life events at follow-up (36%), as well as Hispanic Americans (45.5%) and Asian Americans (50%). Overall, it appears that minorities were more likely to experience positive life events at follow-up, but none had reached the levels of positive experiences reported by Caucasians.

An inspection of negative life events revealed that at impact phase slightly more than half of the Caucasian sample experienced high negative life events (51%). Proportionally more Hispanic Americans experienced high negative life events (72.7%), slightly more than half of the African Americans experienced high negative life events (56%), while Asian Americans had the fewest respondents falling into the high negative life events group (38.9%).

At follow-up, proportionally fewer of the Caucasians fell into the high negative life events category (42.8%). The proportions of respondents who fell into this category at follow-up also decreased for all minority groups (blacks = 44%, Hispanics = 45.5% and Asians = 27.8%). Hispanics initially seemed at greater risk of experiencing high levels of negative life events but this group became closer to the other ethnic groups by follow-up.

As indicated in the chapter 3, classifying respondents based upon level of exposure to positive versus negative stressors created a useful typology. Caucasians fell equally into the Winners and Losers category (24%). At first interview, minority respondents were more likely to fall into the Losers category (low positive and high negative stress) and were somewhat less likely to fall into the Winners category (high positive and low negative stress).

Half of the Hispanic American (50%) and nearly half of the African American sample (45.5%) fell into the Losers category, as did nearly one-fifth of the Asian American respondents (17.6%). Almost one-fourth of the Asian respondents (23.5%) fell into the Winners category. One-third of Hispanics fell into the Winners category, while less than a fifth of African Americans (18.2%) fell into this category. These differences emphasize that minority groups vary in their exposure to negative and positive stressors.

As detailed in chapter 3, the African American Tina Tighter is an excellent example of a minority woman who experienced many negative stressors, few positives ones and moreover little improvement or hope of improvement in her life over time. Childhood stressors, abuse of her children by her former spouse and poor finances were significant features of this sad story.

The situation was also rough for Maria Martinez, but she had personal resources to cope with the aftermath of divorce. Unlike Tina Tighter, Maria was a student in veterinary medicine when we first interviewed her and she went on to become a doctor of veterinary medicine. These accomplishments demonstrate high personal resources, such as motivational and intellectual skills, that can be used in adaptation to divorce. Chances are that Maria wouldn't have as many financial difficulties as Tina but things were not all rosy for Maria. In order to fulfill her dreams, Maria moved to a new city but this change created a significant geographic distance between her and her family. Maria can no longer engage in her "absolute favorite thing" on a regular basis: being with her parents and siblings. Like minorities from intimate families, Maria is cut off from the center of her life and social support system that she identifies as being so critical to her well-being. This physical separation from her family, the mainstay of her social support, makes her sad.

By follow-up the portion of black respondents in the Losers category had gone up (53.3%) but had fallen considerably for the Hispanics (9.1%) and Asians (6.3%). The portion of Winners has gone up slightly in the African (20%), Hispanic (36.4%) and Asian American subsamples (25%). These trends indicate that experiences with positive stressors generally have changed over time, with things improving for the minorities over these years. The African Americans stood apart from the Hispanic and Asian Americans because the proportion of Losers increased rather than decreased over time for African Americans. One possible explanation for this trend is that the African Americans had poorer personal resources such as education and income that would assist them in moderating their experiences with negative stressors and acquiring positive stressors.

Coping Strategies in Divorce

As indicated earlier, minorities experience more negative stressors and less positive stressors over their lifetime. The literature suggests that reactions to stressors are not merely defined by the objective number and type of stressors, but indicate that personality and coping strategies learned over an individual's lifetime and mediators, such as social support and social resources, may systematically intervene to produce an individual's stress reactions. The following section will highlight some of the major trends in predominant coping strategies for minority respondents in the aftermath of divorce.

As defined in chapter 4, certain profiles of coping styles provide useful information about how successful individuals may be in dealing with life and the divorce process. Two of the coping styles, Action Copers and Supercopers, were high on the situation-altering factors of Help Seeking and Active Mastery. It may be remembered that the *Action Copers* were low on the strategies of Situation Redefining and Stress Management. A little over 15% (15.1%) of the Caucasian sample were Action Copers who actively sought help from a variety of people and tried to actively master stressful situations but used little Situation Redefining and Stress Management techniques to deal with their stress. The Hispanic Americans were represented in this group in higher portions as well (18.2%). Asian Americans used Action Coping less frequently (14.3%) and African Americans were under-represented in this coping style (6.7%).

Supercopers were high on all types of coping. Hispanic Americans were the Supercopers of the sample with over one-fourth adopting this technique to deal with their stress (27.3%). Again, 15% of Caucasians used this technique to deal with their stress. A small percent of Asian Americans (14.3%) and an even smaller percent of African Americans (6.7%) adopted this coping pattern to deal with their stress.

Mystics' coping styles represented a small segment of the sample. Mystics were highest in their perception that stress was a growth experience and high on Fatalism and Emotive Action, but low to intermediate on all other strategies. Only 8.5% of the Caucasian sample adopted this technique. No minority group used this technique to handle its stress.

The *Balanced* coper fell in the intermediate range on all strategies. Only 11.6% of Caucasians, Hispanics (9.1%), Africans (6.7%) and Asians (7%) adopted this technique.

The *Noncopers* were lowest or tied for the lowest on all strategies. In other words they did nothing to deal with their stress. They were intermediate on self-blame. The Noncoper strategy was not popular among Caucasians in this sample (7.5%), Africans (6.7%) or Asians (0%). But, nearly one-fifth of Hispanic Americans adopted this technique to deal with stress.

Stoics were high on Fatalism and Emotive Action, and highest on stress management by cognitive control. These Stoics were most likely of all types to use selective ignoring as a coping strategy and which has been found to be the least effective mediator of stress (Pearlin and Schooler 1978). The Asian Americans were most likely to fall into this coping pattern (21.4%), with the African Americans following a close second (20%). No Hispanic Americans and few Caucasians (11.6%) fell into this coping pattern.

Karen Lai is a good example of a respondent who fell into the Stoics category. Cultural and experiential factors may account for a good proportion of people who fell into this category. Many Asian cultural, philosophical or religious tenants encourage a sense of fatalism in people socialized under these beliefs. For instance, a sense of mastery is correlated with the degree of American or Westernized cultural beliefs. Likewise, a sense of fatalism or low mastery is correlated with the degree of Asian cultural beliefs (see Yee [1982] for review). Control over one's emotions has also been linked with Asian cultural tenants such as those of Confucius. It is difficult to determine whether Karen Lai was socialized under these cultural conditions or whether she became that way as a result of her life experiences. Living in poverty and seeing no hope for a better future, coupled with socialization that encourages this philosophy of life, could generate and perpetuate a sense of fatalism in these unfortunate individuals.

Imaginative Escapers were relatively high on situation-altering and situation-redefining strategies but were extremely high on Self-Blame and Wish-fulfilling Fantasy. Note that these characteristics have been associated with problems in adaptation to divorce. Asians fell into this coping pattern in the highest proportion (28.6%), followed by Caucasians (13.1%), Hispanics (9.1) and least by blacks (6.7%).

An examination of the *Unclassified* coping category revealed that minority respondents are overrepresented in this miscellaneous category. This category represented all the people who didn't fit into the other classification categories, including nearly half of the African American respondents (46.7%), followed by Asian Americans (21.4%), Hispanic Americans (18.2%) and Caucasians (17.6%). Perhaps a closer examination of the patterns may reveal other coherent coping styles. It is not so mysterious that many of the minorities fell into this category because the fit does not always work if the categorization system was developed on largely Caucasian samples but applied to different cultural groups.

Self-Concept of Divorcing Persons

As detailed in chapters 7 and 8, the divorce process and subsequent adaptation to this nonnormative transition may have a significant impact on the divorcing person's self-concept. The following section highlights some ethnic differences in the self-concept of these respondents.

Images of the self that have been identified as a personal resource during the divorce process are: Desirable-Engageable Self, Masterful Self and Socially Skilled Self. The only significant difference between Caucasians and minorities are perceptions concerning the Masterful Self. Similar to trends previously reported for locus of control (i.e., feelings of having much personal control or feeling that one is masterful versus control to be outside one's self being or feeling less masterful) ethnic differences in the Masterful Self were found. Minorities (46.79%) felt less masterful than Caucasians (50.68%), with African Americans feeling the least masterful (43.90%). Hispanics (47.70%) and Asian Americans (47.94%) felt higher mastery than African Americans, but lower than Caucasians. Minority males were the only group to have grown in their feelings of mastery from impact to follow-up, but this was not large enough to produce statistical significance because minority males were the exceptions in the sample. In general, and as found in chapter 7 for the whole sample, there is some general overall stability in the self-image over time.

There were no significant ethnic differences for the images of the self that have been identified as resources during the divorce process, except for

Masterful Self. The picture is different when one examines the ethnic group differences in self-concept that have been associated with poorer adaptation.

Images of the self that are reflective of deficits in the self-concept that were included in this study are: Negative Self, Dominant Self, Incompetent Self, Vulnerable Self, Hostile Self, Self-Oriented, Self-Criticism and Ego Diffusion.

There are significant differences between the Caucasian and minority respondents concerning negative feelings about themselves. Minority respondents were significantly more likely to have a negative self-image than their Caucasian counterparts. African Americans felt more negatively about themselves than Hispanic or Asian Americans. African American females, in particular, felt extremely negative about themselves compared to other groups.

Minority respondents were significantly less likely to describe themselves as having dominant aspects of the self. Hispanics felt the least dominant, with African Americans in the middle, then Asian Americans feeling the most dominant in comparison to other minorities, but still significantly less than the Caucasian group. Although not significant statistically, minority women felt more vulnerable than all other groups, with Asian Americans feeling most vulnerable, then African Americans, and Hispanic Americans feeling the least vulnerable.

Although not significant, trends suggest nonetheless that minority respondents felt more incompetent than their Caucasian counterparts. Hispanic Americans felt the most incompetent, then African Americans, while Asians felt the least incompetent of the minority groups. This suggests that a substantial segment of the minority population undergoing the divorce process may experience feelings of low self-esteem and might benefit from clinical intervention. The patterns of self-images presented by some of the minority respondents indicate that minority individuals undergoing divorce may have a higher vulnerability to stressors during the divorce process and may need special assistance to cope with this transition.

Ego Diffusion Describes Ambiguity and Diffusion in the Self-Image. It appears that there were no significant ethnic differences in Ego Diffusion at time one, but at time two the minority respondents were significantly more confused and unsure about their self-image than the Caucasian group. The significant upward trend in Ego Diffusion among minority respondents suggests that at least some minority individuals became more confused about themselves over time and may require assistance in their adaptation to divorce. Many of these minority respondents were still traversing through the liminal stage in divorce adaptation and are at greater risk for psychological disturbance.

Clinical literature and an earlier chapter has highlighted parental identification as having a critical role in adjustment. As described in chapter 8, high parental identifiers had less negative feelings about themselves and saw themselves as socially skilled. Nearly half of the African American respondents (46.7%) saw little similarity between either parent and themselves. More than half of the Asian American respondents (54%) felt this same way, while just over one-fourth of the Hispanic Americans saw low similarity between either parent and themselves.

In contrast, nearly a third of the Caucasian sample highly identified with both parents. About a fourth of the African American (26.7%) and Hispanic American (27.3%) samples fell in this category. Only 8% of the Asian American sample highly identified with both parents. This suggests that perhaps there might be some acculturative differences, intergenerational distancing or cultural conflicts between immigrant parents and children for the Asian American sample. As a result, normative parental identification processes break down between generations for these families. Foreign-born parents are seen as very different from a person born and raised in the United States or who has been socialized in American culture. The potential for intergenerational conflict is great because different rates of acculturation occur and create wide intergenerational gaps in these immigrant families (Yee and Hennessey 1982; Yee 1989).

As seen in the case presented in chapter 8, Cheryl Chang was a mixture of Asian and Western influences. Cheryl's case illustrates the wide generational gap in many Asian families living in the United States. Cheryl didn't receive support from her parents during the divorce process, and describes her former spouse and father in strikingly similar but negative terms. These characteristics could be described, although somewhat stereotypically, as traditional Asian male gender roles. Cheryl is rejecting the traditional Asian gender roles and interaction patterns that accompany these beliefs. She claims to be a feminist and that her mother doesn't understand these beliefs or behaviors associated with these beliefs. Cheryl solves these cultural issues by establishing a live-in relationship with a Caucasian American male.

Views of Social Supports

The literature on social support suggests that adequate social support buffers individuals from the extreme negative consequences of the divorce transition and aids in adaptation to divorce. In work conducted mainly with African American samples, minority individuals dealing with marital discord, separation and divorce have been reported as having more support than their Caucasian counterparts because marital dissolution in these minority families is quite common. One implication is that there would be more support for single parents and divorced individuals in the African American community; whether this greater social support comes from African cultural roots, family structures or adaptational strategies of African Americans living in the United States is yet to be identified.

We used several indicators to study social resources from a minority perspective. As we found in chapter 9, an active network, including whether or not the individual had a confidant, had a significant influence on the impact of divorce on the individual. There were several differences in the active network of minority respondents. Visits to relatives and proximal availability of parents were not significantly different between minority and Caucasian respondents but minorities were more likely to have parents living nearby. Fewer minorities reported proximity to parents at time two, which may indicate that the importance of parent proximity during the crisis resolution phase was more significant for minority respondents than for Caucasians. The frequency of mentioning that parents lived nearby didn't change from impact to follow-up for Caucasians. Having parental social support during marital dissolution may have a cultural component because marriage can be such a central part of an adult person's life, especially for Hispanic and Asian cultural groups.

Minorities had slightly more relatives living nearby than Caucasians. A component of social support is family cohesion. There is no evidence that minorities suffer from more family dissolution than Caucasians in the sample. Minorities and Caucasians were about equal in the incidence of divorce among their parents and their siblings.

Having a confidant is a critical predictor of life satisfaction and coping with divorce successfully. There were significantly more friends available to Caucasian respondents than to minorities in the sample at impact, but this lessened by the second contact. At follow-up there were more friends living nearby for the minority group than at impact; the situation for Caucasians in the sample stayed relatively the same. The significant difference among ethnic groups narrowed at follow-up. By then, minority respondents found a confidant or friends to provide social support.

Another indicator of social support is whether the divorced individual is currently dating. Although not a significant difference, fewer minorities were dating at first contact. All these trends indicate that Caucasians had a larger social support system at impact for both romantic and platonic friendships than minorities, but these differences grew smaller at follow-up.

Overall the results indicated that minorities had significantly less social supports during the impact phase than their Caucasian counterparts in the study. This difference shrunk at follow-up by which point the social supports of minorities had improved in both quality and quantity.

Control over Divorce

Control has often been reported to play a powerful role in mitigating stress effects. Control over the divorce might be such a mediator, as indicated in chapter 10. In brief review, two categories of control, general and situational, have been linked with adaptation. General control is conceptualized as an aspect of personality, but has mainly been defined as perceptual control rather than actual control. In contrast, situational control is seen as control over specific problems or in specific situational contexts or spheres. For instance, control over one's ability to perform well in problem solving versus control over one's health.

The relationship between types of control and divorce adaptation we found complex and the current literature does not reflect this complexity. The literature indicates that control over the separation is associated with successful adaptation to divorce. Little or no relationship is seen between general control and divorce adaptation except indirectly by influencing an individual's coping strategies to handle life's problems.

When we compared minority and Caucasian respondents with regard to general control and control over the marital separation, the differences were not quite significant. However, minority respondents felt less general control than Caucasian respondents. That minorities felt less general control than their Caucasian counterparts mirrors the result in studies that examine general control in a variety of ethnic groups (see review in Yee 1982). The lack of significant ethnic differences found may be due to the nature of the sample. Hispanic and Asian Americans came from primarily middle- to upper-middle-class and more highly educated populations—factors linked to a more internalized general control. Hispanic Americans in this sample felt the least general control, African Americans fell somewhere in the middle, with Asian Americans feeling more general control than the other minority groups, but still less than their Caucasian peers.

Surprisingly, Caucasian and minority respondents were about equivalent in their control over the marital separation. Both Asian and Hispanic Americans felt that they had slightly more control over the decision to separate than their Caucasian peers. Blacks and Caucasians had roughly the same amount of control over the decision to separate.

These trends, although not significant, suggest that minority respondents fell into a pattern of control that was associated in chapter 10 with lower morale and more symptoms, coupled with poorer adjustment over time. Minority respondents fit the pattern of lower general control coupled with high situational control leading to considerable unhappiness at having made the decision to separate, but having few resources to deal with being divorced and/or being a single parent. Minority women in the sample fit this pattern much more closely than minority men. Having higher general control as a significant aspect of one's personality prior to separation leads these individuals to have more effective coping skills and as a result they are less at risk for poor divorce adaptation.

Issues for Heterosexual Marriage and Gay Divorce

Diminishing sanctions against homosexuality and gay lifestyles in our society may result in a lower incidence of "heterosexual" marriage involving a bisexual or gay partner and a higher prevalence of divorce resulting from such marriages when they do occur. However, a countertrend may be appearing. In a book entitled *Uncommon Lives: Gay Men and Straight Women* Whitney (1990) discusses why straight women are deliberately choosing to marry gay men. Whitney suggests that these women handle loneliness by marrying gay men, but there are no empirical studies which tell us how prevalent this trend may be. An examination of the literature reveals an absence of empirical work in this area. The meaning of divorce and subsequent correlates of adaptation to divorce may be quite different for heterosexual versus homosexual divorcées.

The majority of research examines the impact of parental homosexuality in child custody cases and does not focus on the divorce process, except as it relates to child custody, nor on divorce adaptation of either the homosexual or heterosexual partner. The large majority of studies that focus on issues dealing with child custody and status of the children do underscore the additional problems faced by homosexual parents.

Kleber, Howell and Tibbits-Kleber (1986) reviewed the literature on the impact of parental homosexuality on child development. The authors conclude that there is no consistent evidence to support the view that parental homosexuality has detrimental effects on child development. Moreover, Lewis (1980) found that marital discord and consequent divorce were more upsetting than finding out that their mother was gay. Lewis does state that it is difficult to separate the impact of divorce from the impact of the mother's lesbianism because denial of homosexuality may bias results.

In a comparative study of heterosexual and lesbian mothers, Pagelow (1980) found that lesbian mothers felt oppressed to a greater extent than heterosexual mothers because they experienced conflicts or were more at risk for potential conflicts regarding child custody, housing and employment discrimination. There are strong negative outcomes for homosexual females once separated or divorced because their gay lifestyle is more evident and creates problems with the heterosexual world.

Gay lifestyle is also problematic for gay fathers. Having children puts them at a disadvantage in a culture that covets a free lifestyle (Pagelow 1980). Gay fathers have more restrictions on their time and with their finances and living arrangements, especially if they have custody or are restricted by visitation rules. This could put gay fathers at a significant disadvantage in the gay world. Historically, fatherhood and its accompanying responsibilities were considered stigmatizing in the male homosexual culture. The stigmatizing effect of having children may now be overshadowed by the spectre of the AIDS epidemic.

Empirical Patterns in the Divorce Process and Adaptation among Gays

In our study there were nine persons who identified themselves as being gay, of whom none were members of minority groups. This might be attributable to the stigma attached to homosexuality by many minority communities. As a group, the homosexuals were slightly more educated, had slightly more income than heterosexuals and had significantly fewer children. There were no significant differences between the homosexual and heterosexual respondents on symptomatology at baseline. At follow-up the homosexual respondents demonstrated a slight increase in symptoms as contrasted to the heterosexuals who showed a significant decline in symptomatology. This divergence in trends produced a significant difference and led us to conclude that the risk for poorer adjustment is higher for the homosexuals than their heterosexual peers in the aftermath of divorce. It is very difficult to tease apart the effects of divorce versus the negative effects of a more public display of the gay lifestyle. As highlighted earlier, lesbian mothers may experience much job and housing discrimination if the public becomes aware of their homosexuality. Herek (1989) sees a trend of increasing antigay hate crimes.

Gays in the sample were hassled by their spouse and neighbors slightly more often than their heterosexual counterparts. These hassles could be a result of child custody and visitation or housing discrimination issues. On the more positive side, they were less hassled by finances, time pressures and social activities than heterosexuals in the sample.

There were no significant differences between homosexuals and heterosexuals in happiness at the first contact, but at follow-up gays in the sample were slightly happier than heterosexuals. Gays in the sample experienced slightly more negative stressors and significantly more positive stressors at follow-up than heterosexuals in the sample, indicating that their lives had improved over time. This trend makes sense since dissolving a heterosexual marriage should allow freer expression of self-identity and of lifestyle than would have been the case in their married life.

Illustration of this last point is provided by Ambrose Pierce. As presented in chapter 3, Ambrose is a Winner in the Stress Typology. Life for Ambrose had been pretty noneventful while in his heterosexual marriage. His life had changed significantly after his divorce. Once he revealed his gay self, he was much happier and seemed to blossom. The case study of Ambrose Pierce's adaptation to divorce was typical of gays who were leaving a heterosexual marriage.

CASE STUDIES: MINORITY LIVES

In general, the minorities experienced greater difficulty in adapting to the divorce process for reasons that may be linked to factors such as histories of childhood stress that may create life-long problems in adaptation and attachments, fewer resources, fewer social supports, lower education and occupational levels and more negative life events. Many of the cases that have been reviewed in previous chapters document these problems. Emmy Lou Danford is a case in point. Obviously not all minority group members are devastated by divorce, and the two cases to be presented here are of minority respondents who showed strengths as well as weaknesses. The first case is of a Hispanic man and the second of a black woman.

Bill Loudon: The Best is Yet to Come

Bill Loudon is a tall and thin 50-year-old Mexican American who manages a postal station. Like many of the northern California Hispanics, Bill is well educated with a B.A. as well as a number of refresher courses specific to his work. He says the most important aspect of his work is the gratification of being able to provide a finished product. At follow-up he reported considerable upward mobility in his career.

Bill reports a high number of childhood stresses, including a long separation from his parents when under 13, having to work to help support his family, separation from his father due to desertion, and the frequent absence of his mother. His Life Evaluation Chart, however, does not reflect any perceived childhood stress.

Bill's troubles did not end with childhood. As a young adult he endured a major stress in adulthood—his first wife died after ten years of marriage and left him with two sons. Later, after 10 years of single parenthood, Bill at the age of 47 married a 30-year-old woman of European descent. After only two and a half years Bill and his new wife are separating. According to Bill, the decision to separate was based on "a series of events which showed each of us our inability to respect each other." Most specifically, Bill complains about "my wife's demands on my time—be home or else, false accusations of infidelity, and arguments over nothing." Another reason Bill cites for the marital separation is "My children from my first marriage—the friction, arguments, animosity, jealousy between them and my wife."

At the first interview Bill describes the separation as involving "a traumatic change. The adjustments have been difficult. There has been loneliness, inconveniences including more responsibility for myself in home duties, and no companionship." He reports feeling more distant from others and very often feels that he is feeling without anyone to talk to about himself.

Although Bill is very troubled by the separation, he reported only four psychological symptoms at the first interview and two at the second. As he looks back on his life, Bill talks about not only the stresses but also how much he has grown from having to deal with loss. In this he seems to demonstrate the strengthening influence that successful resolution of earlier experiences can have.

Other strengths that are evident in Bill's life include his ability to create a more harmonious relationship with his former wife, begin dating, continue his interest and hobbies, and develop a successful career. Although the separation was "very stormy," even by the first interview he feels "no animosity or bad feelings—everything was very neutral." In fact, he describes a meeting to discuss support money as being "friendly, conciliatory, altruistic. Just a casual get-together." Asked if there is a chance of reconciliation, Bill said: "Our personal good feelings for each other haven't been completely demolished. There is still a chance. She has requested a reconciliation, but I have not agreed to it." Instead, Bill enumerates some of the benefits of separating, such as "the peace of mind" and "the freedom of movement" and "the latitude to make decisions without having to consider anyone except myself."

Bill began dating even before the separation and is now going out with two women. Asked to describe the one he likes the best, he said: "I met Jill before my marriage and we were friends. We renewed the relationship and it became a more intimate relationship after separation." He likes the fact that there are "No heavy responsibilities and that he enjoys feeling good being around her," enjoys her companionship very much and the mutual satisfaction of sex. "Sex during marriage was often an imposition on me. Now I don't feel obligated to perform."

In addition to dating, Bill has a fairly large social network to call upon. He said that he and his sons are closer now and that "there is more understanding and communication." About four times a month, Bill visits with parents, brother/sisters, aunts/uncles, and cousins. He gets together with one of his four friends about twice a month. Bill also reported having both a cousin and a friend as confidants.

Another strength Bill brings to the divorce process is his goals and his interests. His goals for the next years are to: "completely readjust my personal life, travel, simplify my life with less involvement in obtaining positions, and possessions." He enjoys reading contemporary literature, politics, and fiction. He enjoys the "ability to leave the present and get into someone else's thoughts." His second favorite thing is to "listen to music, classical guitar music" and enjoy the "personal good feelings."

By the second interview Bill can report being promoted to the central post office and has been traveling quite a bit more. Now he is not at all troubled by the divorce and he thinks his life is much better than that of other divorced persons. He is "pretty happy" on the Bradburn Scale and felt pleased and proud several times during the past week. He sees his ex-spouse every two months but does not think there is a chance of reconciliation. He has been dating the same person for over three years now; in fact, she is the same person he described at our first interview. He is not sure if he would consider marrying Jill, but feels certain a marriage with her would be better than his last one. He feels the best is yet to come.

Nancy Nelson: A Survivor

A superficial examination of Nancy Nelson's life would suggest she has very little going for her. Nancy is a 40-year-old, unemployed African American who dropped out of high school to marry her childhood sweetheart. The mother of four children ages 10, 13, 16 and 20, she reports 16 psychological symptoms at the first interview and says she visited the doctor 100 times in the last year, for her "nerves," foot surgery and a host of other problems. Although Nancy was willing to answer all the questions, the interviewer had to repeat and explain many of the questions because Nancy had problems understanding the meaning of words.

In contrast to these details, she comes across as vibrant and full of life. She is slim and tall, and styles her long black hair beautifully. Nancy wears a pants suit, high heels, and has a confident walk and air about her. She acts very relaxed and comes across as a woman who has control of her life. She was, in fact, the one to initiate the divorce. Her decision was made six months before actually separating, allowing her time for anticipatory coping. She recalls that her greatest difficulty was "Trying to make up my mind whether I wanted the divorce or not and I kept coming back to the same answer: 'Yes!' "

When asked what kinds of things influenced her decision to separate, Nancy says it was "Arguments. There was no communication. That's it. If you can't communicate, you can't have a marriage. You can't deal with arguments, disagreements. I prefer it to be a 50-50 thing, but you can't find a man you can do this with." She also feels she "wasn't recognized as a wife. I felt like a robot. We couldn't communicate or have any understanding. He acted like he was always right. I have a chronic illness. He resents me seeing the doctor regularly."

It was not until the follow-up interview, however, that Nancy reveals the most important reasons for seeking a divorce. "I don't believe in a busted jaw and broken ribs and teeth. Can't no man tell me he loves me and do that to my body." Nancy was surprised when she herself became physically violent. Asked at follow-up what was the most stressful thing that happened during divorce, she said "I attacked him—something just snapped in my head." Asked how she handled it, she said: "I filed for divorce."

During the period of separation what she misses most is "The good time we did have before we started having problems." The separation has changed the way she feels about herself: "I feel better about myself. I feel now I can deal with working problems out—things that I would want to do and was unable to do before. I was more in a rut and had no motivation." Although she feels more distant from "past mutual friends," she is now less disappointed in life, and feels more in control of her life and more responsible. As she explained: "Now I can do things he [her husband] wouldn't allow, like my working. I can go when I want to and come when I want to and do what I want to when I want to."

Continuing this theme, Nancy said: "I feel more content—no pressure, no demands, much freer." She expects her life "will improve—my health will improve, my children will feel better—they have gotten nervous as a result of my conflicts." When Nancy told her children about the impending divorce, they said: "Good idea! This is the best decision you made in a long time. How soon?" Her new life has greater freedom. "With my spouse not around I don't have to devote my energy to tasks to please him. I can do the things I want to do." Her most important goals are: "My health and my kids."

Nancy's ability to work towards and accomplish many of these goals by the second interview is living evidence of her personal strength. Beginning with her goal of being a good mother, we see that Nancy continues to consider her children a top priority. For example, she now says that one of her favorite things to do is: "talk with my children." She says that she does this every day and feels that the most important thing about this is "good communication together." She daydreams about the present and the future and specifically "about doing things with my children—taking them places." Asked about any changes in her relationship with her children, she said: "We've gotten closer."

Now divorced for over two years, Nancy is enrolled part-time in school, taking courses in "Sociology, Math, English and Business. I started out going for a degree in Social Work, but I changed my mind. Now I want to deal with Psychology." For the last two months, she has been working full-time as a "receptionist, filing, doing general paperwork for a publishing company." She has just enough money to make ends meet, but expects the future to be much better. In fact, Nancy said that "her finances are getting better by the day."

Nancy has been able to upgrade her general health from being "poor" at first interview to "excellent" at follow-up. She now reports having seen a doctor only twice during the past year, both times for a cold. She said: "But before that I was in the doctor's office at least twice a week. I was there constantly. He got tired of me. He told my husband that I was a hypochondriac and he gave me sugar pills just so I'd have some pills to take."

Her psychological health has improved as well, going from 16 symptoms at first contact down to 10 at follow-up. On the Bradburn Scale she reported being "very happy" and reports slightly more positive emotions than she did when first interviewed. Another source of strength has been Nancy's ability to develop new supportive relationships. However, her relationship with some of her married girlfriends has gotten worse, primarily because they have opted to remain in troubled relationships and she has gotten out. She also lost "friends on my husband's side," but she has made five new friends and reports having more than one person who she can count on for advice and understanding. Not even thinking of dating when we first met her, she now is dating someone that she met through a friend. She said that she relies on him very much for companionship and guidance, but not at all for money or practical matters. Although she does not want to remarry right away, she thinks she knows what she wants. "I want everything good. First we must be able to communicate. Give me half of what I want—financially, fairness sexually—put that on the top. I should be able to go when I'm ready. He should be able to deal with me."

Working is the activity that she feels has helped the most "because that way I'm not able to just concentrate on problems—I'm not here at the house giving myself time to think and feel sorry for myself." She also enjoys hobbies such as sewing because: "it's very relaxing. I get a chance to create things because I can design what I want to wear and I get a kick out of wearing it and having people say: 'Oh, that's so nice.' " Her absolute favorite thing to do is revealing: "To just lay down on the bed and watch TV and don't answer the door or phone—to not be disturbed by anyone or anything." Asked the most important thing about it, she said: "Because I don't get a chance to get into myself to find me."

SUMMING UP

Overall, the results support the notion that minorities may be at greater risk of health problems in the context of divorce, but emphasize how different minority groups are not only from the Caucasian population, but from each other. By and large, for example, the African Americans seem to have been the group most at risk, while Hispanic and Asian Americans had specific problems but fared relatively better than the blacks.

Symptomatology decreased for Caucasian American males and females, Hispanic and Asian American males over the three and a half years of study. In contrast, symptomatology increased for African American males and Hispanic American females or stayed the same for African and Asian American females. The Caucasian respondents were happier than minority respondents at impact. The gap in happiness closed at time two. These data suggest that quality of life in the aftermath of divorce improved with time for most respondents, but for some groups of minorities, especially females, this trend was not evident. Interventions should be directed at these vulnerable groups.

Minorities as a group, but especially African Americans, experienced more childhood stressors which made them more vulnerable to stressful life events and influenced the nature of their adult attachments. Exposure to positive and negative stressors is represented quite nicely by the Stress Typology. Winners and Losers also show evidence that minorities are at greater risk in the aftermath of divorce. This Stress Typology also demonstrates differences within each ethnic group as well. There were clearly Winners and Losers in each ethnic group.

Coping strategies used by minorities and Caucasians differed. There were clear patterns of coping that have been linked with cultural features that encourage or discourage use of certain coping styles. Both cultural and experiential factors help explain the prevalence of these coping patterns among the various ethnic groups. As demonstrated in this and other research, there are clearly certain adaptive coping strategies that more effectively deal with life problems. Further research will be necessary to investigate and examine the precursors of these Stress Typology personalities and coping styles in order to create appropriate intervention strategies to help vulnerable individuals.

Minorities not only perceived themselves as less masterful, hence lacking a resource for positive adaptation, but had more images of themselves that have been identified as deficits of the self-concept. Minorities in the sample described themselves as more vulnerable, incompetent, and confused about who they were than their Caucasian counterparts.

At least at the impact phase, minority respondents had fewer friends to draw upon and especially lacked a confidant to provide social support. By time two this difference lessened. There were no differences in availability of family in close proximity for minority and Caucasian Americans.

Minority respondents felt less general control over life than Caucasians in the study. This study replicates findings found in many other studies. There were no ethnic differences in situational control over the divorce. This leaves minorities with high situational control over the decision to divorce, but with fewer resources of general control to deal with the consequences of that decision, thus leading to greater unhappiness among minorities.

As discussed in this chapter, several critical factors helped us understand differences in the divorce process and adaptation among ethnic groups. First, cultural differences and the acculturation of individuals to traditional beliefs either hindered the divorce process or provided support for these individuals. Second, racism and discrimination systematically influence the types of resources, such as educational or socioeconomic status, which are available for divorcing individuals. As demonstrated in this chapter, minorities had less resources to cope with the aftermath of divorce. Third, the characteristics of marriage and divorce have changed dramatically over the last decade. We need more research to examine how these marriage and divorce trends influence minority families.

The critical factors for gays leaving a heterosexual marriage are different. Leaving a heterosexual marriage may be experienced as revealing one's true self to the world or releasing a great weight from around one's neck. Gays showed some increased distress in the aftermath of divorce but that may be the result of secondary hassles such as child custody and not of the divorce itself. These secondary hassles may represent the negative fallout of revealing a gay sexual orientation. Clearly, these factors are different from those experienced by minority respondents. More research is needed to examine divorce and divorce adaptation for both gay and straight partners.

12

RISK FACTORS IN DIVORCE: A LIFE
COURSE PERSPECTIVE

David A. Chiriboga

Although there are many things that can be said about divorce, perhaps the most general is that few go through the experience without emerging as a different person. "Stripped to its bare essentials," as Maury and Brandwein (1984, 193) notes, "divorce is a major change." The changes are pervasive, and involve both self and one's relations with the outer world. The multiple demands placed upon individuals as a result of these changes, may be ignored, denied or confronted, but ignored, denied or confronted, each response is a step towards shaping a new life. In this chapter we will review some of the changes associated with divorce, as well as the factors that may place individuals at risk when the changes occur. We also discuss the implications of our findings for developing instruments designed to identify people at risk.

DIVORCE AS A FORCING HOUSE FOR CHANGE

One of the most startling findings we uncovered in this excursion into the realm of divorce concerns just how much change actually is going on during the period of time surrounding the marital separation. A clue to the amount of change comes from the life event measures. Our Life Events Question-naire was designed to assess change from the individual's status quo, an orientation that owes a debt to the research and theories of stress developed by Holmes and Rahe (1967). Items in the questionnaire essentially center on changes in everyday things such as eating habits, the number of arguments with coworkers or supervisors, job status and the like.

For the one-year period prior to their first interviews, participants in the Divorce Study reported many more life events than did Transitions Study participants on nearly all of the 11 different domains in which we assessed the incidence of life events. Perhaps more significantly, this greater incidence was not limited just to negative events. The divorce participants reported more negative and more positive events, at all ages.

These results underscore the idea that life simply does not remain the same for people going through a divorce. For many people, marriage was the first step in a natural and seemingly inexorable progression that included children, the PTA, family dog, station wagon, saving for the children's education, worrying about day care and the like. Being in such an expectable progression creates a visualizable future, predicated on marker events such as the birth of each child, entrance of successive children into day care, pre-school, kindergarten, elementary school, intermediate school, high school, college, marriage, and so forth.

At first, the impact of the divorce process seemed greater for older partici-pants in the study. Recall that the average morale score for both men and women decreased progressively with each decade of life as we looked in on them with our first interviews. Among the women, especially those in their 40s or older, weaned on more traditional philosophies concerning the role of women, the idea of seriously working for a living and depending on their own abilities for survival, was often the very furthest thing from their minds prior to their marital separation. Plunging headfirst into the upheaval created by marital separation, most of the middle-aged women experienced hardship but ended up, three or more years later, reasonably intact and living reason-ably well. And, we might add, often amazed at their survival. They were in fact doing better than the younger women, in part because the latter were often faced with the sometimes conflicting demands of raising children and reentering the world as a single person.

For men, much the same scenario had unfolded. At the first interview the older men were doing less well: as we noted earlier, for both men and women this seemed related in part to the fact that the older people seemed more aware of the consequences of divorce, and also were more deeply entrenched in social networks grounded in the marital role. Those aged 40 and over also stood out as the men most at risk of heightened exposure to stress in many different areas of life, in comparisons between the Divorce and Transitions

Studies. Our conclusion here was that a contagion or spillover effect is strongest among middle-aged and older men who are going through a divorce. This conclusion we based on the fact that in the Divorce Study the middle-aged men were no different from younger men in their high exposure to negative events, while in the Transitions Study, middle-aged men reported fewer life events than younger people (this was true at each of the five contacts). The cross-sample pattern of differences suggests that the transition of divorce elevates normal levels of stress exposure for older men more than it does that of younger men with a net effect of equalizing stress exposure during at least the impact phase of divorce.

By the second interview however, the situation had shifted. Men in their forties had fared particularly well in the aftermath of divorce. They had the highest morale of any age group, and generally were most likely to have adapted well to the new condition. This may be due in part to the fact that, like the older women they were relatively free of the need to raise children, and so forth. That is, they brought less "baggage" with them from their past life and thus were freed to carve out new lives with fewer impediments. At the same time, this particular age group may have the double advantage of having careers still on the rise, a well-established sense of personal identity and a wide selection of dating and marital options. Older men were faced with careers that at the least were at a peak, and also with growing recognition of the aging process. Younger men, like younger women, could not escape from the burdens of the past, and also were faced with the demands of establishing careers and a secure identity.

Change in the Long Run. We found that in the long run the majority of men and women had resolved the problems they were facing during the impact phase of divorce. One criterion of their successful resolution of the crisis is that by follow-up their life event scores by and large were just the same as those reported by participants in our companion study of transitions. The psychological well-being of the divorced participants was also comparable, or even better, than what we observed in the companion study.

What we encountered, as we looked at the lives of these men and women, is that the stress context of divorce often prompts a growth experience. In chapter 3 we talked about the fact that for many people, especially those in the middle years, the course of life had essentially been set when they married. Life scripts had been written, and the expected life course was more or less a certainty. Divorce upset the expectable lives of our participants, adding uncertainty about the future to the troubles they already faced in their marriages.

The immediate consequences were clear. During the impact phase the majority of our participants were distressed, and uncertain about what life held in store for them. In fact, a significant number of participants, especially men, could not project even one year when they were asked to rate how they expected their future lives to be. Three and a half years later, it was a vastly different story. Most participants now seemed to be living reasonably ordinary lives, and we found it hard to distinguish Divorce from Transitions Study participants on our measures. Many, if not most, of these people had responded to the challenge, discovering in the process abilities and strengths they often had been unaware of. As noted in the last section, this seemed most true for women aged 40 and over, and for men in their forties.

Towards the end of this chapter we will discuss in greater detail some of the implications of the changes people encountered in their lives. Next however we will address an issue that came up again and again: gender differences in the experience of divorce.

GENDER DIFFERENCES

There is controversy over who suffers more during the divorce process: men or women. Two extensive reviews of the literature on adjustment to divorce conclude that men have more difficulty than women (Gove 1973; White and Bloom 1981), but other studies suggest women to have greater difficulty, especially if they have children (Wallerstein and Blakeslee 1989). What we ourselves found is that there are marked differences in the ways men and women experience and adapt to the divorce process. There were differences as to which elements in the stress process model were related to psychological adaptation, and there were differences in the level of adaptation itself. Overall, the sources of problems, the context and resolution of problems are very different for men and women. Here we will just consider a couple of examples.

Negative Events and Adaptation

In reviewing just information obtained at the second interview, we found that negative events were associated with symptoms for women, but not for men. Several years after their separation, women reporting more negative stress were more likely to manifest higher symptom scores. These findings parallel conclusions from a number of stress-related studies in which women were demonstrated to have a greater vulnerability to life events (Chiriboga and Cutler 1980; Kessler 1979), especially if they were not married (Thoits 1982). However, the harmful effect of negative events, in terms of women's psychological symptoms at follow-up, may derive not only from their greater vulnerability but also from their greater actual experience of negative events. Indeed, we found that women reported significantly higher overall levels of negative life events at follow-up than did men; at baseline there was no difference.

In other words, during the impact stage of divorce men and women were on a relatively equal footing in terms of the experience of negative events, and men as well as women at that time were adversely affected by them. It may be that when a negative condition like divorce occurs, the chain or sequence of negative events generated for women by the initial crisis is more enduring than it is for men. In the long run, women may be distressed, not so much by the divorce as by its consequences.

These findings then suggest a greater long-term vulnerability of women to divorce. This matches the common assumption that women on the whole suffer greater losses in economic and social status than men. Indeed, in the present sample, men on the average had substantially higher incomes than women. Women also reported higher levels of psychological symptomatology during the first interview, when men and women were both at the crisis or impact stage of divorce.

Both sexes experienced a reduction in mean levels of symptoms from first to second interviews, but women continued to manifest a higher level of symptomatology. This finding was anticipated: women traditionally score higher on indices of psychological symptoms, and more specifically, we found the same kinds of gender differences in our companion study of transitions (Fiske and Chiriboga 1990).

Looking at the total symptoms count may be misleading. When we looked at results from a factor analysis (Chiriboga et al. 1982) of the Symptoms Checklist we found that men and women did not differ in the levels of symptoms reflecting somatization, anxiety, personal and what we called ruminative depression (e.g. "have you felt that life is not worth living?"). Women, however, were more likely to exhibit signs of a less severe form of depression (for example, "feeling moody and blue for no reason"), stress response (e.g., "must you do things slowly in order to make them without mistakes?" "do frightening things keep coming back in your mind?") and personal insecurity (e.g., "do strange people or places make you feel afraid?").

Gender Differences in the Presence and Effect of Support

Differences were found not only in the kinds of social supports available to men and women, but also in the continuity of social supports over time. For men, the structural and behavioral aspects of social support (as reflected by Active Network and Support Seeking) were most stable; for women, the perceptual dimension was highest in stability. We also found that stability in the support system has differing implications for mental health. For women the important thing may be to maintain what they have, since women generally have more extensive and more highly utilized support systems. Our results suggest that the existing support systems of women may generally be more than adequate to provide what is needed during a stress condition such as divorce.

Men on the other hand appear to generally operate with a more bare-bones support system. In fact, we have found that men generally placed great reliance upon their wives for support, and many wished they could turn to her again for help, though recognizing that this would be inadvisable (Chiriboga et al. 1979). Under conditions of stress, satisfactory adjustment seems to follow from an activation and expansion of the support system—an activation that continues for as long as necessary, but no longer.

Support Seeking as an Example of Sex Differences. Support-seeking behavior presents some interesting issues. Why was support seeking associated with a better psychological outcome for men? Men are usually reported to be poor support seekers; they seek medical and psychological help much less frequently than women. One suggestion has been that men tend not to identify their own vague feelings as emotional problems that might need treatment (Kessler 1979). Women do better in problem recognition, and thus are more likely to be able to seek help. And as expected, among the divorcing men and women, women sought more help than men at both time periods.

In another analysis of the current data set, help seeking was related to appraisals of the degree of stressfulness of divorce (Chiriboga et al. 1979). Those who experienced distress over the divorce were the ones who sought help. Although women sought help more than men, men and women were pretty much on a par when it came to stress appraisal. In fact, at baseline men tended to have somewhat higher average scores on distress over the divorce (see chapter 3); there was no difference between men and women in distress over the divorce at follow-up. Among the divorcing men and women, women (as expected) sought more help than men, at both time periods. But the higher help-seeking levels for men were associated with lower symptom scores.

The critical factor seems to be stress appraisal. Under threat of divorce, men may be predisposed to appraise the situation as stressful, which they perhaps are less likely to do in other stress situations. Lazarus and Folkman (1984) found that men and women did not differ in the kinds of coping that they used, in similar contexts of life; they differed in which contexts they experienced stress. Perhaps, divorce in that sense is a great leveler between the genders; both encounter marked changes and assess them similarly as stressful. Divorce may be so cataclysmic for some men that it overcomes their resistance to help seeking; and apparently these men benefit from their efforts, at least as measured by symptom level.

The importance of appraisals or perceptions were not limited to those dealing with the specific stress conditions being faced. The perception of support was another critical element in understanding how people fared, and seemed to be one of the most powerful of the social support measures. Regardless of the actual circumstances, people who feel supported seem to do better. Unfortunately we know little concerning the factors that affect how people view the quality and quantity of support they actually receive. Perceptions are by their very nature relative and subjective. The same amount of "support" that evokes a feeling of adequacy in one person may leave another person profoundly dissatisfied. Thus the issue of perceived support is difficult and complex, and remains largely unexplored. The individual personality and social situation of the receiver act as essential filters, which interpret and transform the meaning of the "support" that is given. It is this process of interpretation and transformation that determines, in the last analysis, the efficacy of social support.

The Value of Androgynous Lifestyles

In a series of analyses published elsewhere, we found that men and women who fared better during the divorce seemed to show more evidence of what might be called an androgynous lifestyle (Chiriboga and Thurnher 1980). Those who maintained less traditional roles and activities during their marriage were generally happier after their separation. We also found that people who maintained separate interests, hobbies and social activities were happier. All in all these results seem very compatible with what we found for another set of variables: those dealing with control. People with less traditional perspectives on how members of their sex should behave, and people who maintained relatively independent activities and interests during their marriage were also the people who scored highest on general feelings of control.

MINORITY STATUS

Although we are all familiar with the demographic studies indicating that members of minority groups, especially African and Hispanic Americans, tend to have a higher divorce rate than whites, the extent to which various minorities are impacted by divorce was somewhat unexpected. In part, but only in part, their excess vulnerability appears to be linked to a generally lower income status. Clearly, there are other factors involved.

One such factor is childhood stress. The racial and ethnic minority groups generally had a greater likelihood of certain childhood stressors, such as having to go to work to help support the family. In addition, African American participants were indicated to have more childhood stressors that were related to family conflict and disrupted families. Perhaps because of their high levels of childhood stress, minorities and again especially African Americans in our sample also seemed less likely to identify strongly and securely with their parents.

Whatever the cause, the symptomatology evident among certain groups, especially African American males and Hispanic American females, actually increased from the first to second interviews. For these people it would appear that the escape from marriage provided little in the way of relief from problems. However, when we looked at Winners and Losers in the Stress Typology we found conflicting evidence for greater disruption resulting from marital separation and divorce. At the first interview, Hispanic and African Americans were far more likely to fall into the Losers category (low on positive events, high on negative) than were Caucasians. Hispanic Americans were more likely to be Winners (high on positive events, low on negative). African Americans were the least likely to be Winners during the impact phase.

The special vulnerability of African Americans, both male and female, is reemphasized when we turn to data from the second interview. The proportion of African Americans falling in the Losers category went from about 46% at first interview to over 53% at the second. For everyone else, the proportion in the Losers category had gone down substantially. We also find that in the analyses of coping, the African Americans emerged as least likely to use strategies of active mastery and most likely to be classified as Stoics. In short, their coping efforts seemed to reflect a sense of powerlessness in which the best strategy was deemed to be avoidance.

A Word on Gay Divorce

While gays may represent a minority group from the perspective of numbers of people, they are extremely heterogeneous in terms of social and ethnic backgrounds and it was difficult to draw any generalizations about them. Our sample of gays was also definitely small: we had only nine who identified their sexual orientation at one or the other of the interviews. Recalling that these individuals had been involved in heterosexual marriages, the overall conclusion that can be reached is that the majority of these men and women did quite well in both the short- and long-term phases of divorce. This may result from a greater fit between sexual orientation and lifestyle being established after the separation.

RISK FACTORS IN DIVORCE

In each of the preceding chapters we have discussed issues and questions that, at least from a theoretical perspective, had seemed relevant to answering the questions of who is most at risk in the aftermath of marital separation and divorce. Given that the topics had been selected for investigation only after extensive pilot testing and literature review, it was not very surprising that they all were shown to actually figure in some important way in the process of divorce. Some were the initiators of change: the things that "go bang in the night." Some were modulators of change. Some represented the change itself, in terms of how well people were functioning. As we reviewed the findings, one overall conclusion we drew was that a screening instrument, given to people when they first surface in the legal system, has the potential of identifying with reasonable accuracy those in need of either short-term or long-term interventions.

Risk and Beneficial Factors: Towards a Screening Tool. One of the dilemmas facing those in the helping professions, particularly in time of increasing economic constraints, is how to serve those people most in need most effectively. In the case of divorce, we encounter a rather unique opportunity to develop strategies of early identification of people at risk since one or the other of the couple will have to file a petition for marital dissolution. At that point, not only is at least one member of the couple usually present, but information is obtained on residences of both. Hence, instituting a procedure of mail or telephone surveys becomes possible.

Such a survey or screening would of necessity need to be relatively brief. Although we have devoted many pages to each of the basic topics covered in this book, the actual measurement procedures that underlie each chapter are not overly long. In other words, if we just consider those measures that were found to assist in the prediction of symptomatology, they are in fact few in number and relatively brief in administration. A life-events inventory, symptoms inventory and questions concerning progress along the transition of divorce, social supports and control would require approximately 20 minutes to be completed.

The fact that a brief inventory can include fairly powerful predictors of later disruption lends itself to clinical interventions. Our research has indicated that the number of people in great need is in fact not that great. Since it seems possible to develop an efficient screening tool to identify those at greatest risk, in either the short or long run, it also seems possible that clinical services could maintain intervention programs at relatively little cost. The key to the success of such programs of course would be early identification of the at risk population. This early identification, we feel, could be facilitated if a screening tool was made part of the process of completing the first sets of papers required for marital dissolution.

ON THINGS THAT GO BANG IN THE NIGHT

Life events and other stressors are generally thought of as chance circumstances that intrude on our lives: things that go bang in the night. Students of adult development and aging have only just begun to appreciate the role of life events and other stressors as factors that can affect the entire trajectory of life. One of the truisms that seems to be emerging is that expectable changes, whether cast in terms of transitions or life events, exert less of an influence on people's lives than do relatively unanticipated changes.

In the research we have reviewed in this book, we were fortunate enough to have at our disposal data from a 12-year longitudinal study of men and women undergoing what are sometimes called "normative" transitions. They are seen as normative because transitions involved in activities such as first job, parenthood, the empty nest and retirement have a high probability of occurring at certain points in the life course.

Stress as Definers of a Transition

A particularly intriguing finding from chapter 3 dealt with the multiplicity of stressors in the lives of divorcing persons. When we compared persons going through the process of divorce to those going through more normative and expectable transitions, it was clear that for every age-group divorcing men and women were experiencing more events. This was true not only for negative events, which might be expected, but also for positive events. Perhaps more important, by follow-up these differences between samples no longer obtained.

One implication of these variations is that life events may be useful as definers of the presence and magnitude of a transition. In a sense one can chart the magnitude of effect by considering whether people are experiencing more than their share of stress events and hassles across different spheres or domains of life. People whose life events exceed the norm only in the area of married life, for example, represent those who have managed to "contain" the impact of the transition. The majority of participants in our study, of course, reported elevated scores across multiple domains, thereby providing empirical evidence that divorce truly does have a pervasive impact.

TRANSITIONS: AN OVERARCHING THEORETICAL MODEL FOR DIVORCE

Throughout this book one of our goals has been to examine issues that have not received a great deal of attention in the literature, but which seem to have some clinical and practical significance for the lives of individuals who are confronted by a major life challenge: the challenge posed by a failing marriage and the possible need to divorce. Remember that when we first interviewed our study participants, not too long after they had separated from their spouse, the facts were for the most part unclear. The separation was recent, the possibility of divorce real but still for many an elusive concept.

An underlying theme of nearly all the chapters we have presented has been that separation and the ultimate dissolution of marriage are experiences that disturb the equilibrium of most people. For example, we report in the third chapter that, especially during the period surrounding marital separation, divorcing persons seemed to experience more stressors, both positive and negative, than did a comparison group undergoing more normative transitions. In that same chapter, it was pointed out that one of the major theoretical models of stress involves the idea that the degree of stress can be measured by the extent to which the equilibrium or homeostasis of the individual is disturbed.

In chapters on transitions, similarly, we found that divorce is a transition that robs people of social involvements that form the basis not only of validation of one's position in society but also of one's sense of identity: who one is. And a theme of disturbance in identity was also noted in chapter 7 on self-identity, although here (as with the stress chapter) it was emphasized that the experience of divorce is not necessarily one that is completely negative in short- or long-term consequences.

In short, we continually found evidence to support the notion that the process of marital dissolution is associated with a major disruption in many if not all spheres of life. As the research team began to put together the variety of findings, from all these divergent spheres, the transitions model again and again was found to be highly appropriate as a means of understanding and perhaps explaining what was happening to our subjects. This model, originally developed by anthropologists working in rather primitive agrarian regions of the world, is based on the twin ideas that how one views oneself is heavily influenced by social involvements and that one's self-image lies at the core of what might be called social health.

The anthropological model of transitions, as formulated by van Gennep and Turner, we found to provide some clarity of focus in understanding the lives of men and women going through the kinds of changes posed by divorce. This model does warrant modification when applied to the more amorphous and ill-defined transitions of the modern world. For one thing, our studies strongly suggest that people can be facing and dealing with the demands of all three stages of the transition simultaneously. This would be unheard of in the more traditional transitions. Another modification, we suggest, is the need for an additional, fourth phase to the transition. This new phase, a preparatory or anticipatory one, assumed considerable importance in our investigations into the significance of timing. Implied in the work of Goode (1956), this is the critical period following the point where the person realizes in his or her own mind that a divorce is probably inevitable. Of particular importance: women who take a month or less to pass through this stage, but who then take considerable time from separation to the point of filing for a divorce, may be especially at risk. This type of passage seems to be associated with a more impetuous and less thought-out approach to divorce, and one marked by indecision and personal distress as well.

Reconciliation as a Special Case. When we looked at the participants several years after they had first separated, we found them to be quite spread out in terms of where they were in the marital career. Some had reconciled, others were still "hanging fire": separated and still not divorced. On the other hand, a handful had already remarried and divorced again! Of all our participants, the reconciled stood apart as a category that deserves special attention from those of us in the health professions. Reconciliation for many represented the failure of a transition. Unable to cope with the demands and problems of separate living, the known problems of an unsatisfying marriage became more appealing.

DIVORCE: CRISIS, CHALLENGE OR RELIEF?

As we conclude this book, the final point that we would like to emphasize is that marital separation and divorce, in the long run, is not the solution to problems, but only the beginnings of a solution. For many it was a relief from the chronic duress of an unhappy marriage, for some it was also a crisis, but for all it posed a challenge: to forge for themselves a new life. The process initiated by the decision to divorce in essence is the beginning of a transition that is successfully concluded only with the construction of a new and more satisfying life.

REFERENCES

Abraham, K. 1927. *Selected Papers of Karl Abraham, M.D. with an Introductory Memoir by Ernest Jones*, translated by D. Bryan and A. Strachey. London: Hogarth Press.

Abramson, L., M. E. P. Seligman, and J. Teasdale. 1978. Learned helplessness in humans:.Critique and reformulation. *Journal of Abnormal Psychology* 87:49–74.

Adams, R. 1937. *Interracial Marriage in Hawaii*. New York: Macmillan.

Adler, A. 1969. *The Practice and Theory of Individual Psychology*. Totowa, N.J.: Littlefield, Adams.

Aguirre, B. E., and W. C. Parr. 1982. Husbands' marriage order and the stability of first and second marriages of white and black women. *Journal of Marriage and the Family* 44:605–20.

Albrecht, S., H. Bahr and K. Goodman. 1983. *Divorce and Remarriage: Problems, Adaptations, and Adjustments*. Westport, Conn.: Greenwood Press.

Ambert, A. 1989. *Ex-Spouses and New Spouses: A Study of Relationships*. Greenwich, Conn.: JAI Press.

Aneshensel, C. S., and R. R. Frerichs. 1982. Stress, support, and depression: A longitudinal causal model. *Journal of Community Psychology* 10:363–76.

Arnold, M. B. 1960. *Emotion and Personality*. New York: Columbia University Press.

Averill, J. R. 1973. Personal control over aversive stimuli and its relationship to stress. *Psychological Bulletin* 80:286–303.

Bandura, A. 1989. Human agency in social cognitive theory. *American Psychologist* 44:1175–84.

Barrera, M. 1981. Social support in the adjustment of pregnant adolescents. In *Social Networks and Social Support*, edited by B. H. Gottlieb. Beverly Hills, Calif.: Sage.

Bengtson, V., and J. A. Kuypers. 1985. The family support cycle: Psychological issues in the aging family. In *Life-span and Change in a Gerontological Perspective*, edited by J. M. A. Munichs, P. Mussen, E. Olbrich, and P. G. Coleman. Orlando, Fla.: Academic Press.

Bernard, J. 1972. *The Future of Marriage*. New York: Bantam Books.

Birtley Fenn, C. E. 1981. Divorce, self-concept and psychological functioning: A longitudinal study. Ph.D. diss., Department of Psychiatry, University of California, San Francisco.

Blair, M. 1970. Divorces adjustment and attitudinal changes about life. Ph.D. diss., Florida State University.

Block, J. 1961. *The Q-Sort Method in Personality Assessment and Psychiatric Research*. Springfield, Ill.: Thomas.

Blood, R. O. 1969. *Marriage*. New York: Free Press.

Bloom, B., S. J. Asher and S. W. White. 1978. Marital disruption as a stressor: A review and analysis. *Psychological Bulletin* 85:867–94.

Bloom, B., W. F. Hodges, M. B. Kern and C. S. McFaddin. 1985. A preventive intervention program for the newly-separated: Final evaluations. *American Journal Orthopsychiatry* 55(1): 9–26.

Bloom, B. L., S. W. White and S. J. Asher. 1979. Marital disruption as a stressful life event. In *Divorce and Separation: Context, Causes, and Consequences*, edited by G. Levinger and O. C. Moles. New York: Basic Books.

Bohannan, P. 1970. The six stations of divorce. In *Divorce and After*, edited by P. Bohannan. New York: Doubleday.

Bondurant, S. B. 1977. The divorce process and the stress of separation. Ph.D. diss., University of Cincinnati.

Borgatta, E. F. 1964. The structure of personality characteristics. *Behavior Science* 8:8–17.

Bornstein, P. E., P. J. Clayton, J. A. Halikas, W. L. Maurice and E. Robbins. 1973. Marital disruption as a stressful life event. In *Divorce and Separation: Context, Causes, and Consequences*, edited by G. Levinger and O. C. Moles. New York: Basic Books.

Bowlby, J. 1977. The making and breaking of affectional bonds. Part I: Aetiology and psychopathology in the light of attachment theory. *The British Journal of Psychiatry* 130:201–10.

———. 1980. *Attachment and Loss*, vol. 3: *Loss, Sadness, and Depression*. New York: Basic Books.

Bradburn, N. 1969. *The Structure of Psychological Well-Being*. Chicago: Aldine Press.

Bradburn, N. M., and D. Caplovitz. 1965. *Reports on Happiness: A Pilot Study of Behavior Related to Mental Health*. Chicago: Aldine Press.

Bramwell, S. T., M. Masuda, N. N. Wagner and T. H. Holmes. 1975. Psychosocial factors in athletic injuries: Application of the social and athletic readjustment scale (SARRS). *Journal of Human Stress* 1:6–21.

Brim, D. G., and J. Kagan, eds. 1980. *Constancy and Change in Human Development*. Cambridge, Mass.: Harvard University Press.

Brown, G. W., and T. O. Harris. 1989. Depression. In *Life Events and Illness*, edited by G. W. Brown and T. O. Harris. New York: Guilford Press.

Brown, P., and B. J. Felton. 1978. Coping with marital disruption in later life: The role of social supports. Paper presented at the 46th annual meeting of the American Orthopsychiatric Association, March, San Francisco.

Brown, P., B. J. Felton, V. Whiteman and R. Manela. 1980. Attachment and distress following material separation. *Journal of Divorce* 3:303–17.

Caldwell, R. A., B. L. Bloom and W. F. Hodges. 1983. Sex differences in separation and divorce: A longitudinal perspective. *Issues in Mental Health Nursing* 5:103–20.

Carter, H., and P. C. Glick. 1976. *Marriage and Divorce: A Social and Economic Study*. Cambridge, Mass.: Harvard University Press.

Catron, L. 1976. Therapies at a halfway house. Master's thesis, University of North Carolina, Chapel Hill.

———. 1983. Childhood stress, transitional status, and adaptation to divorce. Ph.D. diss., Department of Psychiatry, University of California, San Francisco.

Catron, L., D. A. Chiriboga and S. Krystal. 1980. Divorce at mid-life: Psychic dangers of the liminal period. Part I. *Maturitas* 2:131–39.

Cauhape, E. 1983. *Fresh Starts: Men and Women after Divorce*. New York: Basic Books.

Cherlin, H. 1981. *Marriage, Divorce, Remarriage*. Cambridge, Mass.: Harvard University Press.

Chiriboga, D. A. 1972. *The Nature and Effects of Relocation in the Aged: A Comparative Study*. Ph.D. diss., University of Chicago.

———. 1979a. Conceptualizing adult transitions: A new look at an old subject. *Generations* 4(1): 4–6.

———. 1979b. Marital separation and stress: A life course perspective. *Alternative Life Styles* 2(4): 461–70.

———. 1984. Social stressors as antecedents of change. *Journal of Gerontology* 39(4): 468–77.

———. 1986. Transitions. In *The Encyclopedia of Aging*, edited by S. Maddox. New York: Springer.

———. 1989. Mental health at the midpoint: Crisis, challenge, or relief? In *Midlife Myths: Coping Strategies*, edited by S. Hunter and M. Sandel. Newbury Park: Sage.

Chiriboga, D. A., and J. T. Bailey. 1989. Stress and burnout among critical care and medical surgical nurses: A comparative study. *Critical Care Quarterly* 9(3): 84–92.

Chiriboga, D. A., P. Brierton, S. Krystal and R. Pierce. 1982. Antecedents of symptom expression during marital separation. *Journal of Clinical Psychology* 38:732–41.

Chiriboga, D. A., A. Coho, J. A. Stein and J. Roberts. 1979. Divorce, stress and social supports: A study in helpseeking behavior. *Journal of Divorce* 3:121–34.

Chiriboga, D. A., and L. Cutler. 1977. Stress responses among divorcing men and women. *Journal of Divorce* 2(2): 95–106.

———. 1980. Stress and adaptation: Life span perspectives. In *Aging in the 1980's Psychological Issues*, edited by L. W. Poon. Washington, D. C.: American Psychological Association.

Chiriboga, D. A., and H. Dean 1978. Dimensions of Stress: Perspectives from a Longitudinal Study. *Journal of Psychosomatic Research* 22:47–55.

Chiriboga, D. A., and S. Krystal. 1985. An Empirical Taxonomy of Symptom Types among Divorcing Persons. *Journal of Clinical Psychology* 6(4): 601–13.

Chiriboga, D. A., J. Roberts and J. A. Stein. 1978. Psychological well-being during marital separation. *Journal of Divorce* 2:21–36.

Chiriboga, D. A., and M. Thurnher. 1980. Marital life styles and adjustment to separation. *Journal of Divorce* 4(3): 379–80.

Cicirelli, V. 1983. A comparison of helping behavior to elderly parents of adult children with intact and disrupted marriages. *Gerontologist* 24:396–400.

Clausen, J. 1988. *The Life Course: A Sociological Perspective*. Englewood Cliffs, N.J.: Prentice-Hall.

Cline, D, and J. Westman. 1971. The impact of divorce on the family. *Child Psychiatry and Human Development* 2:78–83.

Cobb, S. 1976. Social support as a moderator of life stress. *Psychosomatic Medicine* 38:300–314.

Cohen, F., and R. S. Lazarus. 1973. Active coping processes, coping dispositions, and recovery from surgery. *Psychosomatic Medicine* 35:375–89.

Cohen, S., and S. L. Syme. 1985. Issues in the study and application of social support. In *Social Support and Health*, edited by S. Cohen and S. L. Syme. Orlando, Fla.: Academic Press.

Cohler, B. J., and Stott, F. M. 1987. Separation, interdependence and social relations across the second half of life. In *The Psychology of Separation and Loss: Perspectives on Development, Life Transitions and Clinical Practice*, edited by J. Bloom-Feshbach, S. Bloom-Feshbach and Associates. San Francisco: Jossey-Bass.

Coho, A. 1984. Self and other conceptualizations: Significance for mental health in divorce. Ph.D. diss., Department of Psychiatry, University of California, San Francisco.

Cone, J. D. 1971. Locus of control and social desirability. *Journal of Consulting and Clinical Psychology* 36:449.

Cooley, C. H. 1972. The looking glass self (the social self). In *Social Psychology*, edited by W. C. Sahakian. Scranton, Pa.: Intex.

Cumming, J., and E. Cumming. 1962. *Ego and Milieu: Theory and Practice of Environmental Therapy*. New York: Atherton.

Darsa, S. D. 1976. Initiation of divorce as a function of locus of control, self-actualization, and androgyny. Ph.D. diss., California School of Professional Psychology, Los Angeles. 1977, 37(9-B): 4671, order #77-6294.

Davidson, P. P., and M. J. Bobey. 1970. Regressor-sensitizer differences on repeated exposures to pain. *Perceptual and Motor Skills* 31:711–14.

Davis, D. L. 1985. Psychosocial competence and stress among middle-class, black and white, married and divorced, males and females. *Dissertation Abstracts International* 47:1718-B (University Microfilms No. DA8614218).

Dean, A., and W. M. Ensel. 1983. Socially structured depression in men and women. In *Research in Community and Mental Health*, edited by J. R. Greenley. Greenwich, Conn.: JAI Press.

deCharms, R. 1968. *Personal Causation*. New York: Academic Press.

Despert, L. 1953. *Children of Divorce*. New York: Doubleday.

DiMatteo, M. R., and R. Hays. 1981. Social support and serious illness. In *Social Networks and Social Support*, edited by B. H. Gottlieb. Beverly Hills, Calif.: Sage.

Doherty, W. J. 1980. Divorce and belief in internal versus external control over one's life: Data from a national probability sample. *Journal of Divorce* 3(4): 391–401.

Dohrenwend, B. S. 1973. Life events as stressors: a methodological inquiry. *Journal of Health and Social Behavior* 14:167–75.

Elder, G. 1978. Family history in the life course. In *Transitions: The family and the life course in historical perspective*, edited by T. S. Hareven. New York: Academic Press.

———. 1981. Social history and life experience. In *Present and Past in Middle Life*, edited by D. Eichorn, J. A. Clausen, N. Haan, M. P. Honzik and P. H. Mussen. San Francisco: Academic Press.

Epstein, J. 1974. *Divorced in America: Marriage in an Age of Possibility*. New York: E. P. Dutton.

Feather, N. T. 1967. Some personality correlates of external control. *Australian Journal of Psychology* 19:253–60.

———. 1968. Change in confidence following success or failure as a predictor of subsequent performance. *Journal of Personality and Social Psychology* 9:38–46.

Ferrari, N. A. 1962. Instititionalization and attitude change in an aged population: A field study in dissidence theory. Ph.D. diss., Western Reserve University.

Ferraro, K. F., E. Mutran and C. M. Barresi. 1984. Widowhood, health and friendship support in later life. *Journal of Health and Social Behavior* 25:245–59.

Fine, M. A., and A. I. Schwebel. 1988. An emergent explanation of differing racial reactions to single parenthood. In *Minority and Ethnic Issues in the Divorce Process*, edited by C. A. Everett. New York: Haworth Press.

Fingarette, H. 1963. *The Self in Transformation*. New York: Basic Books.

Finlay-Jones, R. A., R. Scott, P. Duncan-Jones, D. Byrne and S. Henderson. 1981. The reliability of reports of early separation. *Australian and New Zealand Journal of Psychiatry* 15:27–31.

Fish, B., and S. A. Karabenick. 1971. Relationship between self-esteem and locus of control. *Psychological Reports* 29:784.

Fiske, M. 1980. Changing hierarchies of commitment in adulthood. In *Themes of Work and Love in Adulthood*, edited by N. J. Smelser and E. H. Erikson. Cambridge, Mass.: Harvard University Press.

Fiske, M., and D. A. Chiriboga. 1985. The interweave of societal and personal change in adulthood. In *Life Span and Change in a Gerontological Perspective*, edited by J. M. Munichs, P. Mussen and E. Olbrich. San Diego: Academic Press.

———. 1990. *Continuity and Change in Adult Life*. San Francisco: Jossey-Bass.

Fitch, G. 1970. Effects of self-esteem, perceived performance, and choice on casual attributions. *Journal of Personality and Social Psychology* 16:311–15.

Freud, S. [1917] 1957. Mourning and melancholia. *The Standard Edition of the Complete Psychological Works of Sigmund Freud*, vol. 14. London: Hogarth Press.

———. [1933] 1964. New introductory lectures on psycho-analysis. *The Standard*

Edition of the Complete Psychological Works of Sigmund Freud, vol. 22. London: Hogarth Press.

———. [1938] 1969. An outline of psychoanalysis. *The Standard Edition of the Complete Psychological Works of Sigmund Freud*, vol. 23. London: Hogarth Press.

Freund, J. 1974. Divorce and grief. *Journal of Family Counseling* 2:40–43.

Friedman, L. 1984. Social support and divorce: A study of stress mediation. Ph.D. diss., Department of Psychiatry, University of California, San Francisco.

Frisbie, W. P. 1986. Variation in patterns of marital instability among Hispanics. *Journal of Marriage and the Family* 48:99–106.

Frisbie, W. P., W. Opitz and W. R. Kelly. 1985. Marital instability trends among Mexican Americans as compared to Blacks and Anglos: New evidence. *Social Science Quarterly* 66:587–601.

Fromm, E. 1941. *Escape from Freedom*. New York: Holt, Rinehart & Winston.

Furby, L. 1979. Individualistic bias in studies of locus of control. In *Psychology in Social Context*, edited by A. R. Buss. New York: Wiley.

Garmazy, N. 1981. Children under stress: Perspectives on antecedents and correlates of vulnerability and resistance to psychopathology. In *Further Explorations in Personality*, edited by A. I. Rabin and R. A. Zucker. New York: Wiley.

Gerard, H. B. 1961. Some determinants of self-evaluation. *Journal of Abnormal Social Psychology* 62:288–93.

Gergen, K. J. 1977. Stability, change, and chance in human development. In *Lifespan Developmental Psychology: Dialectic Perspectives on Experimental Methods*, edited by N. Datan and H. W. Reese. New York: Academic Press.

Glass, D. C. 1977. *Behavior Patterns, Stress and Coronary Disease*. Hillsdale, N.J.: Erlbaum.

Glick, I. O., R. Weiss and C. M. Parkes. 1974. *The First Year of Bereavement*. New York: Wiley.

Glick, P. 1984. Marriage, divorce, and living arrangements: Prospective changes. *Journal of Family Issues* 5:7–26.

Golan, N. 1986. *The Perilous Bridge: Helping Clients through Mid-life Transitions*. New York: Free Press.

Goldschmidt, W. 1974. Ethology, ecology, and ethnological realities. In *Coping and Adaptation*, edited by G. V. Coehlo, D. A. Hamburg and J. E. Adams, New York: Basic Books.

Goode, W. J. 1956. *Women in Divorce*. New York: Free Press.

Gorman, B. S. 1971. A multivariate study of the relationship of cognitive principles to reported daily mood experiences. Ph.D. diss., City University of New York.

Goss, A., and T. E. Morosko. 1970. Relation between a dimension of internal-external control and the MMPI with an alcholic population. *Journal of Consulting and Clinical Psychology* 34:189–92.

Gould, R. E. 1976. Socio-cultural roles of male and female. In *The Sexual Experience*, edited by B. J. Sadock, H. I. Kaplan, and A. M. Freedman. Baltimore: Williams & Wilkins.

Gould, R. L. 1978. *Transformations: Growth and Change in Adult Life*. New York: Simon & Schuster.

Gove, W. R. 1973. Sex, marital status, and mortality. *American Journal of Sociology* 79:45–67.

Gutmann, D. L. 1964. An exploration of ego configurations in middle and later life. In *Personality in Middle and Late Life: Empirical Studies*, edited by B. Neugarten and Associates. New York: Atherton Press.

Gutmann, D. L. 1985. The parental imperative revisited. In *Family and Individual Development*, edited by J. Meacham. Basel: Karger.

Hagestad, G. O., M. A. Smyer and K. L. Stierman. 1984. Parent-child relations in adulthood: The impact of divorce in middle age. In *Parenthood: Psychodynamic Perspectives*, edited by R. Cohen, S. Weissman and B. Cohler. New York: Guilford Press.

Haggard, E. A. 1943. Experimental studies in affective processes: I. Some effects of cognitive structure and active participation on certain autonomic reactions during and following experimentally induced stress. *Journal of Experimental Psychology* 33:257–84.

Hallberg, H., and B. Mattsson. 1989. Life after divorce: A study of newly divorced middle aged men in Sweden. *Family Practice* 6(1): 9–15.

Hansburg, H. G. 1980. *Adolescent Separation Anxiety*, vol. 2, Huntington, N.Y.: Krieger.

Hanusa, B. H., and R. Schulz. 1977. Attributional mediators of learned helplessness. *Journal of Personality and Social Psychology* 35:602–11.

Harvey, O. J., H. H. Kelley, and M. M. Shapiro. 1947. Reactions to unfavorable evaluations of the self made by other persons. *Journal of Personality* 25:393–411.

Henderson, S. 1977. The social network, support and neurosis: The function of attachment in adult life. *British Journal of Psychiatry* 131:185–91.

Herek, G. M. 1989. Hate crimes against lesbians and gay men: Issues for research and policy. *American Psychologist* 44:948–55.

Herman, S. 1974. A grief process. *Perspectives in Psychiatric Care* 12:108–12.

Hersch, P. D., and K. E. Scheibe. 1967. On the reliability and validity of internal-external control as a personality dimension. *Journal of Consulting Psychology* 31:609–13.

Hetherington, E. M., M. Cox and R. Cox. 1976. Divorced fathers. *Family Coordinator* 25:417–28.

Hill, C. T., Z. Rubin, and L. A. Peplau. 1979. Breakups before marriage: The end of 103 affairs. In *Divorce and Separation: Contexts, Causes and Consequences*, edited by G. Levinger and O. C. Moles. New York: Basic Books.

Hjelle, L. A. 1971. Social desirability as a variable in the locus of control scale. *Psychological Reports* 28:807–16.

Hobfoll, S. E. 1988. *The Ecology of Stress*. New York: Hemisphere Press.

Holmes, T. H., and M. Masuda. 1974. Life changes and illness susceptibility. In *Stressful Life Events: Their Nature and Effects*, edited by B. S. Dohrenwend and B. P. Dohrenwend. New York: Wiley.

Holmes, T. H., and R. H. Rahe. 1967. The Social Readjustment Rating Scale. *Journal of Psychosomatic Research* 11:213–18.

Horowitz, M. J. 1976. *Stress Response Syndromes*. New York: Jason Aronson.

Horowitz, M. J., and N. Wilner. 1980. Life events, stress, and coping. In *Aging in the 1980's*, edited by L. W. Poon. Washington, D.C.: American Psychological Association.

Horowitz, M. J., N. Wilner, C. Marmar and J. Krupnick. 1980. Pathological grief and the activation of latent self images. *The American Journal of Psychiatry* 137(10): 1157–62.

House, J. S. 1981. *Work Stress and Social Support*. Reading, Mass.: Addison-Wesley.

Hunt, M. 1966. *The World of the Formerly Married*. New York: McGraw-Hill.

Hunt, M., and B. Hunt. 1977. *The Divorce Experience*. New York: McGraw-Hill.

Huntington, D. S. 1986. Fathers: The forgotten figures in divorce. In *Divorce and Fatherhood, The Struggle for Parental Identity*, edited by J. W. Jacobs. Washington, D.C.: American Psychiatric Association.

Ilfeld, F. W., Jr. 1982. Marital stressors, coping styles, and symptoms of depression. In *Handbook of Stress: Theoretical and Clinical Aspects*, edited by L. Goldberger and S. Breznitz. New York: Free Press.

Isaacs, M. B., and G. H. Leon. 1988. Race, marital dissolution and visitation: An examination of adaptive family strategies. In *Minority and Ethnic Issues in the Divorce Process*, edited by C. A. Everett. New York: Haworth Press.

Iu, C. R. 1982. Ethnic and economic correlates of marital satisfaction and attitude towards divorce of Chinese American women. *Dissertation Abstracts International* 43:1293-A (University Microfilms No. DA8219695).

Jacobs, J. W. 1986. Involuntary Child Absence Problem: An Affliction of Divorcing Fathers. In *Divorce and Fatherhood: The Struggle for Parental Identity*, edited by J. W. Jacobs, Washington, D.C.: American Psychiatric Association.

Jacobson, G. F. 1983. *The Multiple Crises of Marital Separation and Divorce*. New York: Grune & Stratton.

James, W. 1950. *Principles of Psychology*. New York: Dover Press.

James, W. H., A. B. Woodruff and W. Werner. 1965. Effect of internal and external control upon changes in smoking behavior. *Journal of Consulting Psychology* 29:184–86.

Janis, I. L. 1974. Vigilance and decision making in personal crisis. In *Coping and Adaptation*, edited by G. V. Coelho, D. A. Hamburg and J. E. Adams. New York: Basic Books.

Jenkins, C. D., M. W. Hurst and R. M. Rose. 1979. Life changes: Do people really remember? *Archive of General Psychiatry* 36:379–84.

Joe, V. C. 1972. Social desirability and the I-E Scale. *Psychological Reports* 30: 44–46.

Johnson, C. L. 1988. *Ex Familia: Grandparents, Parents, and Children Adjust to Divorce*. New Brunswick: Rutgers University Press.

Joreskog, K. G., and D. Sorbom. 1981. *LISREL: Analysis of Linear Relationships by the Method of Maximum Likelihood*. Version V. University of Chicago, Ill.: International Educational Services.

Jourard, S. 1964. *The Transparent Self*. New York: Van Nostrand Reinhold.

Kagan, J. 1980. Perspectives in continuity. In *Constancy and Change in Human*

Development, edited by O. G. Brim, Jr., and J. Kagan. Cambridge, Mass.: Harvard University Press.

Kagan J., and H. Moss 1962. *Birth to Maturity*. New York: Wiley.

Kaplan, G. A., R. E. Roberts, T. C. Camacho and J. C. Coyne. 1987. Psychosocial predictors of depression: Prospective evidence from the Human Population Laboratory Studies. *American Journal of Epidemiology* 125(2): 206–20.

Kelly, E. L. 1955. Consistency of the adult personality. *American Psychologist* 10(1): 659–81.

Kessler, R. C. 1979. Stress, social status and psychological distress. *Journal of Health and Social Behavior* 20:259–72.

Kiefer, C. W., and J. Cowan. 1979. State/context dependency and theories of ritual. *The Journal of Psychological Anthropology* 2(1): 53–83.

Kitano, H. H. L., and L. K. Chai. 1982. Korean interracial marriage. *Marriage and Family Review* (Special Issue: Intermarriage in the United States) 5:75–90.

Kitano, H. H. L. and W. Yeung. 1982. Chinese interracial marriage. *Marriage and Family Review* (Special Issue: Intermarriage in the United States) 5:35–48.

Kitson, G. C. 1982. Attachment to the spouse in divorce: A scale and its application. *Journal of Marriage and the Family* 44:379–93.

Kitson, G., and H. Z. Lopata. 1978. Divorce and widows: Similarities and differences. Paper presented at the 16th annual meeting of the American Orthopsychiatric Association, March, San Francisco.

Kitson, G., and M. Sussman. 1967. The process of marital separation and divorce: Male and female similarities and differences. Case Western Reserve University, Cleveland. Unpublished manuscript.

Kleber, D. J., R. J. Howell and A. L. Tibbits-Kleber. 1986. The impact of parental homosexuality in child custody cases: A review of the literature. *Bulletin of the American Academy of Psychiatry Law* 14(1): 81–87.

Klein, M. 1984. Mourning and its relationships to manic-depressive states. *International Journal of Psychological Analysis* 21:125–32.

Kobasa, C. S., S. R. Maddi and T. Covington. 1981. Personality and constitution as mediators in the stress-illness relationship. *Journal of Health and Social Behavior* 22:368–78.

Kotlar, S. L. 1965. Middle-class marital role perceptions and marital adjustment. *Sociological and Social Research* 49:282–93.

Krantzler, M. 1973. *Creative Divorce: A New Opportunity for Personal Growth*. New York: M. Evans.

Krystal, S., D. A. Chiriboga and L. Catron. 1980. Divorce at midlife: Psychic dangers of the liminal period. Part 3, Clinical considerations. *Maturita* 2:141–46.

Lachman, M. 1977. Dating: A coping strategy during marital separation. Paper presented at the 57th Annual Convention of the Western Psychological Association, April 23, Seattle.

Lazarus, R. S. 1966. *Psychological Stress and the Coping Process*. New York: McGraw-Hill.

Lazarus, R. S., and S. Folkman. 1984. *Stress, Appraisal, and Coping*. New York: Springer.

Lazarus, R. S., and R. Launier. 1978. Stress-related transactions between person and environment. In *Perspectives in Interactional Psychology*, edited by L. A. Pervin and M. Lewis. New York: Plenum Press.

Lazowick, L. M. 1955. On the nature of identification. *Journal of Abnormal Social Psychology* 51:175–83.

Leary, T. 1957. *Interpersonal Diagnosis of Personality*. New York: Ronald Press.

Lecky, P. 1945. *Self-Consistency*. New York: Island Press.

Lefcourt, H. M. 1966. Internal versus external locus of reinforcement: A review. *Psychological Bulletin* 65:206–20.

———. 1972. Recent developments in the study of locus of control. In *Progress in Experimental Personality Research*, vol. 6, edited by B. A. Maher. New York: Academic Press.

———. 1976. *Locus of Control: Current Trends in Theory and Research*. Hillsdale, N.J.: Erlbaum.

Lenihan, G. O. 1979. Patterns of response to the first year of divorce: Illustrative case studies of persons married 10 years or longer. Ph.D. diss., University of Illinois at Urbana, Champaign.

Lester, D., and A. T. Beck. 1979. Early loss as possible "sensitizer" to later loss in attempted suicides. *Psychological Reports* 39:121–22.

Levinger, G. 1976. A social psychological perspective on marital dissolution. *Journal of Social Issues* 32(1): 21–46.

Levinger, G., and O. C. Moles. 1979. *Divorce and Separation: Context, Causes, and Consequences*. New York: Basic Books.

Levinson, D. J., C. N. Darrow, E. B. Klein, M. H. Levinson and B. McKee. 1978. *The Seasons of a Man's Life*. New York: Alfred A. Knopf.

Lewis, K. G. 1980. Children of lesbians: Their point of view. *Social Work* 25:198–203.

Lieberman, M. A. 1982. The effects of social supports in response to stress. In *Handbook of Stress: Theoretical and Clinical Aspects*, edited by L. Goldberger and S. Breznitz. New York: Free Press of Glencoe.

Liem, G. R., and J. H. Liem. 1978. Social class and mental illness reconsidered: The role of economic stress and social support. *Journal of Health and Social Behavior* 19:139–56.

Lifton, R. J. 1971. Protean man. *Archives of General Psychiatry* 24:298–304.

Lind, A. W. 1964. Interracial marriage as affecting divorce in Hawaii. *Sociology and Social Research* 49:17–26.

Lindgarde, F., M. Furu, and B. Ljung. 1987. A longitudinal study on the significance of environmental and individual factors associated with the development of essential hypertension. *Journal of Epidemiology and Community Health* 41:220–26.

Lopata, H. Z. 1979. *Women as Widows*. New York: Elsevier North Holland.

Lowenthal, M. F., and D. A. Chiriboga. 1972. Transition to the empty nest: Crisis, challenge or relief? *Archives of General Psychiatry* 256:8–14.

Lowenthal, M. F., and C. Haven. 1968. Interaction and adaptation: Intimacy as a critical variable. *American Sociological Review* 32:20–30.

Lowenthal, M., M. Thurnher, D. A. Chiriboga and Associates. 1975. *Four Stages of Life*. San Francisco: Jossey-Bass.

Luborsky, L., J. P. Docherty and S. Penick. 1973. Onset conditions for psychosomatic symptoms: A comparative review of immediate observation with retrospective research. *Psychosomatic Medicine* 35:187–204.

Luckey, E. B. 1960a. Marital satisfaction and congruent self-spouse concepts. *Social Forces* 39:153–57.

———. 1960b. Marital satisfaction and its association with congruence of perception. *Marriage and Family Living* 22:49–54.

———. 1960c. Marital satisfaction and parent concepts. *Journal of Consulting Psychology* 24:195–204.

Maccoby, E. E. 1990. Gender and relationships: A developmental account. *American Psychologist* 45:513–20.

Mandler, G. 1979. Thought processes, consciousness, and stress. In *Human Stress and Cognition*, edited by V. Hamilton and D. Warburton. New York: Wiley.

Mandler, G., and D. L. Watson. 1966. Anxiety and the interruption of behavior. In *Anxiety and Behavior*, edited by C. D. Spielberger. New York: Academic Press.

Maretzki, T. W. 1977. Intercultural marriage: An introduction. In *Adjustment in Intercultural Marriage*, edited by W. Tseng, J. F. McDermott and T. W. Maretzki. Honolulu: University Press of Hawaii.

Marguia, E., and R. B. Cazares. 1982. Intermarriage of Mexican Americans. *Marriage and Family Review* 5:91–100.

Marris, P. 1975. *Loss and Change*. Garden City, N.Y.: Anchor Books.

Maslow, A. H. 1954. *Motivation and Personality*. New York: Harper.

Maury, E. H., and R. A. Brandwein. 1984. The divorced woman: Processes of change. In *Marriage and Divorce: A Contemporary Perspective*, edited by C. C. Nadelson and D. C. Polonsky. New York: Guilford Press.

McCrae, R., and P. J. Costa. 1984. *Emerging Lives, Enduring Dispositions: Personality in Adulthood*. Boston: Little, Brown.

McCubbin, H. I., and M. A. McCubbin. 1988. Typologies of resilient families: Emerging roles of social class and ethnicity. *Family Relations* 37:247–54.

McCubbin, H. I., C. B. Joy, A. E. Cauble, J. M. Patterson and R. Needle. 1980. Family stress and coping: A decade in review. *Journal of Marriage and the Family* 42:855–71.

McFarlane, A., G. R. Norman, D. L. Streiner and R. G. Roy. 1983. The process of social stress: Stable, reciprocal, and mediating relationships. *Journal of Health and Social Behavior* 24:160–73.

Mead, G. H. 1934. *Mind, Self, and Society*. Chicago: University of Chicago Press.

Mechanic, D. 1974. Social structure and personal adaptation: Some neglected dimensions. In *Coping and Adaptation*, edited by G. Coelho, D. Hamburg and J. Adams. New York: Basic Books.

Melges, F. T., and J. Bowlby. 1969. Types of hopelessness in psychopathological process. *Archives of General Psychiatry* 20:690–99.

Melichar, J., and D. A. Chiriboga. 1985. Timetables in the divorce process. *Journal of Marriage and the Family* 47:701–8.

————. 1988. Significance of time in adjustment to marital separation. *American Journal of Orthopsychiatry* 58(2): 1–7.

Meyers, J. C. 1976. The adjustment of women to marital separation: The effects of sex-role identification and of stage in family life, as determined by age and presence or absence of dependent children. Ph.D. diss., University of Colorado.

Mika, K. S. 1980. Adjustment to separation among formerly cohabiting men and women. Ph.D. diss., University of Colorado.

Miller, S. 1989. Invited presentation, Conference on Adult Stress and Adaptation. Trier, Federal Republic of Germany.

Monroe, S. M. 1983. Social support and disorder: Toward an untangling of cause and effect. *American Journal of Community Psychology* 11:81–97.

Morse, S., and K. J. Gergen. 1970. Social comparison, self-consistency, and the concept of self. *Journal of Personality and Social Psychology* 16(1): 148–56.

Murphy, L. B. 1974. Coping vulnerability and resilience in childhood. In *Coping and Adaptation*, edited by G. V. Coehlo, D. A. Hamburg and J. E. Adams. New York: Basic Books.

Murphy, L. B., and Associates. 1962. *The Widening World of Childhood: Paths toward Mastery*. New York: Basic Books.

Myers, J., J. Lindenthal and M. P. Pepper. 1971. Life events and psychiatric impairment. *Journal of Nervous and Mental Disease* 152:157–59.

National Center for Health Statistics. 1990. Births, marriages, divorces and deaths for 1989. *Monthly Vital Statistics Report* 38(12): 1–20.

Neugarten, B. 1968. Awareness of middle age. In *Middle Age and Aging*, edited by B. L. Neugarten. Chicago: University of Chicago Press.

Nevaldine, A. 1978. Divorce: The leaver and the left. Ph.D. diss., University of Minnesota.

Norman, C. E. 1963. An analysis of meaning. *Psychological Review* 79:293–302.

Norton, A. J., and P. C. Glick. 1979. Marital instability: Past, present and future. *Journal of Social Issues* 32:5–20.

Norton, A. J., and J. E. Moorman. 1987. Current trends in marriage and divorce among American women. *Journal of Marriage and the Family* 49:3–14.

Nunnally, J. 1967. *Psychomatic Theory*. New York: McGraw-Hill.

Nystrom, S. 1980. The use of somatic hospital care among men in the community of Borlange. *Scandinavian Journal of Social Medicine* (Supplement 17): 1–48.

O'Connor, N. D. V. 1976. An exploration of the effects of anticipatory grief versus acute grief on recovery after loss of spouse among divorced and separated women. Ph.D. diss., University of Oregon.

Osgood, C. E. 1962. Studies of the generality of affective meaning systems. *American Psychologist* 17:10–28.

Osgood, C. E., G. J. Succi and P. H. Tannenbaum. 1957. *The Measurement of Meaning*. Urbana, Ill.: University of Illinois Press.

Pagelow, M. D. 1980. Heterosexual and lesbian single mothers: A comparison of problems, coping, and solutions. *Journal of Homosexuality* 5:189–205.

Pais, J. S. 1979. Socio-psychological predictors of adjustment for divorced mothers. Ph.D. diss., The University of Tennessee.

Parkes, C. M. 1971. Psycho-social transitions: A field for study. *Social Science and Medicine* 5:101–15.

————. 1975. What becomes of redundant world models? A contribution to the study of adaptation to change. *British Journal of Medical Psychology* 48:131–37.

Parkes, C. M., and R. S. Weiss. 1983. *Recovery from Bereavement.* New York: Basic Books.

Paykel, E. S., J. K. Myers, M. N. Dienelt, G. I. Klerman, J. J. Linderthal and M. P. Pepper. 1969. Life events and depression. *Archives of General Psychiatry* 21:753–60.

Payne, R., and B. B. Pittard. 1969. Divorce in the middle years. *Sociological Symposium* 1:115–24.

Peacock, J. 1976. *Consciousness and Change.* New York: Wiley.

Pearlin, L. I. 1985. Social structure and social supports. In *Social Support and Health,* edited by S. Cohen and L. Syme. New York: Academic Press.

Pearlin, L. I., and J. S. Johnson. 1977. Marital status, life-strains and depression. *American Sociological Review* 4:704–15.

Pearlin, L. I., and M. A. Lieberman. 1976. Interview schedule. Life events and Adaptation in Adulthood project. University of Chicago, Committee on Human Development. Unpublished manuscript.

————. 1979. Social sources of emotional distress, *Research in Community and Mental Health* 1:217–48.

Pearlin, L. I., M. A. Lieberman, E. G. Menaghan and J. T. Mullan. 1981. The stress process. *Journal of Health and Social Behavior* 22:337–56.

Pearlin, L. I., and C. Schooler. 1978. The structure of coping. *Journal of Health and Behavioral Science* 19:2–21.

Persson, G. 1980. Relation between early parental death and life event ratings among 70-year-olds. *Acta Psychiatrica Scandinavica* 62:392–97.

Peskin, H. 1972. Multiple prediction of adult psychological health from pre-adolescent and adolescent behavior. *Journal of Consulting and Clinical Psychology* 38(2): 155–60.

Peskin, H., and N. Livson. 1981. Uses of the past in adult psychological health. In *Present and Past in Middle Life,* edited by D. H. Eichorn, J. A. Clausen, N. Haan, M. P. Honzik and P. H. Mussen. San Francisco: Academic Press.

Phares, E. J. 1965. Internal-external control as a determinant of amount of social influence exerted. *Journal of Personality and Social Psychology* 2:642–47.

Phares, E. J., D. E. Ritchies and W. L. Davis. 1968. Internal-external control and reaction to threat. *Journal of Personality and Social Psychology* 10:402–05.

Pierce, R., and D. A. Chiriboga. 1979. Dimensions of adult self-concept. *Journal of Gerontology* 34:80–85.

Porterfield, E. 1982. Black-American intermarriage in the United States. *Marriage and Family Review* (Special Issue: Intermarriage in the United States) 5:17–34.

Price-Bonham, S., and J. O. Balswick. 1980. The non-institutions: Divorce, desertion, and remarriage. *Journal of Marriage and the Family* 42(4): 959–72.

Quentin, D., and M. Rutter. 1976. Early hospital admissions and later disturbances of behavior: An attempted replication of Douglas' findings. *Developmental Medicine and Child Neurology* 48:447–59.

Rabkin, J. G., and E. L. Streuning. 1976. Life events, stress and illness. *Science* 194:1013–20.

Rahe, R. H. 1968. Life crisis and health change. In *Psychotropic Drug Response: Advances in Prediction*, edited by P. R. A. May and J. R. Wittenborn. Springfield, Ill.: Charles C. Thomas.

Rank, O. 1945. *Will Therapy*. New York: Alfred A. Knopf.

Rankin, R. P., and J. S. Maneker. 1988. Correlates of marital duration and Black-White intermarriage in California. *Journal of Divorce* 11:51–68.

Raschke, H. J. 1974. Social and psychological factors in voluntary postmarital adjustment. Ph.D. diss., University of Minnesota.

———. 1977. The role of social participation in postseparation and postdivorce adjustment. *Journal of Divorce* 1(2): 129–40.

Rice, J. K., and D. G. Rice. 1986. *Living through Divorce: A Developmental Approach to Divorce Therapy*. New York: Guilford Press.

Rodin, J. 1986. Aging and health: Effects of the sense of control. *Science* 233: 1271–76.

Rogers, H. S. 1978. Sexual attitudes and behavior of people in the process of divorce: A study of sexuality and its association with loneliness. Ph.D. diss. The Institute for the Advanced Study of Human Sexuality, San Francisco.

Rogers, C. R. 1951. *Client Centered Therapy*. Boston: Houghton Mifflin.

———. 1961. *On Becoming a Person*. Boston: Houghton Mifflin.

Rosenberg, M. 1979. *Conceiving the Self*. New York: Basic Books.

Ross, H. L., and I. V. Sawhill. 1975. *Time of Transition: The Growth of Families Headed by Women*. Washington, D.C.: The Urban Institute.

Roth, S., and L. Kubal. 1975. Effects of noncontingent reinforcement on tasks of differing importance: Facilitation and learned helplessness. *Journal of Personality and Social Psychology* 32:680–91.

Rotter, J. B. 1966. Generalized expectations for internal versus external control of reinforcements. *Psychological Monographs: General and Applied* 80:1–28.

———. 1990. Internal versus external control of reinforcement: A case history of a variable. *American Psychologist* 45(4): 489–93.

Rutter, M. 1977. Individual differences. In *Child Psychiatry: Modern Approaches*, edited by M. Rutter and L. Hersov. Oxford: Blackwell Scientific.

———. 1979. Protective factors in children's responses to stress and disadvantage. In *Primary Prevention of Psychopathology*, vol. 3 of *Social Competence in Children*, edited by M. W. Kent and J. E. Rolf. Hanover, N.H.: University Press of New England.

———. 1981. Stress, coping and development: Some issues and some questions. *Child Psychological Psychiatry* 22(4): 323–56.

Ryckman, R. M., and M. F. Sherman. 1973. Relationship between self-esteem and internal-external control for men and women. *Psychological Reports* 32:1106.

Sanborn, K. O. 1977. Intercultural marriage in Hawaii. In *Adjustment in Intercul-*

tural Marriage, edited by W. Tseng, J. F. McDermott and T. W. Maretzkipps. Honolulu: University Press of Hawaii.

Schaefer, C., J. C. Coyne and R. Lazarus. 1981. The health-related functions of social support. *Journal of Behavioral Medicine* 4:381–406.

Schlossberg, N. K. 1984. *Counseling Adults in Transition: Linking Practice with Theory*. New York: Springer.

Schulz, R., and D. Aderman. 1973. Effect of residential change on the temporal distance to death of terminal cancer patients. *Omega: Journal of Death and Dying* 2:157–62.

———. 1974. Clinical research and the stages of dying. *Omega: Journal of Death and Dying* 5:137–43.

Schwertfeger, M. M. 1982. Interethnic marriage and divorce in Hawaii: A panel study of 1968 first marriages. *Marriage and Family Review* 5:49–59.

Seeman, M. 1963. Alienation and social learning in a reformatory. *American Journal of Sociology* 69:270–289.

Seligman, M. E. P. 1974. Depression and learned helplessness. In *The Psychology of Depression: Contemporary Theory and Research*, edited by R. J. Freeman and M. M. Katz. New York: Winston.

———. 1975. *Helplessness: On Depression, Development and Death*. San Francisco: W. H. Freeman.

———. 1989. Research in clinical psychology: Why is there so much depression today? In *The G. Stanley Hall Lecture Series, Vol 9*, edited by I. S. Cohen. Washington, D.C.: American Psychological Association.

Sells, S. B. 1970. On the nature of stress. In *Social and Psychological Factors in Stress*, edited by J. E. McGrath. New York: Holt, Rinehart & Winston.

Selye, H. 1974. *Stress without Distress* New York: Signet.

Sobota, W., and A. Cappas. 1979. Semantic differential changes associated with participation in a public lecture series describing the emotional and behavioral consequences of divorce. *Journal of Divorce* 3(2): 137–51.

Spanier, G. B., and R. F. Castro. 1979. Adjustment to separation and divorce: A qualitative analysis. In *Divorce and Separation: Context, Causes, and Consequences*, edited by G. Levinger and O. Moles. New York: Basic Books.

Spanier, G. B., and R. A. Lewis. 1979. The measurement of marital quality. *Journal of Sex and Marital Therapy* 5:288–300.

———. 1980. Marital quality: A review of the seventies. *Journal of Marriage and the Family* 6:825–39.

Spencer, P. 1965. *The Samburu: A Study of Gerontology in a Nomadic Tribe*. Berkeley: University of California Press.

Stack, S. 1989. The impact of divorce on suicide in Norway, 1951–1980. *Journal of Marriage and the Family* 51:229–38.

Staples, R. 1985. Changes in black family structure: The conflict between family ideology and structural conditions. *Journal of Marriage and the Family* 27:1005–13.

Staples, R., and A. Mirande. 1980. Racial and cultural variations among American families: A decennial review of the literature on minority families. *Journal of Marriage and the Family* 42:887–903.

Steele, G. P., S. Henderson and P. Duncan-Jones. 1980. The reliability of reporting adverse experiences. *Psychological Medicine* 10:301–6.

Streib, G. F. 1971. New roles and activities for retirement. In *The Future of Aging and the Aged*, edited by G. L. Maddow. Atlanta: SNPA Foundation.

Strickland, B. R. 1989. Internal-external control experiences: From contingency to creativity. *American Psychologist* 44:1–12.

Stryker, R. 1964. Marital satisfaction: Perception of self and spouse. *Journal of Marriage and the Family* 25:117–24.

Stuckert, P. R. 1963. Role perception and marital satisfaction—a configurational approach. *Marriage and Family Living* 25:415–19.

Symonds, P. M. 1951. *The Ego and the Self*. New York: Appleton-Century-Crofts.

Taeuber, C., and V. Valdisera. 1986. Women in the American Economy. *Current Population Reports, Special Studies* Series P-23, No. 146. Washington, D.C.: U.S. Government Printing Office.

Taylor, A. B. 1967. Role perception, empathy and marriage adjustment. *Sociological and Social Research* 52:22–34.

Teachman, J. D. 1986. First and second marital dissolution: A decomposition exercise for whites and blacks. *The Sociological Quarterly* 27:571–90.

Tennen, H., and S. J. Eller. 1977. Attributional components of learned helplessness and facilitation. *Journal of Personality and Social Psychology* 35:265–71.

Thoits, P. A. 1982. Conceptual, methodological and theoretical problems in studying social support. *Journal of Health and Social Behavior* 23:145–59.

Thurnher M., C. Birtley, J. F. Melichar and D. A. Chiriboga. 1983. Sociodemographic perspectives on reasons for divorce. *Journal of Divorce* 6(4): 25–35.

Tinker, J. N. 1982. Intermarriage and assimilation in a plural society: Japanese Americans in the United States. *Marriage and Family Review* (Special Issue: Intermarriage in the United States) 5:61–74.

Trovato, F. 1987. A longitudinal analysis of divorce and suicide in Canada. *Journal of Marriage and the Family* 49:193–203.

Tryon, R. C., and D. E. Bailey. 1970. *Cluster Analysis*. New York: McGraw-Hill.

Tschann, J. M., J. R. Johnston and J. S. Wallerstein. 1989. Resources, stressors and attachment as predictors of adult adjustment after divorce: A longitudinal study. *Journal of Marriage and the Family* 51:1033–46.

Turner, R. J. 1981. Social support as a contingency in psychological well-being. *Journal of Health and Social Behavior* 22:357–67.

Turner, R. J., B. G. Frankel and D. M. Levin. 1983. Social support: conceptualization, measurement, and implications for mental health. In *Research in Community and Mental Health*, Vol. 3, edited by J. R. Greeley and R. G. Simmons. Greenwich, Conn.: JAI Press.

Turner, V. 1967. *The forest of symbols: Aspect of Ndembu ritual*. New York: Cornell University Press.

United Nations. 1987. *Demographic Yearbook*. New York: United Nations.

Vachon, M. L. S. 1976. Grief bereavement following the death of a spouse. *Canadian Journal of Psychiatric Association* 21:35–42.

Vachon, M. L. S., P. Clayton, S. Demaris and G. Winokur. 1968. A study of normal bereavement. *American Journal of Psychiatry* 125:168–78.

Vaillant, G. E. 1977. *Adaptation to Life.* Boston: Little, Brown.

———. 1978. Natural history of male psychological health: VI. Correlates of successful marriage and fatherhood. *American Journal of Psychiatry* 135:653–59.

van Gennep, A. 1960. *The Rites of Passage.* London: Routledge & Kegan Paul.

Vernick, S. K. 1979. Selected correlates of divorce and post-marital attachment. Ph.D. diss., University of Florida.

Veroff, J., E. Douvan and R. Kulka. 1981. *The Inner American: A Self Portrait from 1957–1976.* New York: Basic Books.

Vinokur, A., and M. L. Selzer. 1975. Desirable versus undesirable life events: Their relationship to stress and mental distress. *Journal of Personality and Social Psychology* 32:329–37.

Wagner, R. M. 1988a. Changes in extended family relationships for Mexican American and Anglo single mothers. In *Minority and Ethnic Issues in the Divorce Process,* edited by C. A. Everett. New York: Haworth Press.

———. 1988b. Changes in the friend network during the first year of single parenthood for Mexican American and Anglo women. In *Minority and Ethnic Issues in the Divorce Process,* edited by C. A. Everett. New York: Haworth Press.

Waldron, J. A., J. W. J. Ching and P. H. Fair. 1986. A children's divorce clinic: Analysis of 200 cases in Hawaii. *Journal of Divorce* 9:11–121.

Waller, W. 1930. *The Old Love and the New: Divorce and Readjustment.* New York: Horace Liverwright.

Wallerstein, J. S. 1978. Children who cope in spite of divorce. *Family Advocate* 2(5): 35–39.

———. 1986. Women after divorce: Preliminary findings from a ten year follow-up. *American Journal of Orthopsychiatry* 56:65–77.

Wallerstein, J. S., and S. Blakeslee. 1989. *Second Chances: Men, Women & Children a Decade after Divorce.* New York: Ticknor & Fields.

Wallerstein, J. S., and J. B. Kelly. 1980. *Surviving the Breakup: How Children and Parents Cope with Divorce.* New York: Basic Books.

Wallston, K. A., G. D. Kaplan and S. A. Maides. 1976. Development and validation of the "Health Locus of Control" (HLC) scale. *Journal of Consulting and Clinical Psychology* 44:580–85.

Warhime, R. G., and M. F. Foulds. 1971. Perceived locus of control and personal adjustment. *Journal of Consulting and Clinical Psychology* 37:250–52.

Weintraub, M., J. Brooks and M. Lewis. 1977. The social network: A reconsideration of the concept of attachment. *Human Development* 20:31–37.

Weiss, R. S. 1974. The provisions of social relationships. In *Doing Unto Others,* edited by Z. Rubin. Englewood Cliffs, N.J.: Prentice-Hall.

———. 1975. *Marital Separation.* New York: Basic Books.

———. 1976. The emotional impact of marital separation. *Journal of Social Issues* 32(1): 135–45.

———. 1979. *Going it Alone: The Family Life and Social Situation of the Single Parent.* New York: Basic Books.

Weitzman, L. 1976. Interview Schedule. University of California, Divorce Law Research Project, Center for the Study of Law and Society, Berkeley. Unpublished manuscript.

White, R. W. 1959. Motivation reconsidered: The concept of competence. *Psychological Review* 66:297–333.

———. 1960. Competence and the psychosexual stages of development. In *Nebraska Symposium on Motivation*, edited by M. R. Jones. Lincoln, Nebr.: University of Nebraska Press.

———. 1973. *Ego and Reality in Psychoanalytic Theory: Psychological Issues.* III(3), Monograph II. New York: International Universities Press.

———. 1979. Competence as an aspect of personal growth. In *Primary Prevention of Psychopathology. Vol. 1: Social Competence in Children.* Hanover, N.H.: University Press of New England.

White, S. W., and B. L. Bloom. 1981. Factors related to the adjustment of divorcing men. *Family Relations* 30(3): 349–60.

Whitney, C. 1990. *Uncommon Lives: Gay Men and Straight Women.* New York: New Area Library.

Wilder, H. B. 1981. Perceptions of general and situational control: Their relevance to adjustment in divorce. Ph.D. diss., California School of Professional Psychology, Berkeley.

Wiseman, R. 1975. Crisis theory and the process of divorce. *Social Casework* 56:205–12.

Wohwill, J. F. 1978. The age variable in psychological research. *Psychological Reviews* 77:49–64.

Wolf, S. 1954. Reactions in the nasal mucosae: Relation of life stress to chronic rhinitis and "sinus" headache. A. M. A. *Archives of Otolaryngology* 59:461–75.

Wolff, H. G. 1968. *Stress and Disease.* Springfield, Ill.: Charles C. Thomas.

Wortman, C. B., L. Panciera, L. Shusterman and J. Hibscher. 1976. Attributions of causality and reactions to uncontrollable outcomes. *Journal of Experimental and Social Psychology* 12:301–16.

Yarrow, M. R., Campbell, J. D. and R. V. Burton. 1970. Recollection of childhood: A study of the retrospective method. *Monographs of the Society for Research in Child Development* 35(5): 1–83.

Yee, B. W. K. 1982. Control in British and Asian elderly women. *Dissertation Abstracts International* 43: No. 3 1983 (University Microfilms No. DA8216699).

———. 1989. Loss of homeland and culture. In *Coping with the Losses of Middle Age*, edited by R. Kalish. Newbury Park, Calif.: Sage.

Yee, B. W. K., and S. T. Hennessey. 1982. Pacific/Asian families and mental health. In *Perspectives on Minority Group Mental Health*, edited by F. U. Munoz, and R. Endo. Washington, D.C.: University Press of America.

Zeiss, A. M., R. A. Zeiss and S. M. Johnston. 1980. Sex differences in initiation and adjustment to divorce. *Journal of Divorce* 4:21–33.

Zybron, G. 1965. Role consensus, need complementarity and continuance of marriage. Ph.D. diss., Western Reserve University.

INDEX

313

Strickland, B. R., 226
Stryker, R., 176
Stuckert, P. R., 176
Succi, G. J., 175
Suicide, 38
Sussman, M., 6, 126
Syme, S. L., 196

Taeuber, C., 2
Tannenbaum, P. H., 175
Taylor, A. B., 176
Teachman, J. D., 251
Teasdale, J., 238
Tennen, H., 237
Thoits, P. A., 92, 195, 204, 211, 284
Thurnher, M., 235, 286
Tibbits-Kleber, A. L., 271
Timing issues, 41, 125–47, 251–52, 291
Transitional status, 47, 97–124, 125–47, 290–92
Trovato, F., 38
Tryon, R. C., 80
Tschann, J. M., 38
Turner, R. J., 195, 197
Turner, Victor, 100, 101, 102, 104, 291

Uncommon Lives: Gay Men and Straight Women (Whitney), 270
United Nations, 38
U.S. Bureau of the Census, 2

Vaillant, G. E., 17, 147
Valdisera, V., 2
Van Gennep, A., 100, 138, 139, 291
Vernick, S. K., 106
Veroff, J., 196, 206
Vinokur, A., 227

Wagner, N. N., 227
Wagner, R. M., 252, 257
Waldron, J. A., 254
Waller, W., 2, 38, 229
Wallerstein, J. S., 6, 18, 38, 39, 155, 160, 211, 212, 229, 234, 235, 236, 245, 283
Wallston, K. A., 228
Warhime, R. G., 226
Watson, D. L., 224
Weber, R., 6
Weintraub, M., 139
Weiss, R. S., 2, 39, 40, 56, 93, 101, 104, 105, 106, 111, 146, 153, 154, 155, 160, 161, 197, 204, 211, 224
Weitzman, L., 5–6
Werner, W., 226
Westman, J., 147
White, R. W., 17, 152, 156, 163, 225, 229
White, S. W., 2, 211, 212, 215, 283
Whitney, C., 260
Widowhood. *See* Bereavement
Wilner, N., 36, 46
Wiseman, R., 153, 154, 155, 171
Wohlwill, J. F., 133
Wolf, S., 227
Wolff, H. G., 227
Woodruff, A. B., 226
Wortman, C. B., 237

Yarrow, M. R., 14
Yee, B. W. K., 260, 264, 267, 269
Yeung, W., 249

Zeiss, A. M., 38
Zeiss, R. A., 38
Zybron, G., 234